PRAISE FOR *SHE'S SO COLD*, FIRST EDITION

"It is unimaginable what our justice system does with juveniles. I hope the changes you have suggested are made."

—*Linda Starr, Executive Director*
Northern California Innocence Project

"An eye-opening and shocking insight into the inner workings of a complex case that sent three innocent young boys to criminal court for murder."

—*Crime Traveler*

"*She's So Cold* is one of the most harrowing stories I have read. . . . This is a gripping tale of law enforcement gone lawless."

—*English Plus Blog*

"Painful to read as a parent. Fortunately, the truth came out. Five Stars."

—*Nikki V., NetGalley*

"This is a fascinating look at a broken 'justice' system, interrogation techniques, false confessions, and the rights of the accused in general and children in particular."

—*Littoral Librarian*

"It was never going to be rated anything BUT five stars! . . . An absolutely fantastic read. Up there with *In Cold Blood* by Truman Capote. I enjoyed it THAT much."

—*Yassemin T, NetGalley*

"McInnis uses clear, descriptive language to describe all aspects of the case. That makes the book read more like a novel than a work on nonfiction. I think that those who like true crime or legal works will enjoy this book."

—*Amy's Scrap Bag*

"Outstanding book" that gives "a clearer understanding about the interrogation process as a whole. A Five-Star book."

—*Keith C., NetGalley*

"She's So Cold shows in excruciating detail how fragile the human psyche is and the power law enforcement wields to manipulate us. It's an excellent case study in how, under the wrong circumstances, fact can become fiction and fiction fact. Thanks to Donald McInnis for an unsettling but necessary look at the dark and sometimes obscure motivations that produce misbehavior by the police and false confessions to crime."

—*Men's eNews*

"So who killed Stephanie? I will leave this to the reader to discover. Hers actually becomes a secondary crime to that perpetrated on these boys. In defense of the police, they must deal every day with the dregs of society who all declare their innocence. The detectives must have methods and ways to tenaciously get at the truth. However, to use what falls dangerously into the realm of torture is surely not the answer, particularly on teenagers."

—*Book Loons*

"As I was reading this book, I did feel and experience injustice as well as anger. The type of harassment that the three boys endured was horrible. It is no wonder that they would and did say anything that the authorities wanted them to say. It is lucky that Mr. McInnis was assigned to represent one of the boys. If not, the boys may never have been released."

—*Cheryl's Book Nook*

"Even though the events of this book are highly maddening, I recommend this book. It is extremely interesting to read about all of the things surrounding Stephanie's death, the investigation, the trial, and the outcome."

—*Grandma Ideas*

"I learned a lot from this book. I recommend those that like true crime read the story. They will get so much more from it than just the mess that the police and others made trying to get a confession."

—*J Bronder Book Reviews*

"This was one of those cases the mass media love and for which they effectively convict the accused in the minds of the public. This was in 1998 in San Diego, and the original victim's name was Stephanie Crowe. But there were more victims, including Stephanie's brother, two of his friends, and the three boys' families. The trauma willfully and knowingly inflicted on them by the police and prosecutors was limited by the fact that so-called 'confessions' by two of the three boys were videotaped. I haven't watched the videos, but reading them is like watching violence in slow motion."

—*Let's Try Democracy*

"If you enjoy mysteries you will love this. If you want to see why we need more people like Donald McInnis working for us, you will enjoy this. . . . Mr. McInnis does a wonderful job of laying out the facts without prejudice. He simply states what happened. Fascinating read!"

—*Maria's Space*

"With a perfect balance between dialogue and description, the story flows through the pages and is easy to follow and understand without complicated police jargon."

—*SA Examiner*

"The unethical psychological and emotional manipulation of three young boys that coerced false confessions establishes groundbreaking need for change. If you are interested in true case studies of the wrongfully accused or an advocate for children's rights, maybe even a newly appointed attorney, this is a must read. It changed the lives of fifteen people and it might even change yours."

—*My Shelf*

"If you are interested in interrogation techniques, children's rights, and/or wrongful convictions, this book is for you. Highly recommended reading!"

—*Defrosting Cold Cases*

SHE'S SO COLD

The Stephanie Crowe Murder Case

A Defense Attorney's Inside Story

DONALD E. MCINNIS

ISBN: 978-1-7323-222-5-7

Library of Congress Control Number: 2020920442

TRU002000   TRUE CRIME / Murder / General
LAW026010   LAW / Criminal Law / Juvenile Offenders

Second edition. The previous edition, by J&E Publications, was released in 2019.

This book is for informational and entertainment purposes. The author or publisher will not be held responsible for the use of any information contained in this book.

DISCLAIMER
In researching this book, material was gathered from a wide variety of resources, including newspapers, academic and forensic papers, and other sources and material both online and offline. To the best of our knowledge, the material contained is correct. Neither the publisher nor the author will be held liable for incorrect or factual mistakes.

What follows in these pages is taken directly from police files, transcripts, videotaped interrogations and the defense attorneys' own case files. Dialog is presented as recorded in such official documents, but minor editorial changes have been made, strictly to enhance readability.

Printed in the United States of America

www.donaldmcinnis.com

IN MEMORY OF
EDWARD AND JOSEPHINE McINNIS

• CONTENTS •

• AUTHOR'S NOTE •

This is an updated edition of *She's So Cold*. It has been revised and restructured to highlight the relevancy of this case to current police and justice-system reform efforts and the Black Lives Matter movement.

This provides a greater focus on the criminal-justice system, the inability of children to understand their constitutional rights, and the harm police officers and prosecutors can, and do, inflict upon impressionable and easily manipulated youth who are treated as though they have the experience and mental capacity of adults.

• INTRODUCTION •

The system let them down.
The families have been paying for it ever since.
Think this couldn't happen to your child? . . . Think again.

She's So Cold **is a true story.**

In January 1998, the idyllic town of Escondido, California, was horrified by news that twelve-year-old Stephanie Crowe had been found brutally stabbed to death in her own bedroom. As there was no sign of a home break-in, and a lack of any physical evidence indicating who committed the crime, the police zeroed in on her fourteen-year-old brother Michael and two of his friends.

Two of the youths, Michael and Joshua, confessed to the heinous crime. They did so without the benefit of legal counsel. Michael made repeated requests to speak to his parents, which under juvenile law is tantamount to invoking his Fifth Amendment right to remain silent. While Michael was pleading to see his parents, his mother and father weren't even aware that their son was being interrogated. In the case of Joshua, the police lied to his father and persuaded him to have his son take a truth verification test. That test was then used to pressure Joshua into confessing.

The parents initially encouraged the boys to speak to police because they trusted the system. They couldn't have been more wrong. Despite the fact that another suspect was in the area, the youths were railroaded into a nightmare which few could have prepared for—one that shattered the lives of everyone involved.

As the defense attorney for one of the boys involved, I found the investigation process and the inquisitions which followed unfair, unethical, and terrifying in their potential.

She's So Cold is a true story. In creating this book, I scrutinized thousands of pages of police, crime lab, and physical evidence reports, as well as court transcripts and many hours of videotaped interrogations. My objective from the start was to ensure the accuracy of what I assembled in this book.

I have faithfully reproduced the language used by the police, the attorneys, the suspects, and others involved, but in some instances I have had to condense some of the exchanges. Minor editorial changes have been made, strictly to enhance readability. I have also kept my personal observations and asides as brief as possible.

The Crowe murder case, in every respect, is a tragic set of events. But, at the heart of this tragedy is justice denied. The ultimate legal results of this case are directly attributable to how the police investigated the murder. In particular, the investigation hinged upon the psychological interrogation techniques they employed against the three boys: Michael Crowe, age fourteen, Joshua Treadway, age fourteen, and Aaron Houser, age fifteen. Equally at fault is the investigators' supposition or belief that only these boys could have committed the murder.

THE REID TECHNIQUE OF INTERROGATION

There are always mind games in the interrogation process, whether played by the suspect or by the police interrogator. However, in 1962 a controversial method of criminal interrogation was developed by polygraph expert John E. Reid and criminologist Fred E. Inbau. The method of interrogation was built around sound psychological techniques but employed trickery and deceit. This method of psychological interrogation is called the Reid Technique of Interrogation, and it was first published in 1962 by Inbau, Reid and Buckley. Their book laid out a psychological process of interrogation designed to get a suspected criminal to confess his or her crime.

Today the Reid Technique is taught to and used by thousands of crime interrogators and police departments throughout the country. There are three stages to the technique. Stage One, "The Fact Analysis," involves the collection and analysis of the crime's facts. Stage Two, "The Behavior Analysis Interview," is a non-accusatory interview designed to gather facts and behavioral information about the possible suspects. At the heart of the Reid Technique is Stage Three and its "Nine Steps of Interrogation." The nine steps employ an accusatory process wherein the investigator tells the suspect that the evidence clearly shows he committed the crime. The claim of evidence may be truthful, mild conjecture, or false. As the interrogator weaves the narrative, he or she comes across as a non-demeaning, understanding, and always patient interviewer, with the goal of making the suspect feel comfortable with telling the truth. All the while, the interrogator uses sets of psychological constructs or themes as potential moral justification for why the suspect did what he did.

In my opinion, the theme developed by the investigator through interaction with the suspect is the key to the psychological interrogation. The theme gives the impression to the suspect that it minimizes the suspect's responsibility for the crime and its perceived legal consequences.

The danger of this form of interrogation is that children as well as adults can be led to falsely confess, as was the case of the New York Central Park Five in 1989. Five teenage boys, all of them Black, were wrongly tried and convicted of the rape and brutal beating of a white female jogger, based in part on coerced confessions. Thirteen anguishing years passed before they were exonerated.

• • •

No better examples can be found in how the police investigate a crime—and in particular how police apply their views and prejudices to those they interview and investigate for a crime—than the manner in which the cases of the Crowe murder and the New York Central Park Five were handled.

These cases, among many others, illustrate why children should never be interrogated by police without the presence of a parent and without first consulting a lawyer. That's why I propose a new Miranda warning for children and a Children's Bill of Rights, which are included it in Appendix II of this book. I hope that this will bring attention to important changes needed in our legal system. If such improvements, even modest ones, do come about, I will be gratified.

—Donald E. McInnis
San Diego, California

PART ONE

Murder and Mind Games:
Stephanie and Michael

1

• SHE'S SO COLD •

The Crowe Family

Day One: Escondido, California
January 21, 1998
6:30 A.M.

Judith Kennedy stirred in her bed, awakened by an irritating buzz she couldn't identify.

Slowly, still not fully awake, she realized it was her granddaughter's alarm clock. It was time for Stephanie and the other two children to get up and start getting ready for school. Judith lay quietly for a few seconds, collecting her thoughts. *Come on, Stephanie, wake up! Turn off that gosh-darned alarm!*

Reluctantly, Grandma Judith Kennedy pushed back the covers and groped for her robe. She could see Shannon, still fast asleep, on the other bed. Stephanie's ten-year-old sister had not been disturbed by the alarm, and neither had anyone else. There were no signs of movement from any part of the house—the home of her daughter and son-in-law. Judith was sharing Shannon's room, as she always did when staying with the Crowes.

Still groggy, Judith made her way down the hallway. She was barely able to see. It was early and still not light outside. Twelve-year-old Stephanie's bedroom doorway was inset in a shallow alcove, so there was even less light there. She felt for Stephanie's partly open door, found it, then pushed it open further with her hand. Softly calling Stephanie's name, she moved into the room, striking something with her foot—something large and soft. She fumbled for the light switch and gasped.

On the floor lay Stephanie. She appeared to be covered with mud. *Mud!* Judith's mind madly screamed the instant assessment, while part of her knew that was absurd.

"Oh, my God!" she cried out in horror. "Cheryl! Steven! Come quick. It's Stephanie! She's covered in mud. Hurry, she's covered in mud!" Over and over she shouted the same thing, waking all the others.

All except Stephanie, who remained motionless on the floor.

Steve Crowe flew out of bed and raced down the hall. Reaching Stephanie's doorway, he collapsed to his knees. Still half asleep, he stared at his daughter in shock. His thoughts were a tsunami—he couldn't make any sense of what he was seeing: his daughter lying prone in a pool of brown, her sightless eyes wide and glassy.

Shuddering uncontrollably, he bent over her body and cradled her head. Her eyes were so vacant; her body stiff and cold. It wasn't mud that covered her body, but blood. He quickly scanned her body, unable to believe what he was seeing. Stephanie was covered in blood.

No! his mind screamed. Steve howled like a wounded animal. "No. No!" he cried out.

He couldn't stop his screams as tears poured down his face. "No. No. No!" His screams were agonizing.

The sound penetrated the very soul of his wife, Cheryl, who had climbed out of bed and made her way to the awful scene. Over Steven's shoulder, she took in the hideous view from the doorway.

Why was Stephanie all covered in brown stuff? Why was she just staring like that? Why was Steve screaming?

Cheryl melted to the floor and lifted her daughter's lifeless body into her arms. Cradling her fiercely, her mind pushed away all coherent thought. She was shaking so severely, she could barely form words.

"Stephanie, it's Mommy . . . Please talk to me, baby."

Gently, she stroked her daughter's face, which she could barely see through her wall of tears. "Mommy will make it all better," she whispered into the dead eyes of her daughter as she rocked back and forth.

I need to warm Stephanie up. That's all I need to do is make her warm again. Once she's was warm, she'll be fine, her tormented mind kept telling her.

Her wail was horrific. "*God, please help me get her warm again,*" she sobbed. She looked up at her mother through tear-drenched eyes.

"Oh, Mom, she's so cold!" Cheryl Crowe wailed, pulling Stephanie more tightly against her. Rocking back and forth, back and forth, she fiercely clutched her daughter to her chest. "We're warm now . . . we're warm now . . ." she babbled, her eyes filled with terror.

When the paramedics arrived, Cheryl Crowe was still clutching her daughter's cold body to her breast, drowning in desperation.

Her face a map of anguish, Cheryl refused to let go of Stephanie. The paramedics gently coaxed her until she finally relented. But they may as well have let this mother cling to her child's body. There was nothing to be done by any medic.

Stephanie had been dead for more than six hours.

So began that dreadful day for the Crowe family. And so began a terrible and protracted ordeal that started with the brutal murder of a beloved child and spiraled into a law enforcement and judicial nightmare, indescribable in its impact and its cruelty.

It was the soon-to-be infamous "Crowe Murder Case."

2

• PSYCHOPATHIC KILLER •

San Diego, California
February 13, 1998

The *San Diego Union Tribune* and the *North County Times* carried front-page stories of the Crowe murder case with explosive headlines. Everywhere I went, people were talking about the three evil boys who killed a twelve-year-old girl, but on February 13, 1998, I still didn't know much about the case, other than what I had read about or heard on TV or radio.

By all accounts, it seemed the police had done a great job, and the guilty kids—Stephanie's older brother, Michael Crowe, and two of his friends, Aaron Houser and Joshua Treadway—had been caught. But then I got a call from Ron Sealey, a retired deputy sheriff with whom I had a good relationship. He asked if I'd be willing to meet with one of the boys' parents to talk about legal representation, so I agreed, and met with Gregg and Susie Houser, the parents of Aaron. Adam, Aaron's older brother, also sat in the meeting.

While it's true that prospective clients scrutinize the attorney they are thinking of hiring, good attorneys also analyze each prospective new client. I was extremely cautious the day I met the Housers—skeptical, even. First off, there's nothing unusual about loving parents believing their son or daughter incapable of criminal behavior. No parent intentionally raises their child to

Michael Crowe, Joshua Treadway, and Aaron Houser
at their arraignment.

do bad things, and there's a natural tendency to be protective no matter what
the kids have done.

Gregg and Susie Houser were convinced their 15-year-old son had been
falsely accused and unjustly arrested and jailed.

But two of the boys had confessed.

Of the three boys accused in the Stephanie Crowe murder, only Aaron
had refused to confess.

Confessions lead to convictions, and though I told the Housers this, as
an attorney I also knew that not all confessions are valid. Only a crazy person
would confess to a crime when actually innocent, especially murder, so I was
intrigued but not optimistic. Two confessions had been extracted, both of
them implicating my prospective client. Not the best situation for building
a strong defense.

As a general rule, I am good at reading people. Susie Houser was easy to
read. Her anger and pain were intense, but she was sincere and open. Gregg
Houser, however, was not such an easy read, and he contained his anger. One

of the points made by Mrs. Houser that day played heavily on my decision to take the case. Aaron had never been in trouble, she told me. He was an excellent student, played in the school band, loved to read and was well liked, was even admired by his teachers. This was not enough to convince me of his innocence, but there was something about Susie Houser herself, something that told me she knew her son well. And she had an unwavering faith in him. Some parents don't know their kids as well as they think they do, of course, but it was apparent Susie was a hands-on parent, a good mom. There was this special kind of concern in Gregg's tone as well. This anxious couple had every reason to seek help.

They had been told to be in the district attorney's office for a meeting the next day. The evidence against their son would be presented to them at that time. They felt they should have an attorney present, and I readily agreed to go with them.

As we assembled at the Hall of Justice in San Diego, thirty miles south of Escondido, everyone seemed apprehensive. Gregg talked nervously, while Susie said very little.

We rode the elevator together up to the public reception area of the district attorney's office on the twelfth floor. After a few minutes, Deputy District Attorney Gary Hoover, the fair-haired, hard-charging favorite prosecutor of District Attorney Paul Pfingst, greeted us. He seated us in a conference room, where Detective Claytor was present. The detective did not seem at ease. He scowled often.

Hoover told us he was saddened by Stephanie Crowe's murder and the involvement of Aaron. What quickly became evident, however, was that the purpose of the meeting was to convince the Housers their son was guilty. They were actually told the police and the DA himself had very grave concerns for their safety—Aaron could be a threat to his own parents.

Susie Houser, horrified, asked why they felt that, and Hoover, with a politician's guile, said, "I can't explain it all right now, but that's why we brought you down here."

"But you said you wanted us here to explain why our son was arrested, what the evidence is against him," Gregg Houser pleaded.

Hoover responded thoughtfully: "Yes, we will explain all the evidence against your son, and why we know he was involved in the murder of Stephanie Crowe." As would later come out, Hoover knew that, beyond the confessions by Michael and Joshua, there was not a shred of hard evidence, not even a murder weapon. But it didn't seem to matter. Hoover was not about to get too far into the subject of evidence, at least not then. He said, "Before we do that, however, District Attorney Paul Pfingst would like to meet with you."

The five of us—Hoover, Claytor, Susie, Gregg, and I—walked out of the conference room and rode the elevator up to the thirteenth floor of the Hall of Justice, where the district attorney's private suite was located. We entered through two large doors, and Hoover told the receptionist we were there to see Paul Pfingst. The DA's office was impressive and overbearing, a symbol of bureaucratic stature and power. Paul Pfingst walked out and greeted the Housers warmly, but he seemed surprised to see me. I had played a key role in Judge Larry Sterling's run against this man for the DA position. Pfingst's reaction was obvious when I told him I was representing the Housers. Nevertheless, he invited us into his office.

"The reason we asked you up here is because we're concerned for your safety," Pfingst said, "and we are fearful of you being harmed."

"Harmed by who?" Gregg asked, disbelief in his voice.

"Well, we hate to tell you this, but your son was involved in the Stephanie Crowe murder, and he might harm you."

This was too much for Susie Houser. "There's nothing wrong with my son," she stated flatly. "So why would you say that?"

Pfingst didn't flinch. "We believe Aaron has mental problems and could be a threat to you," he said.

"I know my son," Gregg Houser said, his temper rising. "He is not a danger to us or to anyone else." Susie Houser was fighting back tears.

"Tell us what brought you to the conclusion Aaron is a psychopathic killer," I said. "That is what you're saying, isn't it, that Aaron is a psychopathic killer?"

"What we really want is your cooperation," Pfingst said.

"My clients aren't going to cooperate until you tell them what led you to your conclusions."

Gregg Houser seemed to have had enough. Anger flared in his eyes as he said, "Look, Aaron's a good kid, and he had nothing to do with this murder. So tell us what you know."

It was a simple enough request, one any parent would make. But there was no response. In fact, the meeting was over. Paul Pfingst stood up and said, "I think it best if we don't get into the evidence at this time. Thank you for coming."

This confusing and unhelpful experience set the wheels in my mind turning, and I wondered just how much they really had on Aaron. But it didn't matter; Hoover escorted us out of the DA's private suite and we returned to the twelfth floor, to the conference room where we had been before. By then I was becoming irritated by the treatment of my clients. I told Hoover we were not going to tell them anything until they revealed what evidence they had.

"I can't do that," Hoover said.

"But that's why you asked us here," Gregg Houser snapped. He was right. The false pretense was now evident. There was a long silence, and I repeated the request.

Hoover's answer remained the same: "We're not going to do that at this time," he said, his tone irritating, almost smarmy.

"Then I guess there's nothing more to talk about," I said, and that ended the meeting.

As we left, I was deep in thought. Both Hoover and Pfingst were playing games, and as soon as we were in the elevator I shared my convictions with the Housers. "They brought you down here to pump you for information, and to turn you against your son. Otherwise, they would have told us what evidence they have. They are trying to scare you by saying he's a killer, a psychopath."

The Housers were concerned, obviously, and wanted to know what the point of it all was. I explained that what the prosecutors most wanted was for Gregg and Susie to go to Aaron and tell him to cooperate, to confess. "But you know what?" I said. "They don't have a damned thing on him, or they wouldn't have pulled this trick."

Back at my office we talked more about the events that had led to Aaron's arrest, and I instructed the Housers to tell Aaron not to say a word to anyone until I had talked to him. I determined I'd meet the boy for the first time that very afternoon.

• • •

At San Diego Juvenile Hall there are several rooms surrounded by glass, cubicle conference rooms where lawyers meet with their clients at simple metal tables. While I strongly suspected the police had no concrete evidence on Aaron Houser, I was a long way from assuming his guilt or innocence. For an attorney, guilt or innocence is, or should be, irrelevant. What I cared most about, always do, was that my client would get full representation and the due process of the law, and a vigorous defense. But the guilt/innocence question nagged at me. How could a child kill the sister he played with on a daily basis?

Aaron looked weary when I introduced myself, which was not a surprise, and when we sat down to talk he looked at me with suspicion. Adult authority and the way he'd been treated had soured him. Guilty or innocent, his world had crumbled, so he didn't trust me. He said Juvenile Hall was difficult to deal with, and he missed his parents and his brother. He wanted to know when he could go home.

I didn't hedge. I told him it was probably going to be a long time; he was going to have to deal with his confinement. I told him not to make friends in "juvy" but to get along with everyone, if he could. I was especially firm in my warning not to talk to anyone about his case. I was well aware that the police were apt to set him up with someone whose only purpose would be to get him to confess, or say something incriminating. He said he was isolated, in solitary confinement. Before I left Juvenile Hall that afternoon I asked that Aaron remain isolated and was assured that they would do that.

Aaron told me he was innocent. *Well, so what's new?* Prisoners are known for denying guilt. Yet, there was something about this kid. First, I was very impressed with the way he seemed to think before he spoke—unusual for a child his age. His vocabulary was equally impressive. *A smart kid,* I thought. *Just how smart was he? Was there a killer hiding behind that intellectual front?* The truth was I didn't know enough to make a real judgment. I had a lot of work ahead of me.

• • •

The next day was a Saturday and I went to my boat. There is something profound in the freedom I feel out on the water, and it helps me clear my head. I had plenty to dwell on that day: a murder case in which confessions had already been made; a case that was going to be costly, far beyond the means of my clients' parents. *Why had I done it?*

I began thinking out my strategy and about the defense team. I needed an extremely sharp and experienced motions specialist; that would be Liz Wise. Pat DeLucia was also chosen. He's a private detective highly respected for his expertise. My partner, Greg Garrison, and our associate, Jay d'Amembrocio, would round out the team. On Monday, I called everyone together and began the meeting with an overview. "Our client is Aaron Houser," I said. "He's one of the teenagers accused in the Crowe murder." I waited for a response.

"Is he guilty?" Jay asked.

"He tells me he's innocent, but I don't know at this point. I've taken the case and will defend him regardless. Gut level? Maybe. He's a very, very bright kid. Talking to him was unlike talking to an ordinary teenager with cars and girls on his mind. He impressed me because he thinks before he talks, but he comes across very calculating, maybe even sullen. We'll have to work on that if he's ever to take the stand. The first thing we need to know is how much evidence the DA has. They claim they have evidence, but they refused to share it. That's where you come in, Liz. You'll handle the discovery motions to assure that we get to see all the evidence. We need to do our own DNA testing, hire an investigator and pull in forensic experts, blood spatter experts, the works. The parents can't afford any of this, so we need funding from the county."

I turned my attention to Pat. "I want you to investigate the murder scene and do background checks. I want to know if there are skeletons in the closet. Has the victim's dad or uncle had mental problems, been arrested for anything? You know the process. I also want a background on all potential witnesses. And I want to know all we can about the other two boys involved. Get all you can from their peers, teachers, old friends, new friends. Cover it all."

At our second meeting, days later, we all had had an opportunity to review the case in more detail. We had even seen videotapes of the interrogations and the two confessions. We agreed that though the evidence was flimsy, or worse, the confessions presented us with a challenge. "But I watched the interrogations last night on video," Pat said. "It was atrocious. I hate to think what I'd do if the cops treated my kids like that."

"Nevertheless, confessions are confessions," Greg said with a shake of his head. "The court is not going to disregard someone saying they did it. What do you think, Jay?"

"If someone confesses to murder, it is usually assumed he's guilty. I mean, who would confess to a murder he didn't do . . . except for some nut case, but—"

I interrupted him: "But false confessions are made every day. I'm not saying these confessions are false. I don't really know, yet, but I am saying that the means used to obtain them can be one possible defense for us to take. The tactics used were just horrific. And I believe the police crossed the line of legal methods. I'll get into the details later."

"What about the polygraph tests?" Jay asked.

"They used a CVSA, and an arrogant cop from Oceanside administered it," I said. "I say arrogant because he's supposed to give the test without bias. Hell, he ran a third of the interrogation. He was out to gain confessions and he succeeded, twice. Our boy, Aaron, however, did not confess. What a vocabulary this kid has," I added.

"If it turns out these boys didn't do it, who did?" Liz asked. "If what I've read is true, the house was locked up and there were no signs of forced entry, so that all but eliminates a random homicide. It almost certainly means someone in the house did it, or was complicit."

I nodded in agreement. "That's why the police are so certain the boys are guilty. And the folks over at the DA's office are sure they have a solid case. This brings me to a vital point: The detention hearing is coming up and at this time I'm going to ask that Aaron be allowed to go home."

"If he's guilty, wouldn't that be letting a killer loose on the street?"

"Our job is to do all we can for our client," I answered. "Besides, it would allow us to test the DA's evidence early. The DA will have to reveal why Aaron is involved and should not be released. Right now, I don't see anything that implicates Aaron but Joshua's confession. So why not push? See if they have more."

"Who's representing the other two boys?" Greg asked.

"Paul Blake is Michael Crowe's attorney. I don't know much about him. Mary Ellen Attridge has Joshua, and he's the key here. The DA is already trying to make deals to have him go state's evidence. If that happens, those boys will go to adult court and their lives will be ruined."

Greg chuckled. He knew Mary Ellen Attridge's reputation.

"Look," I said to the others, "what Greg is enjoying is that I'm going to have to be working with Attridge, and he knows that could be difficult."

"She's not a good attorney?" Jay asked.

"She's a great attorney. But she can be a handful; overly tenacious and a pain in the . . ."

"So how do you plan to make it work?" Greg asked in a serious tone.

"We need her if we're going to win this case, so I'll do whatever it takes." The very thought of working with Mary Ellen Attridge was frustrating. But we really did need her; it was her client who seemed willing to save his own neck at the expense of the other two. If Attridge decided not to fight the confession, have Joshua admit his guilt, my client wouldn't have a chance, and neither would Michael Crowe. However, Mary Ellen Attridge wouldn't just roll over. I had to make her believe she had a fighting chance. Otherwise, I'd have no choice but to consider pleading out Aaron.

I spent a lot of time going over the confessions and the other information coughed up by the police, and I saw Aaron as often as I could. By the time I had read all the transcripts of Michael's confession and seen all the videotapes of the three boys' "interviews," I was livid, angry at a system that would allow such injustice.

But there was something even more upsetting, something I would learn later, at Aaron's juvenile custody hearing. During Michael Crowe's interrogation, and just before he broke, officer Sweeney took him out of the room and away from the camera. He told Michael his parents believed he killed Stephanie and they never wanted to see him again. The thought of this was nothing short of sickening. No wonder Michael accepted the officer's fanciful ploy of there being two Michaels—one good, the other an evil Michael.

Aaron and I met several times a week, first getting to know each other and then going over the evidence bit by bit, line by line. As we did, I grew closer to Aaron. Sure, I was experienced enough to know that a clever guilty person, young or old, would try to suck me in. After all, I was his only hope of going home. But I didn't believe this about Aaron. Soon, I became convinced of his innocence, his and that of the other two boys. I was not alone.

Yet, if that were true, that they were innocent, why would Michael Crowe and Joshua Treadway confess to a crime they didn't commit? Their attorneys, Paul Blake and Mary Ellen Attridge, were asking the same question.

3

• HE DIDN'T CRY •

Day One: Escondido, California
January 21, 1998
8:30 A.M.

For Ralph Claytor, the morning started much like any other, but that would soon change. As a police detective in a relatively quiet town, he seldom began his day rushing to the scene of a homicide. A father himself, and a cop with extensive experience working juvenile cases, Claytor was deeply disturbed by the call urging him to hurry to the Crowe house where a child lay dead. He was the one chosen to lead the investigation and the subsequent interrogation of suspects, but he could not have guessed that this case would haunt him forever.

And it would be his last homicide investigation.

The Crowe home was located in one of the most isolated areas of town. A modest four-bedroom single-level ranch, it was nestled on a winding hillside above Valley Center Road. It wrapped around a pool overlooking an eighteen-acre avocado grove on the northeast edge of town. The grove had been mostly ravaged by wildfire several years earlier.

Claytor wound his way up the hillside, through the eerily remote neighborhood, looking for the address. The Crowe property was surrounded by a hive of squad cars and crime-scene vehicles, an odd contrast in such a rural area. Emergency lights swept dully in the growing morning light as two uniformed cops approached his car.

The Crowe family home

"What do we got?" Claytor asked the uniforms. They led him inside, explaining what they knew.

As many times as he had seen it before, it could still be very jarring. The victim lay like a rag doll, blood-drenched and lifeless. It was an obscene contradiction to the playful bedroom glowing in the first rays of daylight.

He squatted for a cursory examination and then rose to his feet. "What about a weapon?" he asked. It was obviously a knife of some sort, but none had been found at the scene.

"Any sign of a break-in?" No. No such sign.

Claytor was read these meager facts from the notebook of the first officer on scene: 1) Body was discovered by victim's grandmother, a temporary guest; 2) Victim's mother Cheryl and victim's brother, fourteen-year-old Michael, reported hearing a vague thumping noise in the night, but neither had investigated; 3) Cheryl Crowe heard her bedroom door open once or twice in the night, and assumed it was the family cat.

Other police officers were checking the house and grounds, searching for clues of any kind. Metal detectors found a buried kitchen knife, but it was quickly eliminated as the murder weapon. Stephanie had been stabbed multiple times about the head, neck, and shoulders. The wounds were deep, too deep to have been inflicted by a mere kitchen knife.

"Keep looking," Claytor ordered.

Claytor himself joined the search and quickly noticed the cobwebs and thick dust that eliminated the front door of the house as the entry point. Similar evidence excluded the windows on the side of the house, even though one window screen was bent back, out of place. Old damage, apparently. An officer informed Claytor that the sliding doors off the master bedroom were open a few inches, and the detective investigated. These doors were poorly maintained and made an awful racket as he moved them, and so did the vertical blinds inside. Since this doorway was no more than a foot from the head of Steve and Cheryl's bed, Claytor concluded that entry there would have made enough noise to awaken Stephanie's parents. As it turned out, Steve Crowe had thrown it open in faint hope of spotting someone, he hoped the killer, on the grassy slopes behind his home.

So this all led Claytor to conclude one thing, something relatively common. This crime had to have been committed by someone already inside the house.

FBI training manuals make this point very strongly: the first suspect in the killing of a young girl is always the father or stepfather, then the mother, then anyone else living in the house. The last option, the least likely, is a stranger.

Claytor asked if Stephanie had been molested, and the forensic specialist declared that it was unlikely, but they would not know for certain until they got the medical examiner's final report.

Claytor eyed Steven Crowe suspiciously, noting his obvious grief. *Was it real, or fake?* It was his job to be suspicious of everyone. He ordered all the family members be kept in the living room, out of the way of the investigating team. They were cautioned not to talk among themselves, and an officer was assigned to ensure their silence. The cops didn't want them influencing each other's stories. Four of the family members all huddled together on the couch, comforting each other.

But Michael remained apart.

For all four of those huddled on the couch, it appeared this was their greatest nightmare. But Michael sat alone on the floor playing a video game. It didn't go unnoticed by the officer watching them. Michael sat in eerie silence, the glow of the TV bathing his face as his thumbs furiously thumped across the video game controller. His stone-cold lack of emotion gave the officer a queasy feeling in the pit of his stomach.

As a defense attorney, I know that any competent forensic psychologist would consider this "self-soothing" behavior, a desperately needed distraction in the face of abject horror.

But to the officer watching the family, Michael's demeanor desperately screamed *GUILT.*

The other family members listened closely as officers conducted their thorough search and performed their many tests. Doors were opened and closed repeatedly. Police technicians dusted for fingerprints and photographed everything. Other techs, wearing orange clothing and protective eyewear, sprayed illuminating chemicals upon which they shone fluorescent lights. And the cops all talked among themselves, in hushed tones, mostly sounding unfriendly and uncaring to the five tormented sufferers.

Detective Claytor finally came to question them. They had already answered many questions, but these would be repeated, and many new ones would arise. The five bereaved were also five suspects in the eyes of Claytor, with Steven as the prime.

Michael revealed that he had gone to the kitchen sometime in the night to get a glass of milk and a Tylenol, having woken up with a headache. When asked what time, he said it was about 4:30 A.M. This raised Claytor's suspicions immediately.

How could he walk past Stephanie's doorway and not see her body? He stared hard at this fourteen-year-old. Something didn't add up here. *Could he be the guilty party?*

Before long, the confused, frightened, and deeply grieving family members were told to go to police headquarters for further questioning. Steven didn't understand, and he felt terrible, leaving the home with Stephanie's body still lying there. But although he wanted to refuse, he finally complied and they were led to waiting squad cars.

Cheryl Crowe was inconsolable as they pulled away from their home, where Stephanie still lay in her doorway.

• • •

Steve Crowe broke into wretched tears again when they were at the police station.

"I couldn't help her," he sobbed over and over. The police officer in the room watched Steve carefully.

Were his tears fake?

Detective Barry Sweeney entered the room with a notepad in his hand. He spoke softly, delicately, assuring Steve he was not under arrest and that he was free to go at any time. Had Steve insisted on going, however, he would have soon discovered that this was not true. After all, he was first on the suspect list, and he wouldn't be going anywhere until the case was sorted out.

Sweeney handed Steve a sketch of the house and asked him to identify the bedrooms. Steve wrote the names of family members on each room in the drawing, starting with the room he shared with his wife, Cheryl. The detective wanted to know if Steve heard any voices through the night, or if he might have gotten up for any reason. Steve said no on both counts.

For forty-five minutes, the officer questioned Steve. He then asked the anguished father to take off his clothing, and his nude body was inspected. He was checked closely for bruises and scratch marks. The officer stared intently at his penis, as if looking for evidence that Steve raped his daughter.

He ordered Steve to extend his arms and hands so the officer could examine his fingers. He turned his hands over and scraped underneath the fingernails, carefully collecting the scrapings into an evidence bag. Steve's nude body was then photographed, especially his hands and anything that looked remotely like a bruise or contusion.

"Get dressed." The officer's curt tone, coming after what he'd been through, enraged Steve, but he held his tongue. A pair of sweats was thrown onto a chair for him to wear, as all of his clothing was placed in large plastic evidence bags.

Each member of the family was questioned and examined in the same manner that morning. Cheryl felt numb as she stood stark naked, holding a card in front of her with her name and identification number on it. The photographer snapped a picture and then began taking close-ups of her body, especially her hands. When she questioned why, the female officer answered, "There could be scratches or bruises, marks left by the struggling victim."

These photographs would be studied thoroughly. Cheryl's stomach tightened in revulsion, but what could she do? Anyway, she didn't really care much about what was happening to her; it was Stephanie who consumed her thoughts. The horrid vision of what she had seen that morning kept flashing vividly through her mind as the police photographer's camera clicked.

Grandmother Judith Kennedy went through the same ordeal, but she demanded the right to leave her bra on. She wore a prosthetic bra because she'd had radical surgery for breast cancer. The children, Shannon and Michael, were allowed to keep their underwear on, but they too were inspected and photographed extensively.

At 5:30 in the afternoon of this first day, Michael Crowe asked if he could make a phone call. He was granted permission and he called his friend, Joshua. He explained to Josh that he was at the police station, and he began to sob, explaining that someone had sneaked into their house during the night and killed his sister. He had seen her body on the floor, he said. Nearby, an officer listened to every word. The name Joshua was written down.

About this time, word began to spread throughout the community: Stephanie Crowe had been murdered.

Soon, the Reverend Earl Guy arrived at the police station. The Escondido Methodist Church was the family's place of worship, and Stephanie had been most actively involved. Earl Guy, an unassuming man, was devoted to his congregation and was shocked and deeply hurt by the news. He had grown to like and respect Stephanie very much, as did so many others. As soon as Cheryl saw the minister she broke into tears, and he tried to console her.

All the family wanted to do was go home and deal with their grief, get away from the frigid, hostile atmosphere of the police station, and somehow try to pick up the pieces of their lives. But they were all told by Claytor that they could not go home, not yet. The adults were to be taken to a motel and the children to a county facility.

Steve finally exploded. He gathered his family and told them they were leaving. They started for the door, but the police stopped them. No one was going anywhere.

Stephanie's parents and grandmother were taken to a motel. They were cautioned not to venture far, and they were not to go near their home. For the first time they realized they were under a kind of incarceration; they were free . . . just as long as they did what the police told them to. Who knew what to think anymore? They were fatigued, emotionally and physically drained, overcome with a sick feeling.

• • •

Shannon and Michael were taken to the Polinsky Childrens Center in San Diego, a place where abused kids were housed, and told they were to be separated for the night. They began pleading to the stern-looking woman standing before them, begging for her to let them stay together. *Why can't we be with our parents?* The Children's Center frowns on a boy and girl sleeping in the same room, but these kids were brother and sister, and they were in the midst of a hellish nightmare. Looking at the two children, clutching each other and in tears, the woman relented and agreed they could spend the night together in the same room.

The police had spent a tedious day at the Crowe house. Stephanie's body was not removed for nine hours, the investigators and forensic specialists going over every minute detail, seeking clues, looking for anything that would lead to a suspect. No evidence had been found that told them who killed Stephanie. But someone, who had already been inside the house, entered Stephanie's room and savagely plunged a knife into her numerous times. Whoever it was must have been in a rage, yet he (or she) had moved quietly through the shadows of the house with knife in hand. And Stephanie had been singled out. This was no killing spree. She was a twelve-year-old someone wanted dead.

The question remained, why?

• • •

At police headquarters, Detective Claytor was busy trying to fit the pieces together. His biggest problem was that a murder weapon had not been found. If the knife had been hidden in the house they would have found it, but the house had been swept clean. Could the weapon have been buried, or thrown away?

Claytor, Sweeney, and several other officers sat in a conference room, tossing around ideas, brainstorming, until one officer said, "Michael, the fourteen-year-old, he didn't cry like the rest."

"What do you mean?" Claytor asked.

"He seemed unemotional and aloof." He explained that while the rest of the family sat together, Michael was off in a corner of the room playing with a video game. Michael's parents would later deny this, but it was enough for Claytor to turn his suspicion toward the boy. Claytor was well aware of the statistics on sibling abuse across the country. Most such abuse is kept hidden, as are other family skeletons, but there are many studies of such abuse, including sibling rape. The U.S. Justice Department has reported that of the roughly 20,000 murders in this country each year, 1.5% are committed by a sibling against another. This amounts to 300 murders by one child against another in the same family every year in the U.S. With this in mind, the Crowe case started to look as if it was going to be cut and dried. If the old man didn't do it, maybe Michael did.

However, Detective Sweeney offered the opinion that Steve Crowe had been faking his sorrow during the interrogation. The options were numerous and baffling. Worse yet, no weapon or physical evidence pointed to a particular person. The officers talked until late that night. More reports came in, and other officers joined the discussion.

Judith Kennedy was very security conscious, one officer said, and she was the one who would always check the doors to make sure they were locked at night. But two doors may have been left unlocked all night. During the questioning of the family it was revealed that Cheryl's brother, Mike Kennedy, had visited the family around dinnertime on the night of the murder. As he left, Judith asked him to lock the door behind him, but no one checked it. Mike was asked if he had a key to the Crowe house, but he did not. Claytor mused about Mike Kennedy.

Obviously none of the family members had been ruled out. But what about Michael Crowe? At 5'2" and weighing 100 pounds, could he have plunged a knife deep enough, strongly enough into Stephanie? All the officers concurred: yes, even a small child could have killed in this way. So Claytor was baffled.

Michael's story of going to the kitchen during the night and somehow not seeing his sister's body in the doorway bothered him. There was another thing: Stephanie had been stabbed in bed. Had she been carried to the doorway, or had she managed to drag herself there, trying to get help? Why hadn't anyone in the house heard anything? All these questions would eventually be answered, Claytor was convinced, and he was determined to put this case to bed early.

On January 22, the day after the murder, the investigation at the house continued. Stephanie's parents and grandmother made arrangements to stay at a relative's house until they were allowed to return home. They shared their experiences at the police station with friends and relatives, telling how they had been taken into separate rooms and questioned over and over about the night before. They were made to undress and felt so terrible as the police looked them over like objects. And they cried again, all of them. Their surviving children were still being held in some awful place, and Stephanie was gone forever. Steven didn't even know when he could bury his lovely daughter.

Claytor attended the autopsy and learned that Stephanie had not been sexually assaulted. But the cuts into her body had been forceful and deep. Nine times she was struck, to the head, neck, and upper shoulder area. Cuts

Michael Crowe

on her hands and on either side of her head seemed to indicate she resisted or moved back and forth as the attacker struck. The girl's clavicle bone and a vertebra in the neck had been cut into, so, like a ballistic marker on a bullet, these cut marks could identify a knife. Once he had the murder weapon, Claytor felt certain he'd have the murderer, but the knife still had not been found. Many knives were found at the Crowe home— twenty-three in the kitchen and sixteen in the garage—but none were the murder weapon.

Finding the weapon remained a top priority.

There were other frustrations. It was beginning to seem as if this murder had been carefully planned.

In cases of extreme rage and the resulting crime, there are always mistakes made by the killer, such as leaving fingerprints or failing to get rid of the evidence. People who act on a sudden impulse tend not to be meticulous in covering their tracks. Most killers tend to panic after committing the crime when it has been one of unleashed passion. But in this case, there had been nothing of significance found at the Crowe house.

So where the hell were the clues?

Inside the house, the search for evidence entered a new phase, one that involved cutting holes in the walls, uprooting toilets, and looking into drains; every possible nook and cranny was explored. Stephanie's room was completely dismantled; wall boards were torn off, and the bed, all her clothing, the drapes, and the carpet were removed. Still nothing. No bloody clothes, no weapon, not a thing that would lead the police to the killer. Claytor made a number of phone calls to the coroner and the lab technicians who had examined the house. Fluorescein, a liquid spray recently used in a new way by a San Diego Police Department forensic technician, had been sprayed throughout the house. Claytor hoped it would illuminate handprints in blood, but nothing of significance appeared. The coroner said he had nothing further to add.

More and more, Claytor felt he should follow his gut feeling that Michael was involved. Around noon of day two, Claytor acted.

He told Sweeney to bring Michael in from the Polinsky Childrens Center.

Institutionalized with strangers, Stephanie's brother and sister were wondering where their parents had gone and what they were doing. The siblings talked, cried together, and held each other . . . but the awful reality did not go away. They had no idea what had happened to Stephanie, but they had seen her dead body, and had seen their parents and grandmother totally devastated. This was all very upsetting for Shannon and Michael. Fear mixed with sorrow, and tears flowed as they waited in silent apprehension. The door opened and a woman beckoned Michael. There was someone there to see him. Shannon grabbed for Michael, but the woman told Shannon she would have to wait alone.

Shannon began to sob as she watched her brother leave the room.

• • •

Michael was greeted by detectives and taken back to police headquarters in Escondido. As they drove, the officers looked at the boy. *Could he? Did he?* In many ways the boy fit snugly into the perfect stereotype of a kid headed for serious trouble. For one thing, he was truly a bright youth with a high IQ. On all standardized tests he was in the ninetieth percentile, and anyone who talked with this 14-year-old recognized the vocabulary of someone much older. It was not only Michael's use of words, but it was also his practical way of thinking. He loved science because he found truth in it, he said. Oddly, someone with a good intellect is a more likely suspect than others, especially when it comes to a murder meticulously planned and carried out—like this one.

In all of us there is an irrational fear of an evil genius. But regardless how widespread the myth about our pride in individualism, anyone who doesn't quite fit the conventional mold is likely to become the focus of blatant mistrust. Michael often wore black clothing. He said it made him feel unique, different from other kids. He wasn't into sports, and by common standards he was pretty much a loner. He wasn't a Boy Scout and he didn't attend church very often. His teachers said he was so advanced he could jump into college early. However, in the current school year his performance and grades had gotten progressively worse. His lessons were simply not challenging enough. Michael complained about the absurdity of being made to copy down the questions for tests, instead of merely writing the answers. All these quirks and qualities played a part in building suspicion around Michael.

But there was something more than his personality traits being considered by the police. Michael wasn't like other kids his age. He had an insatiable appetite for violent video games; he was consumed by them, and the police saw this fixation as bizarre, perhaps even sinister.

When Michael came home from school each day he would usually go to his room and play video games such as *Tomb Raider* or *Final Fantasy VII*.

4

• INTERROGATION •

Day Two: Escondido, California
January 22, 1998
Noon

At the police station, Michael was greeted by Detective Mark Wrisley, who had questioned Michael the day before. Wrisley repeated the *Miranda* rights statement, making sure Michael understood he had the right to remain silent and that anything he said could be used against him in a court of law. Michael said he did understand and agreed to answer the detective's questions anyway, without an attorney present.

Wrisley began the questioning in a friendly manner. He wanted to know if Michael slept okay the night before, and if he'd eaten breakfast.

And so the tone for the questioning was set: Wrisley was there only to gather information. Mostly, Michael was asked to go over what had happened the night before Stephanie's death. He went over the same questions each family member had answered the day before. Michael gave the same answers.

Yes, he thought all the doors of the house had been locked, but he remembered that, after going to bed, he'd heard a knock at one of the doors.

This piqued Wrisley's attention. Was he hearing the truth, or was Michael setting him up, inducing him to think there was a "thief in the night"?

The detective wanted to know if it was a loud knock, or more of a rap.

"How long did the pounding go on?" he asked. Michael was not sure. He said he was half asleep.

"Is that unusual? The knocking, I mean," Wrisley asked.

"Yes. Not many people come by at that time of night."

"You didn't feel compelled to get up and go check it out?"

"I was pretty sure it wasn't any of my friends or anything I needed to be concerned about," Michael said and shrugged.

They talked a little longer about the knocking, and Wrisley wanted Michael to estimate the time.

Michael said he was pretty sure it was sometime before midnight.

Wrisley nodded, but the wheels were turning in his head . . . the time of all these events would be crucial to building their case. He was well aware that the county's chief medical examiner had estimated the time of death as no later than 12:30 A.M., but it could have been as early as 9:00 p.m., depending on the time Stephanie had eaten her salad—her last meal.

Suddenly, Wrisley jumped to another time: 4:30 in the morning, when Michael said he'd awakened with a terrible headache and walked to the kitchen for a Tylenol and a glass of milk. He had turned on his TV set, he told them, so he could see to make his way out of the room.

"I seem to remember your TV has a clock," the detective said.

"Yes."

"Did you turn it on to watch, or what?"

"I turned it on so I could see."

"Kind of like a night light?"

"Yes."

"When you got up, was your door open, or closed?"

"When I went back to sleep?"

"No, when you woke up and went to the kitchen."

"I think I left it open."

"You have to go into the hallway to get to the kitchen, right?"

"Yes."

"How could you see where you were going?"

"I think the light by the front door was on, by the double doors."

"On the outside or inside?"

"The inside."

"How about the hallway light? Was it on or off?"

"I'm pretty sure it was off."

"Your room is right across from Stephanie's room—was her door open or closed?"

"Closed."

"You saw nothing unusual?"

"No."

"And did you go to the kitchen?"

"Yes. I filled a glass with milk."

Michael said he returned to his room around 4:45 A.M., and Detective Wrisley perked up again.

Michael had gone to the kitchen at 4:30. That was an awful long time to down a glass of milk and take a Tylenol. He raised the question, and Michael said he'd had a little trouble opening up the Tylenol bottle. Wrisley returned to the subject of the house lights, fishing to find out how well lit the hall was.

He believed it was impossible for anyone to walk past Stephanie's bedroom door—twice—without seeing her body.

There was only one other discrepancy during this interview. Michael said his bedroom door was open when he awoke, and later had said he was in the habit of closing it at night. Detective Wrisley had not missed this, but he elected not to bring Michael's attention to it. He did not want Michael to start thinking about what he was saying, calculating his answers. He suspected the kid was lying through his teeth anyway.

Michael was asked what he did that morning, after being awakened by the screaming, and he said he had rushed out into the hall and found his mother holding Stephanie. He saw some blood, and had gone to the living room, not wanting to see more. He had never seen his parents so upset.

Wrisley told Michael that they—the police—had gathered a lot of evidence, and wondered what Michael thought should happen to the person who killed his sister.

"They don't deserve to live," Michael said.

"Why?"

"Of all the people I know, Stephanie was the best. She was kind, and she cared more for other people than for herself. If anyone had to die in this world, it definitely wasn't her. It's horrible. If they knew her, and if they killed her on purpose, they don't deserve anything, no mercy at all."

The questioning lasted another twenty minutes. Michael was then returned to his room at the center, where Shannon had been anxiously waiting for his return. She wanted to know when they could go home. Michael didn't know, but under the circumstances, things had gone reasonably well, he told his sister. The police officer seemed nice enough; he was just trying to find out who did this terrible thing to Stephanie.

Little did Michael know what would be coming his way in the days that followed.

• • •

On the second day, the investigation continued at the Crowe house, and the frustration of the police intensified. No physical evidence had yet been found pointing to anyone as the killer. Not even the hair fibers under Stephanie's fingernails were identified, except that some of the fibers were animal hair. It was assumed these were picked up when the girl crawled from her bed toward her bedroom door. So it was back to square one. The conclusion was that whoever murdered Stephanie had a mind for detail and was a calculating person who knew how to put a strategy together and follow it, all the way down to covering their tracks.

The investigation team kept coming back to Michael, the expert at games which demanded fast thinking, lots of planning, and strategic moves. He was in the house, and there had been no sign of forced entry. And he was up at 4:30 in the morning, claiming he didn't see his sister's body in her bedroom doorway. None of the officers believed his story. He had not shown adequate sorrow the morning the body was discovered.

We don't have evidence, but we have Michael, Claytor thought.

• • •

Late in the afternoon of the following day, January 23, Michael Crowe was brought back into the interview room at the police station. This time the police were prepared; a consulting psychologist had been brought in to help guide the interrogation. Michael was told to sit on a plastic chair in a windowless interrogation room with bare white walls and a hidden video camera.

He sat alone, fidgeting, wiping tears from his eyes and sometimes holding his head in his hands. He didn't look as clear-minded as he had the day before. He looked tired, worn, and frightened. He burst into loud sobbing but then composed himself, seeming to think for a while. Then he'd cry again.

The hidden video camera recorded all this as Claytor, Wrisley and Lawrence N. Blum, PhD, a clinical psychologist from Orange County, watched. Finally, Wrisley entered, taking a seat a few feet away from Michael. He seemed friendly, greeting Michael in a sympathetic way; he wanted to know how the boy was feeling. Wrisley asked if Michael had breakfast and so on, and then he read the boy his rights again and wanted to be sure they were understood. Michael said he understood that he could have an attorney present and that he had the right to remain silent.

He also understood that he was a suspect . . . yet he waived his rights anyway.

Wrisley began by asking Michael again about his favorite video games. He wanted to know how they were played. For a moment Michael relaxed. He seemed relieved to have his mind on something other than the police, the murder, and his sister Shannon, alone at the center in Kearny Mesa. Wrisley listened intently as Michael explained how video games were played; the maneuvering, the goals, the obstacles. Wrisley wanted to know how well Michael played these games.

A tiny spark of pride shone in Michael's eyes. "I win a lot," he declared. But a moment later, something else flashed through Michael's mind and he started crying again.

Wrisley told Michael to take a few deep breaths and relax. Michael did his best to follow the instruction. Then Wrisley changed the topic. What was Michael's favorite subject in school? He liked math, he said. What were his major interests? Science, he replied. Did he like to read? Yes. What books? He liked Tolkien's *Lord of the Rings*. He had read the *Prophecies of Nostradamus*, too, and believed some of the ancient predictions had come to pass. Nostradamus is an intellectual challenge for readers of any age, but Michael apparently understood the material. He talked for a moment or two, then he broke into tears again.

He allowed himself to bawl uncontrollably for a few seconds, and then he managed to compose himself. He looked up in his despair, tears running down his face, as Wrisley eyed him. Michael's voice was cracking but audible. He asked why they (the police) thought he killed his sister.

At precisely that moment, the telephone in the room rang. Wrisley answered it and spoke briefly. He explained that he must leave the room and Michael watched him exit, his question unanswered.

So Michael was alone again.

Wrisley went to the adjacent video room to observe him with the others.

"This is it," Claytor said. Dr. Blum agreed, and the three men talked about how they would proceed.

Michael's mind was racing a mile a minute as he sat alone with his thoughts. Maybe the reason the police thought he was guilty was because they had evidence, had discovered something he wasn't aware of.

Suddenly, Michael muttered, "Oh God, please don't let this happen to me."

The door opened and Michael looked up, drying his tears again. But this time it was Detective Claytor, not Wrisley. The detective did not attempt to explain the switch but got right down to business. There was a kind of good-cop/bad-cop game going on.

"You asked a question?" Claytor said, then dropped the hammer: "We have evidence," the detective said bluntly. Michael's response would determine how the rest of the interrogation would be played out.

Michael looked bewildered, worried. *Had they found something that might implicate me? Was that what the detective was saying? That's what it sounded like.*

"I didn't do it!" Michael's voice cracked in a weak-sounding denial, and tears flowed again.

The interrogation continued, and during the questioning, Michael mentioned a school chum he had once been close to: Aaron Houser. Aaron had called him once and asked if Michael had killed his sister yet. The detective asked why Aaron would ask such a question, and Michael said he didn't know. "Probably for a joke," he speculated.

Claytor was quite interested in this incident, but he didn't let his thoughts show. Aaron was a new name on the list. Was he a cohort? Even if he had not collaborated in the crime itself, maybe Michael had confided in Aaron. What reason could there be for this friend to ask Michael if he had killed his sister if Michael hadn't talked about it? Claytor asked if Michael would agree to take a truth verifying test. Michael said yes, he would. By now, Claytor had developed a strong gut feeling. His twenty-three years of experience told him Michael was guilty . . . smart, but guilty.

"I'll cooperate with you," Claytor told Michael, "but you also have to cooperate with me. It's the rules of the game."

There was a little more talk, but Michael came back to his original question. Why did they think he killed his sister? Claytor answered the question with another: "Why do you think the evidence leads me to believe it?"

"I don't know," Michael whimpered. "I didn't do it. The evidence shouldn't . . ." He cried again.

Claytor sat motionless, unmoved by the tears. After a while he spoke softly, even sympathetically. "What I'd like to do is . . ." He paused, then he said, "I'd like you to think about the situation we find ourselves in. Put yourself in my place as a Cloud," he said, referring to a *Final Fantasy VII* character in the computer video game popular with kids. "As a Cloud, I'd like you to answer some of these questions. What are you going to do in the face of this evidence? You tell me which direction you're going to take."

Michael looked confused, his eyes wide in fear. *The police have evidence. What is it?*

Claytor waited, stone faced, eyes boring into Michael. When Michael didn't respond, Claytor broke the silence with a declaration that was barely above a whisper: "We found her blood in your room, Michael."

Suddenly, it was as though the world stopped turning on its axis.

Michael collapsed back, his arms falling to his side.

Wait a minute. His mind raced. *If blood was found in my room, then someone had to leave it there. No one was in my room but me, right? So how could this be? There was evidence.*

This was a blow to Michael's confidence. He was no longer the smart kid, in control, and it was right here that his intelligence began working against him.

In ordinary circumstances, Michael was scientific, mathematical and very logical. He was not the type to simply blurt out, "I didn't put blood there." Instead, he was the poised type who could quickly analyze all implications. He was a fourteen-year-old kid, but one much more together than most adults. Here, though, he was facing a situation he couldn't handle—one far out of his range of experience. Michael was no longer the bright kid with an answer for everything; the freshman student who resented doing homework because it was too easy and it bored him. Now he was confronted with a riddle he couldn't solve. How could he explain blood in his room when he was the only one who could have put it there? The six-foot detective and the five-foot two-inch boy sat across from one another—on opposite ends of the world. Neither spoke.

Wrisley suddenly returned to the room and broke the locked stare between the boy and the detective.

Wrisley sat down, took a few moments to contemplate Michael, and finally said, "You know what I hear when you tell me all this? I hear almost like there are two Michaels. On the one hand, there's the Michael I'm going to say is very compassionate toward his sister, who would defend her, stand up for her, if he had to. He would go out of his way for her. This Michael would allow Stephanie to have her way . . . even at the expense of his own wishes and desires. I mean, Michael, you thought it was alright if she would do whatever it was she wanted to do in her own way. You would go along with that, right?"

"Yes." Michael's voice croaked.

"You would talk to her, help her with homework, those kinds of things?"

"Yeah, I would." Michael's tone reflected relief. This cop was saying good things about him.

"Okay. But there seems to be a real contrast with the Michael who has to encounter this opponent . . . in which he has to take all these different things and defeat this person, you know, with weapons or with swords or whatever it is. You know, you have to make a decision what to use. Does that sound right? I mean, can there be two Michaels? The one Michael who deals with his sister one way, and another Michael who lives in the game world and has to . . ."

"I don't know." Michael wilted, confused by this new line of questioning.

What the detective was suggesting, of course, was that Michael had multiple personalities. He was saying Michael was a great kid, but he lost himself in the video games he played so intently. In doing so, he left the good Michael behind and went into a fantasy world, perhaps letting loose of reality altogether.

Claytor told Michael he thought there were two parts to him. He said, "I think there's a part of you that loved your sister, and did good for her, and you know that. I've heard some of the kids at school razzed her about her weight, right?"

Michael nodded.

"That's something you probably wouldn't tolerate. The good Michael wouldn't. Then there's another Michael that's not so good, and who unconsciously might come out as some sort of a defense mechanism. Would you agree with that?"

"I guess. I don't know."

Michael was now in a deep thought, totally lost in the idea he could have done something without knowing it.

Claytor continued: "You know what? I firmly believe that once we understand, and once everyone else understands about this part of Michael, who isn't quite so good . . ."

"If this is true," Michael said, agitated, "I don't even know he exists."

Claytor finished his thought, " . . . then not only are we going to understand, but people, once they understand, and once they see . . . it's not going to be quite as bad."

Michael was feeling condemned now, and through the tears welling up in his eyes he implored, "What's going to happen to me then, if that's all true? I didn't even know."

The interrogation continued for two grueling hours. Michael was exhausted, physically and emotionally. He had not rested much since the morning his sister's body was found; it had been one fatiguing episode after another. The investigating detectives could see he was weary. But, for a while, Michael stood his ground. Through his tears and despite his fears he kept repeating that he didn't harm his sister, and in the next breath he would say if he did do it, he really couldn't remember.

Michael had completely broken down mentally as well as physically. The long, isolated days had taken their toll. He could not see beyond the accusations to the psychological game being played by the police, and because he was wavering, Detective Claytor felt they were getting someplace at last.

Michael was ready to agree that he might have done it.

Claytor showed some concern and empathy for Michael, saying, "I'd really like to be able to treat the one part of Michael as a victim in this case." *Was Claytor indicating he would even treat me as if the crime was not really my fault?* Michael looked at Claytor and dried his tears.

Finally, Claytor asked again, "Would you have any problems with taking a truth verification exam?"

"No."

"Not at all?"

Michael gave him a sour look. "No," he repeated.

"You act like you're disgusted."

"I told you I wouldn't mind."

"What's the problem then, Mike?"

"I've spent two days away from my family. I couldn't see them . . . I only . . . I'm being treated like I killed my sister, but I didn't. It feels horrible. I'm being blamed. Everything I own is gone. I spend all day in clothes other than my own. Other than that . . . I mean, everything I have is gone. Everything. You won't even let me see my family. It's just horrible."

Claytor's aggressiveness diminished again, and he said, sympathetically, "Mike, you have to trust me on this. This is going to work out. What we are after, and what's important, is that we get to the truth of the matter. Like I told you, I'm not blaming anyone. We want to believe what you're telling us, okay?"

Michael shuddered a nod and said, "Okay."

"We're just trying to get to the truth, okay. Would you hang on for a minute?" Claytor rose and left the room. Soon he returned with another officer, one Michael had not seen before. Claytor introduced him as Chris McDonough, from the Oceanside Police Department.

McDonough was also friendly and had a nice smile. "Hi, Michael," he said.

"He's here in reference to the truth verification exam we discussed," Claytor said. "If you don't mind, I'll leave you two for a few minutes and you can get to know each other. Okay?"

"Okay," Michael said.

Detective McDonough was trained and experienced in the use of the Computer Voice Stress Analyzer, commonly known as CVSA, a machine supposedly able to detect lies. Stress analysis testing is purported to be akin to the polygraph test, but as a seasoned defense attorney, I know that, in reality, the science is highly questionable, and in some circles is maligned. Regrettably, it is used by hundreds of law enforcement agencies even though the results are not admissible in court. The critics say it's a coin toss as to whether this machine can detect lies; others defend the machine as accurate and reliable. Chris McDonough had a reputation for touting its technology.

As Claytor was leaving the room, McDonough turned to Michael and asked, "How're you doing, pal?"

"I don't know," Michael sighed, his head swimming.

As the detective set up the machine, there was a lot of small talk, seemingly friendly chatter. How was Michael doing in school? What kind of subjects did he like? McDonough also wanted to know what kind of video games Michael enjoyed.

"Right now, my favorite is *Final Fantasy VII*."

McDonough showed interest, asking about the object of the game. Michael explained that it was a role-playing game; he had to save the world from a bunch of evil people. He played as a character named Cloud.

"Cool. Sounds like a lot of fun," McDonough said. He asked Michael about his friends. Not in an intimidating way, but rather more conversationally. Michael said Joshua Treadway was his best friend. He mentioned another guy he liked, but didn't know his last name. Raoul was his first name. He also mentioned Aaron Houser again. In referring to Aaron, he said, "I was friends with the guy, but he's turning out to be a real jerk right now."

McDonough was curious, so Michael explained: "If he's around, like you're one on one with him, he's a pretty good guy. But if there's other people, he's not a nice guy."

"A two-timer?"

"Yeah, he'll pick someone to make fun of."

The detective wanted to know how Michael got along with his dad. Michael responded enthusiastically, "Great!"

"Okay. What does your dad do?"

"He paints cars for a living."

"Good. Okay. And you guys get along okay?"

"Great."

"What do you like to do together?"

"I just hang out in the garage with him, and watch him tinker around and stuff. We both have about the same sense of humor, so we like the same jokes. If he's going to pick up something, I'll sometimes go with him."

"Okay, how about your mom?"

"I love my mom. We don't get along all the time, of course, because she's . . ." He shrugged, at a loss.

McDonough interjected, "That's her job. You're fourteen!"

The conversation went on, and the detective kept to the subject of how Michael felt about his family. He loved them all, Michael said, enjoyed them all. His favorite thing about his mom was that she was fair. What he didn't like about her was when she grounded him. The subject was changed and Stephanie was not mentioned.

McDonough asked about school again: "Intellectually you are far advanced, Michael?"

"My tests say I'm somewhere like a freshman in college, or better."

"Okay. Have you taken SATs?"

"No, I haven't. Not yet."

"What tests have you taken?"

"The MAT test."

McDonough seemed impressed. "The MAT test? What were your numbers, do you know?"

"Almost all of them are 99s. I got a couple of 98s."

"In math and science?"

"I think all of them. I think my lowest was 97 the last time."

"Great. I bet you're really proud of that."

"Yeah."

McDonough, watching every emotion, moved the tired boy back and forth in conversation. He changed the subject once again, back to Michael's family. He asked about his grandmother and then slowly drifted into questions about Stephanie. He wanted to know what Michael loved most about her.

"She is a real people person. She had, you know, she was more popular than me, that's for sure. She had a lot of friends. She, you know, she was really liked. I think where I come up short, she's perfect in those areas. I liked almost everything about her."

Smoothly, McDonough seized the opening. "Okay. Let's talk about the things you didn't like."

"She was annoying sometimes. But, you know, that's the same as . . ."

McDonough added, "What sisters do, right?"

Michael nodded and said he had been blessed with a good family; he liked his sisters. Yes, they had their disagreements, but mostly they all got along.

This was followed by questions about what Michael had done the night before the murder. This line of inquiry soon changed to subjects such as what television shows he liked. He was a *Simpsons* fan. Then back to the morning Stephanie's body was discovered. McDonough again wanted to know what Michael saw.

The probing continued, with McDonough trying to make Michael feel as comfortable as possible. The detective had done a good job of putting him at ease. Soon, the truth verification exam would begin; it was important to have him calm.

McDonough said to Michael, "It would not be right for you to sit here and tell mistruths. It wouldn't be fair to you. Do you agree with that?"

Michael agreed.

"Okay. Unless a person was just a cold-hearted, you know . . . what am I thinking . . . what word am I looking for?"

"A cold-hearted, evil person," Michael volunteered.

"Yeah," McDonough agreed. "Yeah . . . which I know we all have the capability of becoming. Do you agree with that?"

"Yes," Michael said.

The detective began to explain the process and the machine.

"This instrument here is what we call a Computer Voice Stress Analyzer. You'll appreciate this, being into computers. What this does is measure FM signals, okay, and as you and I are communicating here, we're sending two types of signals. Am I right?"

"Yeah."

"Okay. There's AM and FM, right?"

"Yes."

"Your mind, your central nervous system, is calculating all of the AM signals coming in, okay. At the same time, an FM signal is being sent, and it's kind of like underneath the AM. You're aware of all this?"

"Yes."

"Okay, this instrument measures that. It was controlled by the government for a long time, okay, because it's so accurate. In fact, they used it to get moles out of government agencies. . . . And that's why I want to talk to you a little bit more here, as we go over the questions, because you and I are going to formulate these questions, okay? And I want you to feel comfortable with the questions, okay?"

"Okay."

The test began.

"Okay. Let's go over these questions here," the detective said. "There's going to be a total of fifteen in all, okay. The first question I'm going to ask you is: 'Is your name Michael Crowe?'"

"Yes."

"Okay. What color are the walls in this room?"

"White."

"Okay. Now this is what they call a control question. I'm going to ask you if the wall is white, and when we get to that question I want you to lie on purpose, okay? I want you to say no, okay?"

"Yeah."

"I'm going to ask are you sitting down, okay? Then, do you know who killed your sister, okay? So what do you think are some of the things we want to learn?"

"If I know who did it? If I did it?"

"Well . . . let's do that, then. Do you know who, let's say, took Stephanie's life?"

"No."

There were a few more questions, then McDonough said, "I'm going to ask you, 'have you ever used a computer,' okay? Now that's an obvious truth, huh?"

"Yes."

"What I want you to do is lie, okay. Will you do that?"

"Yes."

McDonough handed Michael a small microphone to clip to his clothing and they spent a few minutes practicing the tone Michael was supposed to use in answering. McDonough then reminded Michael of the rules: "Now remember, when I ask you about the wall, you're going to lie. When I ask about the computer, you're going to lie. Okay? Everything else from that point on, I want the truth, okay. Are you with me?"

"Yes."

"Okay, here we go. Is your name Michael Crowe?"

"Yes."

"Is the wall white?"

"No."

"Are you sitting down?"

"Yes."

"Say it a little louder. Are you sitting down?"

"Yes."

"Do you know who took Stephanie's life?"

"No."

"Is today Thursday?"

"Yes."

"Do you know who took Stephanie's life?"

"No."

"Am I wearing a watch?"

"Yes."

"Have you used a computer?"

"No."

"Is this the month of January?"

"Yes."

"Do you suspect someone of taking Stephanie's life?"

"No."

"Are we in the state of California?"

"Yes."

"Do you know who took Stephanie's life?"

"No."

"Are you wearing shoes?"

"Yes."

"Did you take Stephanie's life?"

"No."

This same line of questioning continued for a few more minutes, and then McDonough told Michael to relax. McDonough rose and tore off the sheet of paper that recorded Michael's AM and FM reactions. He said he was going to leave the room and look at the printout.

Michael watched the detective leave. The room went silent and felt hollow. The seconds dragged by, then the detective returned. As far as Michael was concerned, his fate was in this man's hands.

"Okay, how are you doing there, son?" McDonough asked as he entered.

"Fine," Michael said with a shrug. He had an anxious look in his eyes.

"Okay, let's go over this here."

The detective was careful not to signal what the truth verification exam had revealed. "What did you think? What were your thoughts through the whole thing?"

"I don't know. I was nervous."

That was not what McDonough wanted to hear. Nervousness could be used as an excuse to invalidate the test. "Nervous? Okay. Let's go over that. What were you nervous about?"

"That it might say I killed Stephanie."

"Okay, and why would it say that?"

"I don't know. Because everyone is treating me like that."

"Okay . . . Well, okay, help me understand what you mean."

"I was told by someone that we're all suspects until proven innocent, so I just feel like I've already been convicted."

McDonough talked to Michael about the instrument in an effort to assure the boy the machine was accurate. "The machine is impersonal," he said, "and it does not lie." He showed his young suspect the graph, pointing out the lines the computer had produced. Michael followed the graph to where McDonough pointed out one of the intentionally false answers. The graph line thickened, became squared. When he told the truth, the graph output was shaped like a Christmas tree. The detective then showed Michael how the CVSA revealed that there was deception shown when he had answered the question, "Do you know who killed your sister?"

Michael slumped.

"Okay. Is there something you know that maybe you're blocking out?"

"No," Michael said quickly.

"Something in your subconscious mind we need to be aware of?"

"That I'm being blamed for something I didn't do," Michael said, fighting back the tears.

"Uh-huh." McDonough wasn't impressed. "Well, what should we do?"

"I don't know." Michael broke down, sobbing. "I don't know why it's saying that."

"Now there's something going on you need to let go of, son," McDonough said. He then warned Michael that holding back the truth would eat away at him "like cancer."

Michael kept saying he didn't know anything. "I swear . . . I swear to God I don't know," he said, looking up to the officer, his face pleading for reassurance.

"Michael, you've got to let it go if it's there."

"It's not there," Michael insisted.

At this juncture, McDonough was more than ever convinced Michael had lied about knowing who killed his sister. His voice deepened and became harsher. "If the evidence at the crime scene points one way, and somebody says something different, as an investigator I'm going to lean on the evidence, okay? And that's what I'm saying here. I don't know . . . I don't want you all of a sudden looking at, you know, all this evidence and saying, 'Oh, my gosh, maybe I should have taken the opportunity to say something.' I'm not saying that's going to happen, but . . ."

Michael spoke up. "But if the evidence is right, they're going to find it. I don't know. Because . . . I . . . I don't know."

"You don't know what?"

"I don't know why it said I lied in the questions. I really don't know. It makes no sense. I'm being told I'm lying, and I'm not lying!"

McDonough followed quickly. "Michael, I'm not saying that. Have you heard me say that?" Michael shook his head and mumbled.

"Okay." McDonough caught his breath. "I'm saying you may have a piece of the puzzle you're not aware of here."

Michael sighed. "I have no clue. I don't know."

McDonough persisted. Again and again he attacked Michael's reasoning and the CVSA's accurate detection of Michael's failure to tell the truth. McDonough no longer effused kindness. Michael was fighting for his mind—for his life.

McDonough looked intently at the boy before him. "Okay," he said quietly, "we're going to take a break for a bit."

Michael watched as the detective rose and left the room. He needed this break, a time to rest his tormented mind, to reorient himself. But his hoped-for relief was brief.

Within minutes, Detective Claytor entered the room. "Hey, Mike, are you with me?"

"Yeah." Michael sighed deeply.

"Do you want a Kleenex?" Claytor shoved a box of tissue at Michael. "I talked to Chris McDonough about the results. I don't think there's any need for us to discuss that anymore."

Michael blinked. *Is he too telling me I lied?*

Claytor pulled back the chair and sat down. "You remember there was a lot of blood? It's very difficult . . ."

Michael's face paled. He buried his head in his hands, but Claytor demanded his full attention. "You need to stay with me, Michael," he said. "It would have been very difficult for the person who did this not to get blood on them."

"Yeah," Michael croaked weakly.

"And not to transfer that blood to other parts of the house. We found blood in your room," he reminded Michael.

"God," Michael whimpered.

"We used a process called—"

"Where did you find it?"

"Pardon me?"

"Where did you find the blood?"

"I'm sure you know," Claytor said. "It's easy to make mistakes in the dark. We do processes, chemical processes . . . you could wipe blood off a wall and clean it up, but there's molecules, protein molecules that remain. There's a chemical process that actually brings that out, okay, and once it's brought out, then we can photograph it. We can actually get fingerprints off it, okay. That's been done."

Michael eyes were hollow as he listened.

"We know who did it," Claytor said sharply. "So what we need to do now is get it over with. We need to get over the fact that it's been done, and get on with our lives. Nothing we can do is ever going to change the fact that Stephanie isn't with us anymore."

"God!" Michael whimpered.

"And it doesn't matter . . . it just doesn't matter what happened at this point. We can't bring her back, but I'll tell you what we can do. What we can do is the right thing by Stephanie, and by yourself and your parents, okay? There are a couple of things we need your help with."

"Okay." Michael's voice quivered in despondency.

"Okay, what I'd like you to do right off the bat, rather than put our team through any more of this, is tell me what you did with the knife."

Michael said, "God, I don't know. I didn't do it. I'll swear to that."

"Does that mean you can't tell me about the knife?"

"I don't know what you're talking about."

"Michael, you've gone from, 'I didn't do it,' to 'I couldn't have,' to 'I don't remember.'" Claytor's tone revealed his impatience, but he waited for a response.

"I don't even know I did it, if I did . . ."

"Look at the inconsistencies we've found," Claytor said, reminding Michael of the "evidence" against him. "I know that there's no way the bedroom door could have been closed at 4:30 in the morning. Our evidence has already shown that, okay? I know about the security lights outside. Those security lights lit up the hallway. I know that."

"They did?" Now Michael seemed uncertain about this.

"Okay, the evidence can't be argued with. What happened is not the issue."

Michael began to sob. "Why are you doing this to me? I didn't do this. I couldn't have. God, God . . . Why?" He could hardly be heard as he fought to speak through his weeping.

"I can't even believe myself anymore," Michael said. "I don't know if I did it or not."

Claytor was noticeably relieved. "I think you're on the right track," he said. "So let's go ahead and think this through now."

"I don't think I did this. I don't remember it. I don't remember a thing."

Claytor lowered his voice, and in an accommodating manner he said, "You know what? That's possible."

"What's going to happen to me? Even though I don't know if I did it. What's going to happen? Does anyone know?"

"I'm going to try and do everything the system will allow to help you through this," Claytor promised Michael.

"I don't even know what's going on anymore. I didn't . . . how am I supposed to tell everybody?" Michael was lost, emotionally drained and out of reserves to fight on. They talked for a few more minutes, then the detective told Michael to take some deep breaths and relax. He'd be back in a few minutes.

Claytor left the room feeling confident. This case was soon to be put to bed. This kid wasn't so bright after all.

• • •

Michael had been under nonstop intense interrogation for more than six hours. He was beaten, mentally and physically exhausted. The officers and psychologist debated what to do next. It was decided to send in McDonough, but this time he should not press hard or threaten. The psychologist stated the boy needed to be persuaded that he could trust McDonough with the truth. Get into Michael's fantasies. Talk about his role-playing in video games. He's a loner. Not many friends. Explore his loneliness.

McDonough reentered the room and Michael looked up at him, perplexed. "I don't remember if I did it," Michael blurted out.

He tried to put the pieces of the puzzle together. He admitted being afraid, and McDonough wanted to know what scared him. Michael said he was afraid of himself. "I don't know what kind of a person would do something like that and not remember."

There was a moment of silence between them. Then Michael told McDonough, "They say they found blood in my room."

McDonough projected himself as a father figure. "Okay, look at me, Michael. I'm not saying I don't believe you, okay? I have a son your age, and he's told me stuff that I know is not true, and eventually he comes around and says, 'Okay, I'm sorry.' You know what? I look at him and go, 'That's all right, son, I understand.' But if you don't know, you don't know. That's not a lie."

"What am I supposed to do?" Michael asked, "I don't even know."

Finally, McDonough admitted they didn't know it was Michael "100 percent." In fact, he told Michael what the police were trying to do was eliminate him as a suspect. That relaxed Michael a little, and McDonough continued, trying to soften up the boy even more, but he stayed on the subject of why it was important to tell the truth, to confess if the confession was true. After Michael kept repeating that he couldn't remember, the detective said not remembering didn't make him crazy, or even a bad kid; it only made him a kid who couldn't remember.

Michael wanted to know if the CVSA said he killed his sister. McDonough gave him the stock answer: He couldn't tell him because it wouldn't be fair to him. Michael couldn't grasp the logic of this, but he knew no matter how many times he asked, he wouldn't be told.

Thus, Michael was left in limbo at the close of that day. The police were holding an ax over his head, and he knew it.

When the Escondido police returned Michael to the Polinsky Childrens Center that night, he was pale and so exhausted he could hardly walk. When he stepped into the room he shared with Shannon, she wanted to know where he had been and all that had happened. He tried to explain, but it seemed so surrealistic, so psychologically confusing and emotionally painful.

Back at police headquarters, Detective Claytor reviewed the taped "interviews." Later he conferred with Dr. Blum, who had watched portions of Michael's previous interview.

Blum offered the opinion that Michael was lying, and Claytor agreed. The detective wanted to know how to pull the truth out of the kid, and Blum suggested that Claytor get into Michael's fantasy world, see what it was all about.

He had to "get into" Michael's loneliness.

5

• FANTASIES •

Day Three: Escondido, California
January 23, 1998
Evening

Detective Chris McDonough studied the CVSA charts with other experts at his own police department in Oceanside. After reviewing the lines on the grid, McDonough concluded there was probable lying. This fortified Claytor's opinion that Michael was the killer. With no physical evidence pointing to a likely killer, the detectives knew gaining a confession was the only way they could solve the case.

Michael was picked up at the Polinsky Childrens Center again and brought in for more questioning. As the police drove him to the police station, the thought of sitting in the interrogation room again devastated him, but he had no choice.

• • •

Meanwhile, Michael's parents didn't even know their son was being interrogated. They didn't know what was happening to either of their surviving children. All they knew was that Michael and Shannon were being held at the Polinsky Childrens Center "for their own good."

Not yet allowed to return to their home, Cheryl and Steve Crowe were still staying at the home of Steve's brother. They had spent another miserable day in grief and confusion, forced to think about a funeral service for their little girl.

The police were working around the clock, still at the house, still desperately seeking evidence. Detective Theresa Ramirez had been assigned to carry out a follow-up investigation. She was at Hidden Valley Middle School, talking to people who knew Stephanie. Carole Hargraves, one of Stephanie's teachers, could not imagine who might have harmed the girl. "Stephanie," she said, "was happy, enthusiastic and a bright kid. She was a good writer, liked theater, was a people pleaser and liked to make people laugh."

And Stephanie's social studies teacher, Katie Peters, described Stephanie as social, warm, verbal and outgoing. Elisabeth Metzer, another teacher, said this: "Stephanie was outgoing, caring, full of life, a people person; an A/B student who loved to sing." No matter who was asked, there was praise for the girl.

• • •

When Michael entered the interview room, he was once again greeted by Detective Mark Wrisley. Wrisley was friendly and showed concern for Michael's discomfort. He began the questioning with easy, non-threatening rhetoric. Where was Michael born? How long had he lived in Escondido? Had he ever moved? What schools had he attended and which teachers did he like? He wanted to know what avenues of science most interested Michael, who told him paleontology and archeology.

Wrisley kept Michael talking on these subjects, showing an interest in him, but slowly the conversation drifted back to the crime. Michael complained that he had been lied to. Wrisley wanted to know who lied. Michael said the police had told him the family would not be split up, and that was a lie. Wrisley was sympathetic and wanted to know if Michael had questions he'd like answered right then and there.

"I just want to know why everyone thinks I did it."

Wrisley told Michael stories of how police respond in different circumstances, and how they were impartial and really only cared about evidence. Finally, after a long session, circling and avoiding Michael's direct questions with indirect answers, the phone in the room rang. Wrisley had to leave for a few moments, he said. He even apologized to Michael because he'd been called away.

Moments later Claytor entered, and soon he was answering Michael's question. The reason they thought he was the killer was because the evidence pointed to him. The clues led directly to him. What else?

"I don't know . . ." Michael said, breaking down again. "I didn't do it, so the evidence shouldn't . . ." He couldn't hold back the tears.

"I know it shouldn't, but it does," Claytor said, making the point strongly. "That has to be addressed."

There was a little more talk and then the detective began his attempt to "get into" Michael's mind, as the psychologist had suggested. Michael described his favorite game, *Final Fantasy Seven*. He played as a character called Cloud, the hero in the game, and eventually had to defeat his nemesis, Sephiroth.

"What I'd like you to do is think about the situation we are in," Claytor said. "Put yourself in my place as Cloud, and answer some of these questions. What are we going to do in the face of this evidence? You tell me what direction you're going to take."

Michael slumped. "I don't know how the evidence can point to me. I didn't do it."

"I'm sorry?"

"I don't know how the evidence can point to me because I didn't do it."

"Take it one piece of evidence at a time," Claytor encouraged.

"Okay, what's the evidence?"

Claytor told Michael to think about it. He was still hoping Michael would disclose some piece of evidence that would be real, maybe the location of the murder weapon.

"You said you found blood in my room?"

"Okay, let's talk about the blood in your room. I have to have an explanation before I go on to the next step."

"Okay."

"What's the explanation, Mike?"

"I don't know. All I know is that you said you found blood in my room. That's all I know about it."

"You asked a question. You gave me your concerns. I gave you an answer."

"Okay."

"I expect one in return."

"That's my answer. I don't know, okay?"

Claytor showed signs of frustration and became more aggressive, authoritative.

"Part of the rules of the game is we can't cop out, Michael. We can't use 'I don't know' as an excuse, because the rules are we have to go from point A to point B and react to the evidence we have. So now you have your rules, and I'm asking you to follow me, just the same as you would, as Cloud, if you were searching out Sephiroth. I'd like you to tell me what my next step is to complete my mission."

Michael queried, "Find out how blood got into my room?"

"How did it get there, okay? You can't say 'I don't know.' That's not part of the rules. That's not part of the game. . . . You asked me a question, I gave you an answer. Your answer is that there's blood in your room. How could that blood get there?"

"I don't know what to think, but I know it isn't right. So what am I supposed to do?"

Claytor reminded Michael that he had a mission to accomplish. "I can't turn it off," he said. "I just can't ignore it."

Michael said, "How am I supposed to tell you an answer I don't have? I can't. It's not possible to tell you an answer if I don't know."

The interrogation continued relentlessly, meandering through the maze of Michael's now befuddled mind. Was he up with current events? Did he read newspapers or magazines? What did he do in his bedroom? How many video games did he have? Then the course of this badgering turned to the evidence against him again, and Michael was again challenged to confront the evidence and either explain it away or admit to it. The only piece of evidence Michael knew, he said, was that he woke up and got some Tylenol.

But Michael was being worn down, so it was time for the switch again.

Claytor left and Wrisley entered. He wanted to talk about Stephanie. Michael agreed.

"What about Stephanie? Did you really like her?"

"She was nice."

Wrisley asked why she was nice, in what way?

"She would . . . Oh, God, she would do just about anything for someone."

"Would she do just about anything for you?"

"Yeah." Michael's voice was cracking again.

"Okay, that's good. What kind of things would you do for her, that you knew she really enjoyed or that she appreciated?"

"I would talk with her, and help her around the house if she wanted."

"I can't hear you, Mike."

"I would help her. I'd do anything she asked me to do. If she wanted to talk to me, I'd talk to her if she wanted. . . . I used to help her with math."

"Okay, what other things would you help her with?"

"Anything," Michael said. Suddenly the sting of it all burned deeper. "Why are you doing this to me?" he asked.

"Why am I doing what?"

Michael murmured something, sobbing.

"Michael, stop for a second," Wrisley said. "It's really important for you and I understand what's going on, okay? I think you understand where I'm coming from. We were talking a little bit earlier about... You had some questions about the evidence, and why we were talking to you, and I was telling you why that was, okay? It's important we all understand what happened."

Michael looked up, drying his eyes.

"The reason I'm asking about Stephanie—I'm not trying to make you feel bad—I just want to understand about you and she. We haven't talked about her very much, and I know you were a good brother, isn't that right?"

They talked about Stephanie and Michael's relationship and eventually the detective steered them to the subject of his friend Aaron Houser.

"Aaron used to make sick jokes," Michael said, "like: 'Why haven't you killed her yet?' And I'd say, 'Come on, Aaron . . .'"

Wrisley wanted to know what made Aaron say such things.

"I don't know," Michael said with a shrug. "He used to make jokes and kid around. I was still trying to be his friend, so I didn't say anything bad about him."

A few moments later, Michael remembered that his buddy Joshua Treadway had told him Aaron also joked with him in that same way.

The detective wanted to know what Aaron said, specifically. "He'd say something like, 'Why haven't you killed her yet?'"

"Help me understand why Aaron would say that. Tell me what's the source of that?"

"Once in a while, to get people off my back, I'd tell them, you know, I didn't know why he was picking on me because I didn't want to be one of those people that might explode. We sort of made a few jokes about that once in a while. But then I stopped and, you know, it was pretty funny, looking back when he used to say stuff like that."

"You said you didn't want to be one of those people who might explode?" Wrisley asked. "Why do you think you are not one of those people?"

"Because I usually . . ." Michael began to answer.

"You usually what?" Wrisley urged.

"If people say something that hurts me, I don't get angry. It just makes me sad."

"Okay, let's pick your favorite game. What's it called?" he asked.

"*Final Fantasy Seven.*"

Michael said he faced opponents that ranged from mutant beasts to soldiers, but he never really killed his human opponents until the very end. To win the game, Cloud attacks and Sephiroth dies.

Michael explained a little more about the challenges of the game and Wrisley listened intently, but then he leaped from the subject of the game back to the possibility of there being two Michaels. This time, however, the idea was that there was not a good Michael and an evil Michael in the same body, but a good Michael and another Michael who lived in "the game." And the one in the game was the one who killed . . .

Michael was obviously shaken by the inference being made, but he didn't respond.

"You know, Michael, we've been up to your house, doing all this evidence stuff and everything." Wrisley's tone was sincere. "In fact, one of the officers up there has been taking Toby [the family dog] for a walk, making sure he's got food, just like the cats."

Michael was appreciative, realizing the police were human, nice people who were making sure his pets were being fed. But by this time Michael looked different, shrunken.

Wrisley left and Claytor returned to the room, and for a time he dwelt on the subject of Cloud and the game, but suddenly he said what he'd said before: "I think there's two parts to you, Michael. The part that loved your sister and did good for your sister, then there's the other Michael . . ."

Michael listened as Claytor speculated on the workings of Michael's mind, and Claytor's theory of two personalities. By this time Michael seemed no longer strong enough to hold his ground. He was at last showing that he was ready to accept the idea there was a part of him who slipped away into some lost reality he didn't remember.

His eyes welled up with tears and he asked pathetically, "What's going to happen to me then, if it's true? Does anyone know?"

At long last the tapestry was coming together, and it matched the preconceived assessment of the detectives: Michael killed Stephanie in an unconscious act.

Claytor attempted to ease Michael's discomfort. "Once it's understood, Michael," he said, "you're going to be treated as if this was an unconscious act. You're fourteen years old, so you'll not be held to the same standards as a criminal. You're going to need some help, though."

There was more chatter, a few minutes of silence, and then Claytor said, "I know there are some extraordinary circumstances going on here, okay? What we have to do is get back to the evidence. And you are going to have to account for some inconsistencies. Like the fact that there was some time between Stephanie lying on the bed, stabbed fatally, and her being moved. Ten to fifteen minutes, okay? What was the purpose of that?"

"I can't tell you."

Claytor paid no attention.

"How are we going to account for that?" he asked.

"I didn't . . . I don't know."

"The rules of the game keep staring us in the face, Michael," Claytor declared. "We have to follow the rules. We have to follow the program here."

"I can't tell you what I don't know."

Detective Wrisley slipped back into the questioning. "Michael, think. Stop for a minute, and listen to Ralph Claytor. What went on between the time she was on the bed and the time she was moved to the floor? We're talking ten, maybe fifteen minutes."

"I don't know," Michael said, sobbing.

"What do you think happened?" Wrisley asked.

"I don't want to think about that. I don't want to . . ."

"Michael," Wrisley said firmly, "the evidence says Stephanie was on the bed. How do you think that could have happened? She was found on the floor. How come?"

"I don't know."

"Were you trying to help Stephanie?" Claytor asked.

"I don't know. I can't remember. I can't remember a thing."

Wrisley reminded Michael of getting up and leaving his room in the night.

"All I remember doing was getting a Tylenol. That's all. I really . . . I wish I could tell you more."

"Michael, think about the part of you that would have been involved in something like this, and imagine what that Michael would have done in Stephanie's room. How would she get from the bed to the floor?"

"She was moved." Michael offered the logical answer.

"Okay, and how would that be accomplished, physically?"

"I don't know. She dropped?"

"Okay . . ."

"I don't know."

"You picked her up?"

"I don't know."

"Is it possible?"

"I guess it's possible, but you told me . . . I don't . . ." Michael shook his head, unable to focus.

Michael was told at this point that he was building a barricade; defending himself, saying he couldn't remember. Michael kept repeating that he loved his sister, and Claytor, seeing this as an opportunity to drag the "truth" up from the depths of Michael's unconscious, said: "You need to protect that love, so tell us what we have to do to help you drop this wall and remember what we need to know. You're the only one who can do it. I could sit here and tell you everything that happened; you know that. You know what the evidence tells us."

Michael turned from the two detectives and looked down, thinking. He spoke, but it was more to himself than to the detectives. "If I did this," he said, "then I must be subconsciously blocking it out. It's worse than knowing I did it. I don't even know if I did it. I don't remember anything. I wish I could tell you otherwise."

"You have no idea . . . I'm over here, Mike," Claytor said, wanting Michael to face him.

Michael managed to look up. "Are you sure I did it?" he asked, pitifully. "Are you sure I did? Please tell me."

Neither of the detectives gave Michael a direct answer, but Wrisley asked, "What's it like to be Michael? Is it fun?"

"Sometimes."

"Why? Tell me about it."

"I can do stuff, like prove I'm smarter in class, win competitions . . ."

"How would you do that?"

"You know, get the best grades in the whole class. You know, when someone asks me what my grades are, and I tell them. I love to see their faces."

"Yeah?"

"Makes me feel like I'm really smart."

"Is being really smart a good thing or a bad thing?"

"It's a lot of pressure sometimes." Michael explained that people expected more out of him. "I get a B-plus and they wonder why I didn't get an A. I mean, not so much this year. A lot of that was in eighth grade, mostly, and the seventh. That's how it was. That's why I like Josh so much. He treats me normally, and I treat him normally too."

"Josh is a pretty good friend?"

"I consider him almost a brother."

• • •

On this same day, two other police officers arrived at Joshua Treadway's home. Tammy Treadway, Joshua's mother, had just left to do some volunteer work at the school, so Joshua and his younger brother, Zachary, were at home by themselves. The two boys invited the detectives in.

The detectives were not aggressive; they were there simply to ask questions, they said, and to hopefully get some information that might help them in the case. Joshua and Zachary were receptive. They had seen enough television shows to understand the situation. They knew the police would likely question everyone who knew the victim's family.

Joshua was truly Michael's friend, as Michael had indicated during his interrogation. Joshua had nothing bad to say about his friend, only that he was quiet, smart and that they shared a lot of the same interests, including soccer; they got along well, he declared. Then Joshua excused himself to go to the bathroom.

While he was gone, one of the detectives noticed a large knife lying on a table next to a woodcarving Zachary had been working on for a school project.

"What's that?" the detective asked, pointing.

"That's Joshua's," Zachary said, thinking the detective was referring to the knife.

A few moments later, Joshua returned to the room and the detective asked him the same question. "That's Zachary's," he said, thinking the detective meant the carving.

The detectives exchanged glances, convinced there was deception, but they continued questioning as if they had not noticed. Most likely Joshua had lied, they concluded.

• • •

Aaron Houser was also questioned that same day. He spoke to Detectives Lanigan and Naranjo.

Aaron didn't reveal the same degree of anger or disillusionment with Michael as Michael had about him. All he said was that he and Michael were friends, but not close. When he went to Michael's house, they would go into Michael's room and play video games. These games were adventure/fantasy games and they would often make up scripts and play the games accordingly. On a few occasions they had written scripts, but mostly they made up their own rules. He added that he did not know Stephanie well, or Michael's parents.

Aaron described Michael as a very controlled person who never lost his temper; in fact, he had never seen Michael get angry about anything. Detective Lanigan mentioned that he and his partner had spoken with Joshua earlier, and Joshua had told them Aaron collected knives. He asked if Aaron had ever loaned Michael a knife. Aaron said he had not, but he had lent him several CDs, and Michael had lost two of them.

"I'd never lend Michael my knives," he said; "they're too valuable."

The police worked hard and as rapidly as possible, doing background checks, interviewing students and friends of Stephanie and Michael and many adults and students who did not know them but knew of them. More of the canine unit's working dogs were scouring the area again, and again the house and grounds were being scrutinized for evidence.

The evidence the police had told Michael they already had was still not available to them.

6

• THE LETTER •

Day Three: Escondido, California
January 23, 1998
Late Evening

Michael's "interview" continued, and the subject turned to murder again. Wrisley wanted to know why Michael had called Joshua from the police station, the day of the murder.

"I just told him what happened. I told him I woke up and found Stephanie dead."

"You woke up and found her dead?"

"I've been trying to tell you, that's all I know."

"What time did you wake up and up find her dead?"

"When I woke up? I don't know, six-something."

"So you came out and found her?"

"No, my grandma did. But it was the first time I saw her."

"What was Joshua's reaction to that?"

"He was really shocked."

"Did you speak to Aaron?"

"No."

"What do you think Aaron's reaction would be?"

"I don't know. I thought I knew him at one time, but I don't anymore."

The dialog continued, but then Claytor seemed to feel the interrogation wasn't going well. He had been observing for a while, and he said, "Mike, a little while ago you told Detective McDonough and me you'd like Stephanie to forgive you. There needs to be some closure here. Could you write Stephanie a letter and ask for her forgiveness?"

"I'm not very good at writing letters."

"This is . . . this is kind of the way you're going to get some of the forgiveness out in the open. Wouldn't you agree?"

Claytor obviously felt that in writing, Michael might reveal something he would not tell them. He handed the boy a pen and paper, and Michael reluctantly began to write.

Dear Stephanie:

I'm so sorry I can't remember what I did to you. It is almost like I'm being convinced of this, more than really knowing it. I will always love you and can still remember you in life. You have always given so much you truly must be an angel. I tried to be as loving as possible to you. I'm still crying for you, and I pray to God that you forgive me for what they say I did.

Sometimes I think it would be better if I could remember, but I don't want to try. The fact that I can't remember is a blessing from God. I only want to remember the way you were when you were with us. I hope you love me forever and that I never forget what you were, a truly loving person.

They are putting me through hell, and I think that's what I deserve. I will always hold you dear to my heart. If I did this I am insane. I hope both you and God will forgive me. We all miss you, and I feel I am being ripped from everything I know.

I never meant to hurt you and the only way I know I did this is because they told me I did and I hope you understand. I don't know what I was thinking. I hope I never remember, because I don't think I could forgive myself if I knew what I did. I want you to know that I was not myself when I did it. They want me to help them, but I can't. I feel because of that I am letting you down. I should help you, but I simply can't. If you

Stephanie Crowe

don't forgive me then I understand. You showed me what God could do for
you and now I have excepted (sic) Him myself. I shall one day see you in
heaven and I hope that I shall have an eternity to serve you for this.
Never forget that I always loved you. Michael.

• • •

The questioning resumed a few moments after Michael finished the letter.
They talked about what Michael had written for a minute or so and Michael's
asking his sister to forgive him for what he did.

"What did you do?" Wrisley asked.

"I don't know. All I know is what you told me."

"What did we tell you that you did?"

"You told me I killed her."

"How?"

"What? I don't know. You asked me if I knew what I did with the knife, so I'm assuming with a knife. That's all I know."

"So what does the knife have to do with it?"

"You asked me to tell you what I did with the knife, but I can't. I don't know. That's all I know."

"Well, if there was a knife, and Stephanie was dead, what role did the knife play?"

"I don't know. It probably killed her."

"How?"

"I don't know."

"Oh, come on, Michael." Wrisley was running short on patience.

"I don't know. God!"

"You've played enough of these games. You know how knives work."

"It cut her!"

"Is that a question?" Wrisley retorted.

"I don't know. How can I tell you?"

"You know how knives work, Michael. That's a little insulting to say, in front of Claytor and me. We investigate these cases all the time, right?"

"I guess."

"You guess?"

"I don't know for sure. I guess it would be."

"So how is a knife used to kill somebody?"

"I guess you stab them."

"Where?"

"I don't know."

"Well, where would you think? If someone was going to die from being stabbed, where would they be stabbed?"

"The head?"

"Okay, where else? Is that the only place?"

"The stomach. I don't know. The chest?"

They stayed on the subject of the knife for a while, but Michael kept on saying he didn't know, didn't remember. And so Wrisley asked if Shannon, or Grandmother Kennedy, or Dad or Mom murdered Stephanie. Michael did not shift the blame—none of these people could have done such a thing, he said.

Then he was asked if Joshua or Aaron murdered his sister. No, he was sure about Josh, but not so certain about Aaron. Not that he said Aaron might have, only that he didn't know. He could have, but who could know?

"How would he have gotten in the house?"

"I don't know."

"Okay, so we pretty much agree that nobody came in from the outside."

"I guess. Well, you're saying so, but—"

"We can prove it, Michael."

"How?"

"Because all the doors were locked. We can prove it by the statements of the people who locked the doors, like your grandma and your Uncle Mike, okay?"

The detectives studied Michael as he absorbed what was being said.

"It's not like you just open the window and step in," Wrisley continued. "You have to climb in. So we know the person who did this was inside the house."

"I don't remember. How many times do I have to tell you? I can't remember, I don't remember doing anything except waking up with a headache."

"And you said Stephanie's door was shut. We know that's not true."

"Did Aaron give you a knife?"

"No. Never."

"He's got a lot of them, right?"

"Oh, yeah."

"What's up with that? Why's he got so many knives?"

"Aaron thinks he's some kind of a collector. He also collects swords."

The detectives listened, but soon the focus was back on Michael and his lapsed memory. They were nearing the end of the fourth hour of that day's interrogation, and Ralph Claytor was apparently anxious to put an end to Michael's game playing.

Claytor and Wrisley kept pressing Michael for "the truth," and telling him he had to deal with "the reality" so as to "go down the proper path."

Michael, overwhelmed, felt his whole world collapsing around him.

Wrisley turned up the knob on the tension: "You ought to do it now, man." Wrisley said it quietly, but his voice thundered in Michael's ears. Both he and Claytor wanted to end the cat and mouse game. And, of course, what a feather in their caps: to solve the case in just three days.

Now more convinced of Michael's guilt than ever, they continued to push. "Tomorrow's not going to work," Claytor said.

Finally Michael said, "You know I'll lie. I'll have to make it up."

"Tell us your story, Michael," Wrisley coaxed.

"You want me to tell you a little story?" Michael asked.

"Tell me the story. What happened that night?"

"Okay. I'm telling you right now, it's a complete lie."

"Tell us the story," Wrisley repeated; his eyes were a laser on Michael.

"Okay. This part is true. I'm extremely jealous of my sister."

"Okay," the detective said and nodded.

Michael talked about how many friends Stephanie had, how popular she was. Claytor wanted to know when he got to the lie part.

"Okay," Michael said, "here's the part where I'll start lying. That night I got pissed off at her. I couldn't take it anymore, okay? So I went and got a knife, went into her room and stabbed her."

"Look up here, Mike. I can hardly hear you."

"Okay. I went to my room, tried to get some sleep. Couldn't."

"I'm sorry?" Wrisley pretended not to hear him.

Michael continued, "I got some Tylenol. Went back to my room and went to sleep, woke up the next morning. That was no lie," he reminded the detectives.

"How many times did you stab her?"

"This is going to be a lie. Three times."

"How many?"

"Three. It's going to be a lie."

"Is it a lie? Go on."

"I don't know. I hate telling you that."

"When you went in, Mike, was she on her back, on her stomach or on her side?"

"On her side. I don't know. I told you it was going to be a lie."

"Well, tell the truth."

"The only reason I'm trying to lie here is because you presented me with two paths. One, I'm definitely afraid of. I'd rather die than go to jail."

"Okay."

"The other one, I—" he said with a shrug, unable to go on.

Claytor had had enough. "No, no. Let me make something clear, Mike. It's like this. You can completely shut up, if you'd like, and say nothing, okay?"

"Okay."

"And what we're going to do with you tonight, I'm going to take you back to Polinsky. We're going to leave you there, okay? There's going to be a court hearing—probably Monday morning. Before Monday, though, all the evidence is going to come rolling in, and you've put us in a position where we're going to prove every minute detail. An avalanche of evidence is all going to come crashing down. You don't have to say a word. We've told you four different times that you don't have to talk to us if you don't want to."

"Back to Polinsky," Michael said barely above a whisper.

"Pardon me?"

"Just take me back to Polinsky."

"You know the direction we're getting ready to go."

"I know I did it, but I don't know how, okay? I don't know when I'm going to be able to tell you anything, okay?"

"How about beginning at the beginning?" Claytor suggested. "Where did you get the knife?"

Michael stared at them blankly.

Wrisley broke the silence by asking when Michael began feeling resentful of Stephanie. Michael went directly into a long string of events, starting in seventh grade, when Stephanie was going to the same school as he was. He talked and talked about how his parents favored her over him, and how she had so many friends, how he became known as "Stephanie's brother," and how he retaliated by calling her fat. He kept adding to his tale of deep-seated anger and contained rage.

But it wasn't only Stephanie, he said. He hated his entire family, and he began escaping into books. He said that was probably the only reason he was friendly with Aaron, because he had a huge collection of books and he could borrow them. He said he loved to read because he could escape. He explained: "I often find myself just sitting there, thinking. I've made up my own fantasy world. It's like I'm three different people."

"Tell me about that, Michael," Wrisley said, his interest sparked.

Michael explained his three personalities. One was Odin—very evil. Another was a passive type, and another was a female, gentle and kind. He said he was these three distinct people, and was even planning to write a book about it. He'd just split himself apart and become these different personalities.

Could they believe him now that he was confessing? Did he really have a rare multiple personality disorder? Is this what he had been lurking behind? And was it Odin who murdered Stephanie, one of the "three faces" of the fourteen-year-old Michael Crowe?

In an unexpected moment, Michael blurted out every angry resentful feeling he could recall. He talked in depth about his jealousies, his feeling of being unappreciated by his family, how he placed the blame of his own failures on his sister Stephanie. He talked and talked and he kept on talking. And during the course of this catharsis he admitted he was positive he'd killed Stephanie.

So Michael admitted murdering Stephanie "in a rage," but he also stated, "I'm not sure how I did it. All I know is that I did it."

Before putting his signature on this confession, however, Detective Wrisley added one more bitter piece of persuasion: "Your parents believe you're guilty, Michael," he said, "and they never want to see you again."

And so, as the clock neared midnight, the lengthy, heartless, and clever manipulations produced the result they wanted. It never occurred to these detectives they had wrought the result themselves. They were only concerned with the fact they had found a way for the supposed "truth" to emerge, the only truth that made sense to them. Their lies about evidence were mere instruments in their eyes; their use justified by a "satisfactory" outcome.

7

• ARRESTED •

Day Four: Escondido, California
January 24, 1998
Early morning

Michael's father and mother, uncle, aunt and grandparents remained in a hellish state, not knowing what was going on, only knowing that their lives had been shattered by some unknown assailant.

Didn't such people have a heart? Didn't they ever take time to look beyond their evil intentions and think how many people's lives they would ruin? What kind of a person would take a little girl's life? Did he not care how much Stephanie wanted to live, to follow her dreams, to celebrate her next birthday?

There were other frustrations adding to their anxiety that day.

When were they going to get their children, Michael and Shannon, back? Why were the police keeping them? And another thing—when were they going to be able to go home and put their lives back in some semblance of order?

There were good reasons why they couldn't go home. For one thing, nothing could be changed, removed, picked up or disrupted in any way until the search was over and all the evidence collected.

In addition, the walls had been sprayed with Ninhydrin, a chemical that makes latent fingerprints visible. It takes a few days for the chemical to work, and no one was allowed to touch the walls during that period. Forensic experts were conducting a Fluorescein examination, hoping to reveal latent bloodstains. The toilets, showers, floors, and sinks had all been sprayed with Fluorescein, but nothing was found outside Stephanie's bedroom. Nevertheless, no family member would be allowed back into the home until all their tests were completed.

The minutes of their lives dragged by slowly, painfully.

Steve Crowe had not slept at all since Stephanie's death and he was at his wit's end. He wanted desperately to sleep; he wanted to get away from the awful truth for at least a few precious hours. Someone suggested sleeping pills, and though he had never been one to need them, he decided to take them on this night.

He swallowed them down eagerly, hoping to escape into the safe haven of elusive sleep.

Just after midnight, the phone rang. Steve fumbled for it in his stupor, knocking it onto the floor. His heart clenched in his chest: news delivered in the middle of the night was seldom good.

But this news would change everything.

He grasped the receiver. "Yes?" he croaked, his voice thick with sleep. Cheryl slid up beside him in the fold-out bed, her eyes twin pools of fear piercing the darkness.

Through his fog, Steve listened carefully. It was the detective on the other end.

"We've arrested a suspect." It felt like an eternity before the cop continued. Steve's heart threatened to shudder to a stop in anticipation. Then he heard the rest: "It's your son."

Steve Crowe's mind scrambled to understand what he was being told.

The police had arrested Michael for murder. Before this point, they weren't even aware Michael had been interrogated.

As he hung up the phone, a paralyzing fear settled on him like a second skin. When Cheryl's hand fell on his shoulder, he nearly screamed aloud. Her face was contorted in horror—*tell me! What's going on?*

How could he?

How could he tell her that a new horror was just beginning?

Steve's fingers madly stabbed at the phone as his wife howled from the other room. Try as his family might, her anguish was inconsolable.

It felt like forever before they put Michael on the phone.

He could barely get out the words as he asked his son if he had done it.

Finally, through sobs, Michael answered, "I don't know what to believe, Dad . . . They say . . . I did it."

Good God! Steve Crowe's mind screamed, *he didn't deny it. He didn't say he didn't do it, so he must have done it. Oh my God in Heaven, how could this happen?*

PART TWO

A Tapestry of Deceit

8

• FINAL FAREWELL •

Day Four: Escondido, California
January 24, 1998
Late Morning

One of the few precious joys Steve and Cheryl Crowe were blessed with was the news that young Shannon was finally allowed to go back with her family.

Michael, of course, was another story altogether.

It had been only a couple of days since they'd seen him, but it seemed like a lifetime. When they arrived at the Polinsky Childrens Center, he looked so gaunt, frail and beaten. Not physically beaten, but emotionally drained. Michael had not only suffered the trauma of his experience, but he was also sick. He had a bout of bronchitis and a temperature of 102. He looked like walking death.

They talked and wept together and by the time their visit was over, both Cheryl and Steve no longer believed the police. They thought Michael must have had some kind of breakdown during the interrogations. Michael agreed that he felt like he was not in control of himself, not his mind or his body. He felt odd, he said, and it was a terrible feeling. As Cheryl and Steve rose to leave, they did not believe him to be guilty, and they would remain convinced of his innocence, despite what the police had told him.

The police, however, felt sure they had their killer. They were also sure they knew where they would find the murder weapon: at Joshua Treadway's house.

Joshua had by then become a suspect.

And the detectives had developed a strategy for how to proceed.

• • •

Back at home, Cheryl Crowe stared into the mirror.

Her face looked ghastly—she didn't recognize the ruin staring back at her. And she wasn't sure what to do with her hands. Those hands were useless. They'd never been trained to prepare for her child's funeral.

That nightmarish conversation with the police kept echoing in her head: "Please, let my son be with his family at his sister's funeral," Cheryl Crowe had begged. "Let him come in shackles if you have to, *but let him be there!*"

But the police had refused.

They wouldn't even allow her to have Stephanie's favorite black dress to bury her in; they needed it for evidence.

Shannon came from behind her. Wrapping her arms around her mother she whispered, "Mommy, you have to get dressed. We have to help Stephanie get into heaven."

• • •

It had been a hellish nightmare of a week for the Crowe family and their friends and relatives. But this day, the seventh day of their ordeal, would involve many other people. This was the day of the funeral, and while Cheryl Crowe was on the telephone, pleading with the police to allow Michael to attend, other people were in their homes, dressing for the sad occasion.

Not far away, Aaron Houser, his brother and his mother were preparing themselves to attend the funeral, as were the Treadways. January 27 normally was a happy day at the Treadway house, it being Joshua's birthday—his fifteenth. But this date was destined to be a permanent reminder of what happened to Stephanie. The Treadways, a deeply religious family, had heartfelt sympathy for the Crowes, and they all prayed many times for them and especially for little Stephanie.

• • •

There is no term in the English language to describe a parent who has lost a child. When one loses a spouse, they are called a "widow" or a "widower." When a child loses both parents, the child is considered an "orphan." But the cruel fate of a child dying before a parent is such an aberration that, through the eons, no English word has been coined to describe its horror.

And no words could describe the overwhelming horror that Cheryl and Steve Crowe felt as they sat beside the grave of their darling Stephanie. Cheryl held little Shannon's hand in a vise-grip, almost subconsciously fearing to let go.

The cruel shadow of Michael's absence, on top of the loss of Stephanie, was one loss too many.

Stephanie Crowe's grave

Six hundred people gathered to bid Stephanie a final farewell. Stephanie's classmates, her friends, and even many strangers had donated money toward the $7,000 burial expenses at Oak Hill Cemetery.

The press was there, along with a few casual observers, drawn to the event in morbid curiosity. Mostly there was a huge outpouring of love and support for the family; most people carried sympathy and real sorrow in their hearts, not just for Stephanie, but for her parents and relatives. They felt a genuine empathy for the Crowes' dual nightmare: the loss of one child and having another accused of her murder.

But, too, there were the whispers—low murmurs of *Can you imagine, her brother did it?*

The Crowes were too ensnared in the vortex of their unimaginable hell to register this.

Their emotional menu swung from catatonic to hysteria as the box containing the ruined remains of their beloved Stephanie was lowered into the ground.

Cheryl felt the overwhelming urge to jump onto the casket and descend with her.

She's never going to have a baby—
She's never going to go to New York—
She's never going to get married—

There was no solace to be had that day.

When the earth swallowed sweet Stephanie, one of the greatest parts of their lives was simply over. But a fathomless void still remained.

And six hundred attendees simply went back to their lives.

• • •

On their drive home, Tammy and Michael Treadway, Joshua's parents, were morbidly silent, but they were grateful their own three boys were alive and healthy. They had always been devoted parents who taught their youngsters positive values. They were religious without being fanatical, community-minded folks who had always tried to raise their children in security and love. They felt especially bad that day because it was Joshua's birthday, and no one was in a frame of mind to celebrate. Joshua sat in the back seat of the car, hardly speaking. He was thinking about Michael, his friend, in jail. He thought about Aaron, too. Aaron was never easy to figure out. Like Michael, Aaron was smart, but unlike Michael, he was aggressive, more verbal, more willing to flaunt his intellect. Although Aaron had a more open personality than Michael, he was still more difficult to get to know.

What the Treadways did not know was that a few days before the funeral, Susie Houser had experienced a sudden inexplicable recall. She remembered that Aaron and Michael had once been close friends, but then, a few months earlier, had fallen out over some missing cash and lost computer games. She knew the murder weapon had not been found, and she had told Aaron to check his knife collection.

Sure enough, a knife was missing. It was a "Best Defense" knife, a heavy hunting knife, the kind of weapon that might have been used in the murder.

As soon as Susie learned the knife was missing, she telephoned the police and reported it.

She mentioned Michael's and Joshua's names and stated they might have had access to the knife. Officers had seen a knife on the table in the Treadway home when they interviewed Joshua and one of his brothers, but it was not believed to be the murder weapon. However, when he heard of Aaron's lost knife, Detective Claytor sent officers to interview Aaron. This latest discovery could explain why the police dogs and all the officers had not found the weapon: it had been secreted at Joshua's home. Claytor had a hunch, and his intuition told him to act. Anyway, this was more than a hunch, so he planned to search the Treadway home.

The Treadways knew nothing of this, of course, and once they returned home from the funeral, Mr. and Mrs. Treadway did their best to create a positive, if not a totally happy, birthday party for Joshua. Opening the gifts would help get their minds off the funeral. Breaking the moment, the telephone rang. It was Detective Claytor. He wanted Joshua and his parents to come down to the police station right away. Their response was understandable: "Good Lord, not today. We've just come from the funeral and it's Joshua's—"

Claytor interrupted, saying it couldn't wait. They had to be at the station immediately.

Claytor's request was confusing to the Treadways, but they assumed the police must need Josh's testimony to clear up some facts about Michael or Stephanie. Mr. Treadway was a man who respected the law. He had two uncles who were career policemen, so he trusted the system and had no real apprehensions as he and his wife drove Joshua to the police station. He certainly did not believe their son had anything to do with the murder of Stephanie.

But Joshua was very nervous. Unlike Michael Crowe and Aaron Houser, he was not strong willed. He was more artistic and sensitive, more open to people, and definitely more naive to the workings of the world.

Immediately after Joshua entered the police station with his parents, he was taken to the interview room and questioned; Mr. and Mrs. Treadway were told to wait in the lobby. It was about 7:00 p.m.

A long time passed before Claytor finally emerged and told Joshua's parents that their house would be searched right away.

Michael Treadway reacted immediately. "What? Please . . . my mother is there, and Joshua's two brothers. My mother isn't well. You'll scare her to death."

A deal was struck. Claytor agreed to wait until the Treadways were back at their house so that they could inform and comfort Michael Treadway's mother, but Joshua was to remain behind for questioning.

Mrs. Treadway felt especially nervous as they drove home, and her husband tried to comfort her. As a professional locksmith, he had been called down to the police station many times and had opened many locked doors for these officers. He saw them as good guys.

"Everything will be fine," he told his wife tenderly. "They're just doing their job. Anyway, Josh wouldn't have anything to do with something like this."

The interview of Joshua did not begin with a soft approach, as Michael's had. Claytor seemed anxious to break the case wide open, and he was straight-faced and rigid with Joshua as the questioning began. There was an arrogant air about him, a kind of "I already know" quality in his attitude.

But Joshua tried to remain calm. He assumed he was there to talk about his friend, Michael. Michael was, in fact, the early focus of Claytor's questions.

"Tell me about your relationship with Michael, Joshua."

"Michael and me get along real well," Joshua said. "He's quiet, you know. A little shy—especially around adults. We have a lot of the same likes, you know, the same interests. I think his favorite sport is the same as mine: soccer. We both . . . um . . . he did a little better than I did in school, sometimes. He applied himself a little more than I did, which I regret. I should have applied myself a little more in the eighth grade."

"You get over to his house much?"

"Yeah, actually a lot. Not recently, though. I got a few bad grades on my last report card, so I'm grounded."

"How long have you been grounded?"

"About six weeks. But Mom made an exception during the Christmas break, so I . . . It's been about a month since I was at Michael's house."

"Why don't you tell me how he and his family get along?"

Joshua told the detective both of Michael's parents were nice. They would even go out of their way to pick him up and drive him home after his visits. He said he really liked the Crowe family. It was hard, seeing them look so sad at the funeral.

Claytor wanted to know some of the things Michael had told Joshua about his family. "Like I said, they had a good relationship. I didn't sense any conflict or anything."

"Okay."

"I mean, occasionally. I can name maybe two times he was kind of mad at his mom."

"Michael?"

"Yeah. His mom had grounded him because he got bad grades on his report card."

"Just recently?"

"The beginning of the school year. He got his PlayStation taken away for two weeks."

"How did he feel about that?"

"He didn't get to talk to me about it because he wasn't allowed to use the phone. But I guess he was kind of upset, you know. He really liked it."

"When was the last time you talked to him?"

"I talked to him Wednesday afternoon, about four-thirty, maybe five-thirty. He called me from here, the police station, and told me about what had happened. It was really shocking because I'm . . . I . . . my school psychologist said the same thing as you. It doesn't happen, you know. Things like that don't happen. I only see 'em on the news."

"Mmm."

"Stuff like that is traumatic, and shocking at first. I didn't sleep much that night, and I still get shaky just thinking about someone being killed in their own home. Even car accidents, or anything, really upset me."

Claytor asked Joshua what Michael had said when he called from the station. Joshua said they talked about Stephanie and the award she had received. Joshua remembered this because Cheryl Crowe had picked up Michael and Josh at their school and then had driven over to get Stephanie. Stephanie had just won the Philanthropy Award, and she had it with her.

Joshua said it was "neat."

The questioning remained conversational, but Claytor seemed eager to get down to the subject of the murder weapon. He told Joshua he had to tell the truth because it was the right thing to do, the legal thing to do. Claytor also explained to Joshua how, in court, the attorneys would pick up on things like embellishing the truth, and how they would exploit any weakness he might show. He told Joshua that once he was on the witness stand he would have to tell the whole truth, no matter how good friends he and Michael were.

Joshua understood, he said. He added, however, that he would hate to think Michael had anything to do with killing Stephanie. Claytor asked him if Michael harbored some animosity toward Stephanie, saying he thought

Michael didn't want to be known as Stephanie's brother. Did Joshua know that?

"Well, I think so," Joshua said. "I think he wanted to be known as his own person. Yeah, he did mention it a couple of times, you know. I guess a couple of kids from Hidden Valley said he was 'Stephanie's brother.'"

"Mmm."

"I guess he just wanted to be known as Mike, you know, not Stephanie's brother."

"How often did you talk about that?"

Joshua said they seldom talked about such things, but he did know Michael was angry with his sister a lot. Claytor focused on this.

"It's just that they don't do normal things, I guess," Joshua said, "Like, I don't know, she'd whine about something and go tell their mom. Shannon or Stephanie would use one of the Blockbuster coupons when Michael wanted to use it, or something such. I don't . . . little things, you know, would kind of make him mad."

"Mmm. And what would he tell you about that?"

"He was upset. Er . . . you feel I'm holding something back right now? I mean . . ."

"No, I feel you're trying to protect your friend. And I think that's admirable." The wheels turned in Claytor's mind. So far, Joshua had confirmed what Michael told them during his confession, but when it came to the possibility of Michael making threatening statements, Joshua said he didn't think Michael meant it. "He was joking about his hit list," he said.

The detective was drinking this all in, but he showed little outward reaction. Joshua was a good candidate for interrogation, willing to talk without hesitation. Claytor turned to questions about Michael and his relationship with Aaron.

"During this year, Mike hasn't been friendly with Aaron. You know, just . . . I don't know . . . high school personalities can mesh well, or not . . . whatever. And there was some deal I didn't get involved in because neither party, Mike or Aaron, wanted me to. But I was friendly with both of them.

Apparently Michael lost some games that belonged to Aaron. You probably heard about that."

"Mmm."

"This is the big feud they had, you know. I guess Michael lost Aaron's games and Aaron wanted money for them. Ever since then they haven't been friends, not the way they were. I wouldn't go so far as to say they're enemies, but they aren't good friends. Aaron even stopped eating lunch with us."

Claytor nonchalantly asked about Michael having a knife. Joshua didn't remember Michael having a knife.

At this point Claytor stood up and asked Joshua to remain, and he left the room on a mission—a mission to search Joshua's home.

9

• MORE TO THIS TRIO •

Day Seven: Escondido, California
January 27, 1998
Late Evening

In the search of the Treadway home, the police found two knives under Joshua's bed: the hunting knife the officers had spotted when they were at the house the first time, and another knife. This second knife had the right dimensions to be the murder weapon. It was a large survival knife inscribed with the words "The Best Defense." Claytor was shown this knife and he smiled—*We've got it!*

Claytor left the house with the suspected murder weapon and drove to the Houser residence. Aaron immediately recognized his knife, and Claytor asked him about Michael and Joshua. Aaron was cooperative, but he seemed a little strange in the way he answered . . . so deliberative. His answers appeared well thought out, and Claytor found this strange for a fourteen-year-old.

As he drove away from the Houser's home, Claytor kept mulling over this short exchange with Aaron. The boy had explained, just as Michael had, that the three of them—he, Michael and Joshua—were all into playing games of medieval sorcery and fantasy. He also had said he'd never seen Michael get angry at anyone "except me." Michael had started calling Aaron an "asshole" around school after their disagreement. Michael had promised he would re-place the lost CDs, Aaron also claimed. Michael had stolen money from him, but Michael denied it. On his birthday, Aaron had received $40 in cash and he left it lying around in his room. Michael visited that day, and when he left, the money was missing. Aaron had no idea when the knife was stolen. He clearly remembered calling Michael and asking him questions such as, "Did you kill them yet?" But that had been a standing joke between them, he claimed. He also added that Michael often joked about killing people he didn't like or was upset with.

Claytor was concerned. There appeared to be more to this trio than had so far surfaced. They were all into Dungeons and Dragons, and who knew where all that took them. Were they all somehow involved in the killing? The scenario of a three-part conspiracy fit into Claytor's stereotypical assessment, and he felt assured that the knife lying in the plastic evidence bag on the seat of his car would tell a lot more of the story, perhaps the crucial details.

Claytor firmly believed Joshua held the key.

• • •

Joshua had been left in the interrogation room all this time, alone with his thoughts.

Claytor returned, after making sure the "murder weapon" had been sent to the lab for processing, and told Joshua that Michael and Aaron had implicated him. He was in big trouble, Claytor told him, but if he cooperated, told the story as it happened, then he'd end up "okay." Claytor warned him that if they had to drag the truth out of him then things could get very tough. He would be subject to the whims of the court, and the system would turn against him. Many years of his life would be swept away. But Claytor was a nice guy, he told Joshua. He didn't want to see such a thing happen, and as long as Joshua told him what he wanted to know, he'd "be there" for him.

All he wanted was the truth.

Joshua was crying when Claytor said, "Well, Joshua, I'll tell you what. We have a little different situation than we had a while ago. So what I'm gonna do is . . . um . . . I'd like to let you know what your rights are, before you talk to me."

Joshua Treadway

"Okay." Joshua tried to show strength in his voice. He didn't want to sound weak or fearful, though plainly he was.

"You have the right to remain silent. You understand that?"

"Yes."

"Okay. Anything you say may be used in court against you. Do you understand that? You have the right to the presence of an attorney before and during any questioning. Do you understand that? If you can't afford an attorney, one will be appointed free of charge. Do you understand that?"

Joshua nodded.

"Do you want to talk to me about what happened?"

"What is this? I'll tell you right now, I didn't have anything to do with Stephanie's death. I'm honest. I didn't do anything." There was determination in Joshua's tone; determination, but also distress.

"Why don't you . . . why don't you just relax? Take a deep breath. You want to tell me the story? Your side of the story, okay. Just go ahead and start from the beginning. Tell me what you think."

Though Joshua tried to keep composed, that composure dissolved quickly. The interrogation had barely begun, but Joshua was presuming the worst, imagining his possible fate. He pictured himself a prisoner in some terrible place for the rest of his life, his dreams never coming true. He tried to control his reactions, hoping to demonstrate to Claytor that he was willing to tell the truth, but he began to struggle for breath. His anxiety was leading to panic. He had to gain control. His actions were starting to convey guilt. Somehow he managed to take a grip on himself, and he began talking about the week that Stephanie died.

"Tuesday night of that week, Michael told me that no matter how sick he was, he was going to be in school the next day, for the final exams. That's what he told me on the phone. I didn't get to talk long because I have a rule in the house, no phone calls." His voice dropped and he muttered something. He then seemed to recover, and he looked at Claytor again as he continued.

"The last time I heard from Mike was on the Wednesday, when he called me from here. I've not heard from him since. The only thing he told me on the phone was that he found Stephanie dead. And I told him I felt sorry for him, asked if there was anything I could do. He told me he was okay. I heard a lot of crying in the background; it was Mrs. Crowe, I guess. She was really choked up apparently. That's all he told me. I asked him how she died, and he said, 'Somebody apparently broke in and killed her.' That's all he told me."

"Anything else?"

"I don't think so. He didn't tell me . . . I mean, if he had anything to do with . . . that didn't even enter my mind at the time, but that's what he told me."

"Okay, Josh, tell me about the knife."

Panic struck Joshua again and the words he uttered came faster and faster. "The knife? I got it from Aaron," he said.

"When?" Claytor asked, trying to nail down dates and times.

Joshua continued, rambling, without addressing the question. "He's had it for a long time, so I, well, I mentioned that I really liked the knife. I know I was wrong, but I took it on the 16th, and it's been sitting under my bed ever since. That knife has been sitting under my bed, I swear, since the night the officer saw . . . that had been . . ."

Joshua mumbled something, pausing, trying to think. He finally continued: "My brother Zachary used it to carve something . . . It was on the couch when the gentleman who was in the car with us was there."

"And you think that's the same story Mike told me?" Claytor asked. This early in the interrogation game, Claytor began suggesting to Joshua that Michael had said something different, something that could be incriminating. It never occurred to the detective that Joshua's discomfort was strictly related to the fact that he'd taken a knife that didn't belong to him.

"I hope he did, because—"

Claytor tightened the screw, interrupting, "What other possible story could there be?"

"I don't know any other possible story. I didn't . . . I didn't touch the knife. I swear it! I'm serious. Seriously . . . I had nothing to do with the killing. I—"

"You know what, Joshua? I happen to know that."

"I didn't give Mike the knife or anything, either, if that's . . . I . . . I just . . . he called me and I heard about it all. And then, on Thursday night, I went to . . . uh . . . service at the church for Stephanie, and I saw her mom there, and that's when I heard from the family that, you know . . . And then I called him, Saturday or Friday. I called Mike's dad because I got a note from Reverend Gary, Stephanie's pastor. He told me Mike was in Juvenile Hall; that he wasn't doing so good. And then I—"

"Calm down now. Just relax."

"And I went to the funeral because it was the loss, and seeing her family." Joshua paused for a few seconds. "Did Mike tell you a different story about the knife?"

Claytor didn't answer. Unlike Michael, who was introverted, deep thinking, Joshua tended to respond impulsively, without thinking. The truth was that Michael never implicated Joshua in any way. In fact Michael, in a moment of reflection, had said he loved Joshua. Joshua was his best friend, he said. But now Claytor was using Michael against Joshua; grinding away with the inference of betrayal.

"Is there any reason Aaron's story would be any different from yours?" the detective said, giving Joshua more to think about.

"Not that I know of. No, I don't."

"This is important, Josh," Claytor said, almost kindly. Almost.

"I understand. It shouldn't be, because all it was . . . I took the knife. That's basically it. It's wrong, I know. Stealing is bad, but I did it. That's what I did. That's it. I haven't done anything else bad. All right, I took the knife and that was it. It was the 16th of January."

"Hmm . . ." Claytor's voice showed his doubt.

"I didn't do anything with the knife. It just stayed under my bed, and that was it. I didn't do nothing with the knife."

They talked about the last time Joshua had seen Aaron, and then Claytor returned to the subject of the knife. "If this is the knife that was used, Joshua, how can you explain it?"

"I can't," Joshua said. "Because I didn't do anything with it. All I can say is that I didn't do anything with it. It's been under my bed."

"But I know better than that."

Joshua responded strongly. "I know it's not the knife that was used, because it couldn't have been. It was under my bed the whole time."

"What if it is?" Claytor kept toying, hoping for a breakthrough.

"Then I don't know how to explain it. It can't be the knife because it was under my bed. How could someone else get it? I mean, it's not . . . It can't be the knife."

"You're saying you took the knife from Aaron, right?"

"Yes."

"Stole the knife from Aaron?"

"Yes."

"Why would you steal a knife? And why that particular knife?" The cat and mouse game continued, with Joshua trying to justify why he stole the knife. But Claytor didn't care about the petty theft; he cared about the knife itself and where the knife was on the night of the murder. He bluntly told Joshua: "The knife got under your bed sometime *after* Tuesday . . . *after* the murder. I think you have far more to tell me . . ."

"Can I make a call to my mom?"

"Excuse me?"

"Can I talk to my mom any time tonight?"

Claytor ignored Joshua's request and resumed his questioning. Joshua was well aware what Claytor was implying, and he became all the more frightened.

Claytor saw this and came down hard on him, returning again to evidence he didn't have, seeking an even stronger psychological grip on the boy, using a combination of guilt and false evidence for Joshua to wrestle with.

"There's stuff I've been able to prove," Claytor said. "Stuff I've been able to locate evidence for, okay? Now, what I have to do, and—and this is really important for you to understand, Josh—what I have to do is, I have to reconcile the differences between what you say and the evidence. These statements of yours don't reconcile with what I know, chronologically. You know what I mean by reconcile? It's like a math problem, okay? Everything has to balance out, okay? If A, B and C on this side tell me that I should expect a D over here, and I don't see a D, then something's wrong with A, B and C. You see what I mean? And what I'm saying is that what you're telling me doesn't fit. It doesn't fit the evidence I'm aware of. It doesn't fit the chronology of events I'm aware of. . . .

"Now, do you want to make me prove it? I don't think you want that, do you? You want to tell me exactly what happened?"

"I'd like to go home."

Joshua, like Michael, had been told there was evidence against him, which was a blatant lie. Innocent or guilty, these assertions were frightening. The guilty suspect would be apt to think, *I'd better tell the truth and come clean,* while the innocent might think, *God! Some kind of evidence is pointing at me. What am I going to do to get out of this mess?* Innocent or guilty, the suspect in such a situation is made to feel that he'd better start thinking of his future.

Claytor liked the position he was in. It opened a door for him to negotiate for the truth, or what he *believed* to be the truth. Here was a kid who, only a short time before, had been making his plans, dreaming his dreams. Now, all of that had been exchanged for a much simpler prize.

All he wanted was to go home.

Getting out of there and going home had become Joshua's only desire, his single wish. Claytor knew this, and he also knew that he was the genie holding the power to grant Joshua's wish. He would use this as a tool.

"Well, I'm going to be perfectly frank with you," Claytor said in a thoughtful way. "Going home really depends on you, okay? Let me explain the juvenile system. In this society we don't run around punishing kids. And you're still a kid, okay? What we want for our kids is to be able to rehabilitate them, okay? Kids make mistakes. We know there's been some serious mistakes made in this case. Unfortunately, a twelve-year-old girl lost her life over a very serious mistake. . . .

"Now the reason I tell you all this is that if you made a mistake, Josh, and all you do is cover it up, well, there's no rehabilitation, see? Do you see where I'm coming from? Okay, your mistake is not as bad as Mike's mistake. And what we need to do is we need to see where you stand on trying to make it right. Trying to face up to your mistake, okay? Now, that being said, do you want to tell me the truth of this matter?"

Joshua nodded.

"I want the truth," Claytor said firmly. "I don't want any fabrication. I don't want any story you've planned out. I want the exact truth, okay? It's gonna be important for you."

Joshua was not the intellectual his two friends were, but he was a long way from being stupid. He had listened to Claytor carefully and he believed what he'd heard. Claytor had said that he knew more of the truth than Joshua was telling him, and this worried Joshua. It frightened him. *What truth did he know?* But there was something else. He had strongly indicated that Michael had told a different story, had implicated him in some way. *Good God, could that be true? Why would he do that?* Maybe he didn't know Michael as well as he thought. Here he was, sitting in the hot seat, this terrible crime hanging over his head because of something Michael had told the police. So Joshua was thinking deeply.

He looked up at Claytor and said, "Can I ask you a question? What's the . . . What's the most serious and most non-serious of both of these deals, for Mike and me?"

"Well, I'm not going to tell you . . . but I'm telling you murder is as serious as you can get."

"I didn't kill anybody," Joshua insisted.

"Okay." Claytor seemed receptive. "You asked me what's the most serious and . . . if you start from there, you can come all the way down. Where you go on the ladder depends on what you're willing to tell me, okay? I know you're not up here," he said as he gestured with his hand above his head. "I happen to know that, okay? Now, are you ready to stop playing games with me and get on with it? I can guarantee it'll be much easier than you think."

"All right," Joshua said. "But this is so stressful for me."

"I understand," Claytor said, seeming sincere. But he felt a sudden surge of relief. This was even easier than he thought it was going to be.

"Where do you want me to start?" Joshua asked. This was not the surrender Claytor was expecting. This was an imaginative kid who had decided to be creative. If the detective wanted to help him, then he would help the detective. Everyone would end up with what they wanted. He'd get off with a hand slap and Claytor would have his story.

"Where do you feel like starting?"

"How about how the . . ." Joshua mumbled something incomprehensible. ". . . the knife?"

"Be my guest," Claytor said, more than receptive. But Joshua did not talk about the knife at all.

Instead, he began reconstructing the case against Michael Crowe. At that moment, this is what he *imagined* Claytor wanted. "Mike didn't have the best relationship with his sister," he said. "I tried not to make it sound bad, at first, but then he did say a lot of stuff like, 'Oh God, I just want to kill my sister.' He did say that a lot."

"Hmm."

"But I never took him seriously. He did say it a lot. A lot! I mean almost every . . . at everything, you know, everything that made him mad. He probably told you this, right?"

"Keep going."

"Okay. Well, I noticed whenever things would tick off Mike, at school, he'd always threaten people, but he never threatened me because I was always his friend."

Joshua kept to the same theme for a few more minutes, but all the while he was thinking . . . thinking hard as he wove the "bad Michael" tale for Claytor.

Then, in an unexpected moment, he looked up and said, "I have a question for you: Is there a way I can take any kind of lie detector for this?"

"That can be arranged. So let's get a little closer to the point, all right?"

"What are you asking for the truth on?" Joshua asked.

"I'm asking for the truth about the knife." There was a tone of decisiveness in Claytor's voice, but also a show of concern for Joshua, a tone of friendliness. But moments later he lost some of his patience. Joshua promised to talk about the knife, but he didn't really say a thing of use to the detective.

"I'm asking for the truth about the knife," Claytor reminded him.

Joshua answered with questions of his own: "Where I got it? How? What Mike wanted me to do with it? That sort of thing?"

"The whole thing," he said. "I'm not here to play games, okay? I'm here to get the truth, and I'll do whatever it takes. I owe it to that twelve-year-old girl, okay? I owe it to this community and ultimately, Joshua, I owe it to you. No more games. Talk about the knife."

Joshua hesitated for a few moments and then, barely able to talk past the lump in his throat, he said, "I got it through Mike. Through Aaron, and through Mike. I'm . . . I'm done lying," he added, very nervous, very weepy. "I just . . ." he paused, "about this whole knife thing. How I got it? How I'm supposed to have hidden it? The reason I'm saying this is 'cause I think you think I hid it, so I just—"

Claytor didn't deny anything. "Well," he interrupted, "you tell me what you were supposed to do with the knife."

Joshua then threw a curve at Claytor: "Okay, I wasn't supposed to do anything with the knife because I don't know anything about the knife, and I'm being honest-to-God truthful with you. I can do a lie detector test right now, because I was just . . . right now, I said all that because I thought I could clear my name by telling you I was hiding the knife. I never got any information, I don't believe, that the knife was the one used to kill Stephanie. I'm not kidding around. I'm willing to take a lie detector test to prove it. I'm serious. I'm not . . . I'm not kidding, and I believe your evidence is the same."

Claytor didn't like the ring of this. His progress seemed to be evaporating.

"You be *very* careful, Joshua, 'cause you don't know what the evidence is, okay? And I do. Okay, now if you want to stick with this . . ."

"I don't know . . ." Joshua was wrestling with what to do.

"You have a choice. Face the truth or face a lie, okay? And the evidence is gonna tell me the truth no matter what. Actually it already has," Claytor continued to lie.

Oddly enough, Claytor's comment seemed not to penetrate. Joshua had heard him, of course, but his mind by then was on something else, something more important to him than the evidence. "When can I talk to my mom? Can I talk to her tonight?" he asked.

"Are you willing to tell me the truth?" Claytor was offering a kind of subtle deal.

"Can I talk to my mom?" Joshua seemed determined.

"Hmm."

"Tonight?"

"Yeah."

"Right now?"

"Do you want to talk about this some more, Josh, or . . . 'cause here's what's gonna happen, okay? If you want to . . . if you want to conclude this conversation, we can do that, okay? But now you're no longer faced with the opportunity of getting the truth out. 'Cause what's gonna happen is, once I leave here, okay, you're gonna be faced with the one thing. The only possible reason you had the knife was to kill a twelve-year-old girl, and it was right there in your bedroom, okay? That's what I can prove. Now, you stop and think about what else I'll have to prove after that. Not much."

Claytor had reversed roles. He had warned Joshua that he was free to stop the interrogation, right then and there; but if he did, the only possible conclusion would be that Josh had the murder weapon for a singular purpose, and he would no longer have Claytor to help him. If that were not enough pressure, Claytor was inferring that he had the proof the knife under Josh's bed was the one used to kill Stephanie.

How could anyone fight the proof of hard evidence, especially knowing his fingerprints would be all over the knife?

Proof, evidence, guilt, innocence . . . questions, questions and more questions. Joshua wanted to talk to his mother. *God, if only he could talk to his mother.* He realized he needed Claytor back on his side.

Claytor could make things go easy for him.

He was the great barrier between Josh and his mother . . . and the rest of a life.

"I . . ." Joshua swallowed, obviously uncomfortable. "I was given the knife," he said. "I was given the knife." He looked dejected.

Claytor was suddenly helpful again. "You need to tell me," he said. "You need to . . . you need to be up front with this, Josh."

Joshua was wrestling with his conscience now. "I just don't know what to say," he said. "Everyone wants me to say this and that . . ."

Claytor knew exactly what to say at this point. "Think about the people who put you in this position. Was it fair for them to do that?"

Now the avenue of escape was presented again: If it weren't for Michael and Aaron, Claytor was suggesting, Joshua wouldn't be in this situation. But there was a silent offering as well. *Since they were not fair to you, why should you be fair to them?* The truth was, however, neither Aaron nor Michael had implicated Joshua at all. All Michael had said about Joshua was that he was his friend, a friend so close that he thought of him as a brother. But Joshua didn't know this.

Claytor now added fuel to the fire. "Okay, then why should it be fair for you to sit here and cover for them, Josh?"

"I don't know. This isn't right." Joshua was near to tears again.

"I agree. It's not right. It's not right to the twelve-year-old girl who's lying dead in her grave."

"What?" Joshua asked. His mind had drifted. "Oh. I thought you said something else. I'm sorry."

Maybe it was Claytor's anxiousness, or maybe he had simply decided to play hardball again: "Yeah? Please don't insult my intelligence," he said. "Just be frank with me. If you have some truth to tell, tell me. If you don't . . ."

"All right." Joshua sounded and looked defeated.

Joshua had agreed to talk, was waving the white flag. But for some reason Claytor decided to stack his bluff even higher. "Okay," he said. "But I'm going to leave here and take the evidence with me."

"Wait, wait," Joshua was terrified. "You're not going to talk to me anymore?"

Claytor hesitated momentarily. "Why? What do you have to say?"

"I was given the knife to hide."

"When were you given the knife?"

"I was given the knife . . . I don't remember."

"Okay." There was suspicion in Claytor's voice. "Can we talk? Was it the day after she died, or two days after?" Claytor had created a safety zone for Joshua. No matter how he answered this question, he'd be cleared of any involvement in the murder. This had not gone over Joshua's head.

"Two days after she died."

"Okay, and who gave you the knife?"

"Aaron gave me the knife."

"And what were you told?"

"I was told to get rid of it. To hide it. Don't let anyone find out about it."

"Hmm. What does Aaron know about it?"

"I don't know what he knows. We didn't talk."

"When did you first find out about the knife?"

"When I received it. I had my instructions and that was it."

"When did you get your instructions?"

"When I got the knife."

"Did you know what was going on when you were given the knife? Before you were given the knife?"

"Not at the time, only when I got it."

"And what were you told?"

"Hide it, and that was all. Just hide it. Get rid of it. Don't let anyone find out about it. Keep it away from everybody."

"Hmm. Why did you put it under your bed?"

"I just thought that was good. No one would look there."

"Hmm. Now I'm confused. Are you telling me the truth now? 'Cause this is like what you said to me a while ago, and all of a sudden you told me it was a big fabrication."

Joshua asked for a drink. His voice sounded dry.

Claytor told him he could have a glass of water, but also warned that he was in no mood for games. "We can stop this right now, if you want," he said, wanting Joshua to remember what would happen if he walked out. He would take the evidence and Joshua would be accused of murder. In effect, it would be all over. "And you can have all the drinks, talk to your mom, talk to your dad, talk to whoever you want," he said. "I'm going to proceed, okay? But you need to understand game time is over. This is not a game. This is very serious business, okay? At your age you can still be tried as an adult," he warned.

"Can you be sent to prison at my age?"

"Absolutely," Claytor said, and then he continued to give the speech again, about how the system merely wanted to rehabilitate him—if he would simply be truthful.

"Can I please talk to my mom before we continue any conversation? I just need to hear words from her, please. Can I talk to her before we continue?"

"Just sit tight," Claytor ordered, and he exited the room.

Joshua was made to wait a tedious eleven minutes, an eternity in these circumstances. By then he was running mostly on adrenaline. It was half-past midnight. *How long can all this keep up?* But soon, he knew, the door would open again and he would be confronted with more of the same.

What he didn't know was that he would actually face a deeper, more penetrating demand for the truth.

10

· I LOVE YOU, DAD ·

Day Eight: Escondido, California
January 28, 1998
12:30 A.M.

Michael Treadway, Joshua's father, had been at the police station all this time, waiting for the police to release his son. He had been praying, sitting in silence, wondering where this night was going to lead. Claytor eventually opened the door to the waiting room and took Mr. Treadway into the interior of the station, where he informed him about his son's possession of the knife and his connection with the gruesome murder. Claytor apprised him of all the "evidence" pointing to his son, Joshua. All this was frightening and heartbreaking to Treadway, a righteous man who tried to raise his children right. He took pride and comfort in the values he raised his family with: God, home and country. It was impossible for him to believe the police would ever lie. In fact, he trusted the police completely. But even if this weren't the case, he was a man who upheld the law, followed the rules, and respected authority. The police asked him to talk to his son and get the truth. They were not "after" Joshua, they told him; they were after Aaron and Michael, who had obviously led his kid astray.

This guileful line was acceptable to Mr. Treadway. If Josh really was involved, he must have been suckered into it by his two friends. He had always wondered about Michael Crowe, anyway, the way he was so quiet and withdrawn. And what of all those crazy computer games the kids were into? All the vivid sex and violence on TV? Yes, if Joshua was involved, these were the causes. *Whatever happened to the time when life was simpler and children grew up building tree houses and playing baseball? God, you read about kids in trouble all the time, but you never think your kid will end up like this. Never!*

The police shared Mr. Treadway's views about the cause of societal decay, but also about Joshua. He wasn't the bad apple here but was just being protective of his friends, the awful murderers who used him to hide the evidence. And so it became Mr. Treadway's job to go in and convince Joshua to tell the truth. All the police wanted was to help Joshua, but unless the boy told the truth then who knew what might happen to him.

Treadway entered the interview room feeling he had the weight of the world on his shoulders. Just seeing his son in the confines of this terrible place was bad enough. But Joshua looked ghastly pale; he had plainly been crying. Their tired eyes met; exhaustion and worry showing in both faces.

"Dad, I love you," Joshua said, and his emotions erupted.

"I love you too, Josh." His father fought his own anxieties, trying to show strength. "God, Josh, tell me what the hell is going on here."

All Joshua could do was choke out, "Oh, Dad . . ."

"Josh, tell me what's going on, Bud. I need to know. I need to know everything, without any bullshit."

"I know." Joshua glanced away. "I love you, Dad," he repeated.

"I'm talking serious, Josh."

"I know . . ."

"What did this little fuckhead get you into?" Mr. Treadway was not a man to swear a lot, but when he did it always sent Joshua the message that he was very upset.

But Treadway had unknowingly become part of the trap. He was becoming the strong liaison between the police and their prisoner. He'd been told not to go easy, to be firm, to get at the truth. In so doing he would be helping his boy. All he wanted to do was help Joshua.

Treadway tried to calm his son down so Joshua would tell him, truthfully, what had happened.

"Dad, I tried. I thought . . ." Joshua composed himself. "He said . . . he said if I come clean on this now, then it can be, you know, less hard on me and I can get rehabilitation and everything because . . ." Joshua could hardly get the words out. "That knife is, like, the knife that killed Stephanie . . . is what he was telling me."

"Okay, was it the knife that killed Stephanie?"

"I don't know," Joshua pleaded.

"Okay. When did you get the knife?"

"January 16th."

"Okay, let's look at the calendar just . . . come on." He wanted Joshua to keep talking.

"That's the truth," Josh pleaded. "But if I tell the false thing, which I know is not right, it's the only way to save myself, and I don't know . . ."

"Josh, you're not gonna—"

"He said this is serious. I can be tried as an adult, Dad." Joshua wanted to make it clear to his father that he was stuck, and his only hope was to tell the police what they wanted to hear. Treadway was listening, but he seemed not to understand his son. The police would not lie; not in Treadway's world.

Treadway knew many of the Escondido officers. They would call him to secure homes and places the officers had raided. He was the locksmith. So, not in his wildest dreams could he believe the police would railroad his son, much less lie to him.

He asked his son about the knife, and Joshua explained that he didn't get the knife from Mike, but from Aaron, before Stephanie was killed. He insisted the knife had been hidden in his bedroom ever since. He just wanted to go home and enjoy what remained of his birthday, perhaps unaware that it was no longer his birthday. But he was scared.

"I've never been this scared in my life," Joshua said.

"Okay, but honest to God, Josh, I'm just going to ask you again, on the Bible . . . If I look around right here, there's probably a Bible. I . . . ."

"I'll put my hand on it, I swear it. I got the knife on the 16th of January, and I didn't kill anybody. I don't know anything about it, Dad, honest!"

"They're not accusing you of killing anyone, Joshua," Treadway insisted.

"But I didn't hide it for anyone else either."

They talked a little more, but finally Treadway told Josh he believed him. And since his dad believed him, Josh said, "I need to tell the guy right now . . . I'm saying no more lies, I don't care if it saves me or not, I have to tell the truth."

"Josh, if you were telling the truth, you never have to backtrack or anything."

"Yeah." Joshua was weighing the consequences again. "Well, what you're telling me right now is putting me on the higher scale," referring to Claytor's scale of culpability and punishment.

"But, Josh, if it's the truth, then it's the truth. Do you know what I'm saying?"

"I sure don't want to be put away." Joshua felt something tighten in his gut again. "Oh, Dad," he said. "I need another hug."

Joshua kept telling his father he wanted to tell the truth. But Mr. Treadway had some remaining doubts. "Don't cover Mike's ass, Josh," he warned.

"I'm not trying to," Joshua blurted out. "I'm just trying to save myself."

"Excuse my language, but fuck Michael, you know what I'm saying? And Aaron . . . has Aaron said anything about this crap?"

"Get the guy in here, Dad," Joshua suddenly demanded. He wanted this thing over with and had made up his mind what to do.

"Just tell the truth, then. That's all I ask."

"All right."

"That's all you gonna do, okay? Honest-to-God truth?" Treadway left the room leaving his son waiting anxiously.

Joshua had asked his father to be with him when Claytor came back, but neither his father nor Claytor returned. After more than five minutes the door was opened by Detective Wrisley. He introduced himself as Mark, a detective. He seemed friendly, even open, but at this juncture the police felt assured that they were now dealing not with one, but with a trio of middle-class killer boys. No matter how the detective seemed, he was there for one purpose: to inspire Joshua into helping put the pieces together and get this case put to bed.

Wrisley then told Joshua the police were talking to Michael and Aaron, who were looking out for their own interests. "Who's to say they're not blaming you for this whole thing?"

Blame me for the whole thing? Oh God, what if . . . what if . . . what if?

"That's what I'm afraid of," Joshua choked.

"Okay, wait, stop. Just relax." It was clear to Wrisley that he'd jarred Joshua, and while he was asking the boy to relax, he was actually pushing Joshua's buttons, stirring his concerns.

"That's why we need to hear exactly what happened, Josh, because we have Michael's story and we have Aaron's; and now we're trying to get yours. . . . We're not gonna sit here all night and play games."

In this, Wrisley reiterated two major ploys inherent in this interrogation. The first was Joshua as the suspect, the accessory, and the second was they were not willing to sit with him all night, begging for information. Joshua knew that if he balked, not telling them what they wanted to know, they might just walk out. And if they walked out, Joshua would go higher on the invisible scale of blame again, and he would be in lots more trouble. However, Joshua, despite all this, stuck with his story.

"I know. That's why I want to come clean, right now," Joshua replied. "But I don't know anything about the knife other than I took it from Aaron wrongfully that day, on January 16th. Saturday or Sunday. It was the weekend. I spent the night at Aaron's place."

"Why did you take the knife?"

Joshua said he loved it, and that he didn't really steal it. He had merely borrowed it. "I just wanted the knife, and I haven't done anything with that knife. I left it under the bed and that was it."

He explained that he only told the story about Aaron giving him the knife and telling him to hide it because Detective Claytor had frightened him. He said he was afraid of being tried as an adult and of going to prison. Once again he offered—no, actually *pleaded*—for the opportunity to take a lie detector test. But of course, this was nothing new to Wrisley. Joshua wasn't the first shrewd little liar to ask for a lie detector test, thinking the police were not about to go to the trouble or expense of actually giving him one. He wasn't the first smartass punk to think he could throw the interrogator off course by asking for a lie detection test.

Wrisley disregarded the question; he simply continued with questions about the knife. Where was it when he took it? How did he take it? Why did he take it? What inspired him to take it? And how was he going to prove it stayed under his bed after he took it?

Then, suddenly, the detective changed the course of his questions. He wanted to know when Joshua last saw Michael. He wanted to hear again about Michael's statements about killing his sister, and asked if Joshua had talked to Michael about having the knife. Then Wrisley had Joshua go over, again, what he knew about the murder, and Joshua told him he knew only what he'd read in the newspaper. The questions continued, and finally they circled back to the knife again. Joshua admitted he couldn't prove the knife was under his bed all the time, but he had shown it to his brother, Zach, who had also seen it under his bed.

Finally, Wrisley reminded Joshua that he had told Claytor that "someone" had told him to hide the knife.

"He made me so scared," Joshua said again. "He said that if I didn't tell him—"

"How could he make you so scared that you'd say something that didn't happen? That doesn't make sense, Josh."

This line of questioning was not going anyplace, and Wrisley knew it. But he was convinced of Joshua's involvement, as were Claytor and others involved in the investigation. Wrisley sat in silence, staring at his young suspect for a few moments; exasperated with Joshua sticking to his story.

Then he stood and offered a subtle warning: "You'd better search your brain and your heart while I'm gone."

But he would not be returning. It was time for Ralph Claytor again. Time to tighten the screws on Joshua.

Claytor did not look pleased when he entered the room six minutes after Wrisley left. The first thing Joshua wanted to know was if the other detective told Claytor what he'd said: that he had stolen the knife; that he had not been given it by either Michael Crowe or Aaron Houser.

Claytor said he knew that, and he told Joshua that, because of this, they were back to square one.

Joshua looked bewildered; his eyes were sunken and red-rimmed. He wondered what was coming next. He was the perfect candidate for applying fear tactics to, and Claytor knew this. What had Joshua said to his father and to Wrisley? How he didn't want to be high on the Claytor's scale of jeopardy where he was likely to be tried as an adult, and that truly frightened him.

Claytor insisted that Joshua was lying, that in fact, the police could prove the knife was the murder weapon. Another detective then entered the room, Sergeant Anderson, to put more pressure on Joshua. He reiterated Claytor's comments.

Something else churned in Joshua's mind as he contemplated his options: the awful fact that his friends, Michael and Aaron, had involved him, pointed the finger at him. Should he be loyal to his friends, even though they had ratted on him (or so he believed), or should he tell the real, honest-to-God truth?

"I have to say . . . the truth is what I told you."

"So your truth, Joshua," Claytor said, "is that the murder weapon was under your bed from the 16th of January." Then he reminded Joshua that the murder did not occur until the 21st of January.

"It never left my room," Joshua stated firmly.

"It never left your room?"

"No."

Claytor said defiantly, "Do you—do you expect people to believe that?"

"I do . . . I do."

"Why? Why do you expect 'em to believe that?"

"Because it hasn't left my room."

Claytor was suddenly at the end of his patience, or he pretended to be. "Okay," he said, standing up, "it'll be Juvenile Hall tonight." And he exited the room.

The thought of Juvenile Hall exacerbated Joshua's fears. He could feel it in the pit of his stomach, he felt it crawling up his spine, and he wanted to scream, cry, or run. In his imagination, Juvenile Hall was a death sentence.

Where could his life go from there? Prison?

Joshua, despite his desires, could not run from himself or from his predicament. What Joshua didn't know, however, was that there was still no evidence, and there had not been any stories told by Michael or Aaron that implicated him. And the knife had certainly not been identified as the murder weapon. Joshua, at that moment, was not at all in jeopardy of being indicted or jailed. A competent lawyer would have yanked him out in no time, and anyway, there was nothing to put him in jail for except, possibly, taking a knife from a friend, petty theft.

• • •

At this same time, Mr. Treadway was in another office; his situation was very different from Joshua's, of course. The police were friendly to him, wanting to help, feeling bad for him, and for his son.

Or that's what they claimed.

In fact, they told him that Joshua was a "good kid." The only problem with Joshua was that those other two bad kids took advantage of Josh, used him and led him astray. They were telling Treadway everything he wanted to hear. And Joshua's father was swallowing nearly all of this pabulum. However, despite these convictions by Mr. Treadway, he was warned that if Joshua did not tell them the truth—confirm some of the "evidence" they had—well then things could rapidly change. What alternative would they have but to categorize him along with Michael Crowe, who had already confessed to the crime?

Mr. Treadway's heart was broken by all this. He might have been naive to the ways and motives of the police, but he was also a man who loved his kids, his Joshua. This was a father who cared deeply and was in pain; a father who, instinctively protective of his children, was now helpless to protect his son.

But the police insisted that if Treadway could convince Joshua to stop "protecting" the other boys, he could protect himself. All he had to understand was that Joshua was a good kid, being foolishly loyal to his friends.

• • •

When the door opened again it wasn't the police, come to take him away, as he expected. It was his father again.

Mr. Treadway looked as frazzled as his son. It had been a long, agonizing night for both of them. They had been taken to the police station before seven that evening and now it was past midnight. *Was it ever going to end? And how was it going to end?*

Neither father nor son could manage to speak in a normal tone. Joshua said, "Dad, I told the truth. That's all I can do."

Treadway shook his head. What choice did he have but to accept this? "Okay, Josh, but do you know what's going to happen to you right now?"

"I don't know."

"Okay, because, my God, another shock. If you're . . . if you're . . ."

"I told them the truth, Dad."

"Okay." Treadway's voice cracked; he was fighting his own emotions. "They're bringing forensic people down to test the knife and . . ."

"I need a hug, Dad. I need a . . ." Joshua was crying again as they hugged. "Thank you for staying," he said in barely a whisper.

"Josh, what else would I do, leave you here? My gosh, you know what I see? This is like *The Twilight Zone*. Do you hear what I'm saying?"

The two of them, father and son, did their best to communicate, but their voices kept breaking. They choked up, unable to speak properly, sorrow and hysteria building in both of them. Joshua told his father he didn't want to answer any more questions. He tried to explain how senseless the police accusations were.

How did the knife get out of the house? How would he have gotten into Michael's house, since there were no signs of entry? Joshua managed to ask his father if the police thought it was a conspiracy.

"If . . . if Aaron gave you the knife, and told you to get rid of it, then, yeah." Mr. Treadway repeated what he'd been told by the police, that this was what had happened.

"He didn't, though."

"Then forever hold your peace."

"I am forever holding my peace, 'cause he didn't." Joshua was firm but not defiant. The conversation continued, and Joshua asked about his mother. Mrs. Treadway was at home and didn't know much of what was going on, Treadway told his son. Joshua wanted another hug. There were tears.

Then, Treadway was parroting the police again. "Well, if the knife . . . if somehow forensics say it was used . . ."

"There's no way," Joshua said, shaking his head. "It couldn't be the knife."

"I'm just . . . but if it was. If Aaron somehow picked it up out of Mike's area, brought it home, thinkin' you got it, because mysteriously . . . hmm . . . and then you got it, after the murder, and now . . . and if that's what happened, and you tell them . . ."

Joshua read between the lines of his father's concern. "Believe me, Dad," he said, "I'm not covering up for anybody else."

The conversation continued and they moved from one topic to another. They talked about the knife, about how the police wanted to hear how Aaron and Michael were involved. And they prayed together.

Then the subject of Joshua taking a lie detector test came up. Joshua wanted to know if such a test would ever go against what a person held as true in their mind.

Treadway tried to explain it as the police had told him. "They look for involuntary auditory something . . ." He tried to remember the terms. "It has to do with your body, if you're lying, even if you could keep a straight face, not blink . . ." He sighed deeply, completely at a loss. "Josh, I don't know what I'm doing. I've never been in a situation like this, okay. So all I can say is that if they come back and say it's the murder weapon, you gotta, you gotta . . . we gotta get an attorney. And we've never planned on anything like that, so let's not—"

Joshua interrupted. He wanted to know how upset Claytor was, and that led them into the subject of Juvenile Hall. Joshua was sure that was where he'd be spending the night, and after that, there would be some sort of hearing.

While Treadway was not a man to defy the system—being the epitome of the law abiding, church going, tax paying, hardworking family man—it was also true that, even in the face of what the police had told him, he was not about to simply take their word over that of his son. So he too wanted the lie detector test to be the real thing, not some pretest or whatever the voice thing was.

The hidden camera was still rolling, of course, and this meeting of minds between Joshua and his father was not producing the results the police had hoped for. They were hoping Treadway would lead his son into admitting his connection with Michael and Aaron in the murder. Treadway wanted the truth, but the police had filled his mind with the idea that Joshua was involved and had been "used" by his two friends. Still, he was not willing to browbeat Joshua into saying something he did not believe.

Actually, the police were hoping for anything that would strengthen their case against Michael Crowe. Michael after all, while confessing to the murder, was still claiming he didn't remember the details. At best it was a confession the prosecutors would not celebrate. The investigators had to have more . . . and they knew it.

During this time Joshua twice mentioned his concern for Michael. He hoped Michael was okay, holding up all right.

Claytor returned and, once Treadway stepped out, Joshua was allowed to speak to his mother.

He was so nervous and excited he could barely dial the phone. He willed his voice not to crack when he heard her answer. "Hello. Is this you, Mom? I just wanna tell you that I love you so much. You don't know how much. How're you doing?"

Mrs. Treadway evidently asked about Josh's father.

"He just left me, said he was going to call you. All right, thanks, Mom. Bye." Hanging up was one of the hardest things he'd ever had to do.

He turned to Claytor, "That was my mom," he said. An innocent way of mentally drawing out the call, which he hadn't wanted to end.

Claytor nodded. "Okay, Josh. Now we're going to book you as a homicide suspect."

• • •

Joshua was led out of the room, down a corridor and into another room where he was made to stand in front of a height ruler for photographs. Joshua willed his entire body not to vomit. This was the real stuff, the booking side of it. This was the part where you stopped owning any part of your life and just did what the police told you to. *After this, they lock you up . . . and that's the end of that.*

JOSHUA TREADWAY, PC-187, booked for murder. The number referred to the section of the California Penal Code for a homicide. But the photograph with the penal code number had nothing to do with anything legal. It was simply another fear tactic the police were using, another psychological ploy to weaken Joshua's resistance.

What they wanted at this point was to scare him to death.

• • •

Joshua was not taken to jail, or to Juvenile Hall; he was led back for more interrogation, as the clock ticked well beyond midnight. Detective McDonough had been called. They wanted Joshua to be given the Computer Voice Stress Analyzer test, the same one they had given to Michael Crowe. McDonough arrived at the station around 2:30 A.M. and he started his interview with Joshua at 3 A.M. McDonough was good at his job, and he maintained a reputation in life as a squeaky-clean, deeply sincere, religious and devoted policeman. Indeed, he was also one of Oceanside Police Department's fair-haired boys.

McDonough's first challenge was to calm the suspect down. As with Michael, he showed signs of concern, and that he was sympathetic with Joshua's fears. He shook his head when Joshua told him he had been taken away from his birthday party and arrested, and he expressed an interest in Joshua's life.

Joshua told McDonough he considered Michael to be his best friend, and he talked about his favorite TV shows. They talked about the games Joshua played. Like Michael, his favorite computer game was *Final Fantasy VII*.

Joshua began to think this guy was okay. He relaxed a little, but it was not all McDonough's charm; it was well past three in the morning and he had been in this pressure cooker for eight hours. He was fatigued and sleepy, and his guard was down.

They talked a little about movies, then McDonough asked about Michael again. Joshua said Michael liked to keep to himself and wore black mostly. He also said Michael was good at problem solving.

McDonough said a criminal case is like a giant puzzle and the investigators are responsible for putting the pieces together. Joshua could help them solve this puzzle by taking the CVSA test. Joshua believed he would pass the test; that the test would prove he was telling the truth.

McDonough's questions went on and on . . . and this detective, whose job it was to be neutral, who was not supposed to involve himself in the investigation beyond the truth verification test, and was not supposed to know anything about the case, was clearly participating in the effort to obtain a confession.

The confession that his cohorts in the Escondido Police Department had failed to squeeze out—*but were still so determined to obtain.*

McDonough had, by this time, become part of the investigation. His assignment was to wring out a confession, and this corrupted his neutrality, his validity as an unbiased CVSA examiner. At this point he had not even started to give the exam. Instead, he was looking for keys he could use to unlock the "truth" of Joshua's presumed involvement.

McDonough explained the test to Joshua and began by assuring the boy how the CVSA was "technology at its finest." He prepped Joshua for the exam, much as he had Michael. He would ask questions and Joshua must answer yes or no. He must tell the truth, except for a couple of "control" questions.

Joshua agreed and, since he said he was ready, he was told to take a deep breath, sit back and relax.

The test took only a few minutes. When it was completed, Joshua felt relaxed—more relaxed than he had for hours.

McDonough then dropped the ax: "I can tell you were stressed on this layout." He went on, as he had with Michael, to imply that Joshua had lied.

At this point, Joshua had been awake for twenty-four hours.

McDonough told Joshua he was going to give him the CVSA test again, to give him another chance to pass. But McDonough had no real intention of repeating the test.

McDonough played the nice guy for a while longer, but then he turned the tables on Joshua. He told the boy he was "out of his league," reminding him the machine "knew" he was lying.

Joshua asked to take the test again, but McDonough reneged, saying, "You're not going to pass, Josh, so I'm not going to do that to you."

McDonough continued to interrogate Joshua. His official assignment had been finished for a long time now, but still he stayed involved, convinced that sooner or later Joshua would admit his guilt. The detective wanted to be part of that triumph.

"Please let me try," Joshua said.

McDonough again refused. "No," he said. "You tell me the truth about the knife and I'll take you through it again."

Joshua offered the same story. He saw the knife in the drawer and took it from Aaron without his knowing it. He stole it, but had the intention of returning it later. . . ."I took Aaron's knife and put it in my backpack."

McDonough lost his charm at this point. "Okay, that's a lie. My experience is telling me you're lying." He continued to preach, reminding Joshua that as soon as he heard the truth, he'd do the test again. "And you'll pass with flying colors."

Joshua was running on pure nervous energy by this time. His body slumped and he looked haggard. Finally he said, "All right, maybe Aaron gave me the knife. But what would happen if Aaron gave me the knife?"

"Don't worry about what would happen." McDonough could now sense he was making headway. He could feel the confession coming. All he needed was a little more time. "Just tell me the truth. Please look at me and tell me the truth. Don't think about it; just let it happen. You're not betraying him, okay. So when did he give you the knife?"

"I don't know, I don't know." His whole body screamed with exhaustion.

"How, when, in what scenario did you end up with the knife?"

"I was at Aaron's place, and he gave it to me."

"What night?"

"It was at Aaron's house . . . I don't know when."

McDonough assured Joshua he wanted him to get through the exam. Joshua looked up, too tired to fight. "You believe I can do it?"

"I know you can. Just put the truth out on the table for me to deal with, okay?"

"Well, at least I've started . . ."

"Exactly. I agree, Josh, thank you. Okay? When you went over there, he gives you the knife. What did he say?"

"He told me it was used."

"Okay!"

"He didn't tell me how it was used. He just told me it was used."

"He told you it was used to do what?"

"Used against Stephanie."

"Did he tell you who used it?"

"Michael."

"What did he say?"

"He said I should hide it."

Joshua was questioned at length for more details, but he had none. He finally said, "Sorry, but all I know is what Aaron told me." He then asked if he could sleep for a bit, but McDonough told him he would first have to finish telling the truth, and then he could take the test again.

"But I have to sleep, sir," Josh pleaded.

McDonough said, "I'll see if your dad's here, okay?" And he left Josh alone.

The boy collapsed to the floor in apparent sleep.

• • •

In the early hours of the morning, a detective entered the room with take-out hamburgers and fries for Joshua, and he awakened the boy gently. They then allowed Mr. Treadway back into the room; he told Joshua to keep telling the truth. So Joshua repeated his story: *Yes, Aaron had given him the knife. No, he didn't have any other involvement. No, he did not hide or wash any clothing. No, he wasn't involved in any conspiracy. Yes, Aaron gave him the knife.*

At long last the detectives agreed to give Joshua the CVSA exam again. Joshua was almost unconscious on his feet by this time, barely able to stay awake. But it was as if a large weight had been lifted from his shoulders. He was desperate to pass the test.

McDonough asked the questions again, and when he finished, Joshua looked up, hopeful. "Did I pass?"

McDonough told Joshua he'd done "real good." Joshua was so relieved, even asked McDonough if he could show his dad the test results.

McDonough said he would show the investigators, first.

"Okay," Joshua said sleepily, but there was a sparkle in his voice for the first time in hours. "Okay, so I'll be able to go home and visit my mom now, right?"

Ten long hours had passed, and Joshua had been awake for well over twenty-five hours. He'd held out for the longest time, and refused to say Aaron had given him the knife, but he had finally wilted and said what they wanted to hear.

The police were tired too, but not too tired to feel great about the success of a long night's work. Claytor summed up: "Okay, we have Michael, with his cock-and-bull story about not remembering, but that's okay. He's in Juvie, and he'll start remembering soon enough. We have Joshua now, and Joshua is usable. He'll help us crack Aaron. Once Aaron is cracked, we've got the trio, and the confessions will be as good as evidence. How the hell did those kids manage to cover up the evidence so well?"

No matter—the confessions were gold.

Case closed.

11

• BEST DEFENSE •

Day Eight: Escondido, California
January 28, 1998
5:30 A.M.

The police informed Joshua Treadway that they weren't going to hold him; Joshua could go home—*now that he had chosen the "right" path.* As Mr. Treadway had told his son, the men wearing a police badge weren't bad guys. They were just doing their job and serving the community.

Joshua and his father were carefully briefed before they were sent home. Joshua was not to see or speak to Aaron nor to Michael Crowe.

The police didn't want his friends to influence Joshua in any way and have him start "lying" all over again.

Joshua was too tired to think about his ordeal on his way home. Too tired to think about anything. Mr. Treadway was equally tired, but he was relieved things had gone the way they had. What he did not realize, of course, was that there was a critical reason for the restrictions on Joshua's contact with Aaron and Michael.

Neither of them had betrayed Joshua, as the police had claimed, nor had they said a word about him being involved in the murder. All Michael had said was that Joshua was his best friend, and that he loved him. At this early stage of the investigation, Aaron Houser didn't even know he was on the suspect list. If Joshua should find out these facts, he might change his story again and then the police would be back where they started.

They had no evidence against these boys, merely a "confession" from Michael that was shaky and might not hold up in court.

When they returned home, they found Mrs. Treadway completely distraught from all the stress she had been going through during her eternal wait. Seeing her son, home at long last, she broke down sobbing. They all talked briefly and then joined in a prayer of thanks. Joshua slammed into bed, completely exhausted. His parents were also tired but were much too troubled to sleep.

• • •

January 27 had turned out to be a troublesome day for more than the Treadways, however.

That morning, prior to the arrest and interrogation of Joshua, Aaron Houser had been "invited" to come to the police station and talk with the police. He was taken, alone, to an "interview room," while his mother waited outside.

Aaron was a loose suspect at that point, but a suspect nevertheless. It was mostly his speech pattern, his way of slowly responding to questions as if he was weighing every word, that bothered the police.

Unlike Michael Crowe, he was not quiet and withdrawn, and yet he was not like Joshua either. He did not say whatever popped into his mind. And while Michael was impressively literary and had a strong vocabulary, Aaron could be even more intellectual. The apparent intellectualism of Aaron gave rise to suspicion that he had the capacity to commit a vicious crime and do so in a meticulous way.

Aaron's first interrogation, which was handled by Ralph Claytor, went far more smoothly than the badgering Michael and Joshua had endured. In fact, most of the questioning was about Michael and Joshua.

Aaron explained how he had met the two, and that they liked to play Dungeons and Dragons. Aaron said he liked to read.

He described Michael as being "calm all the time. He never overreacts," and "isn't what I call social." He usually stays by himself.

Claytor wanted to know if Aaron had ever seen Michael angry. Aaron said that just recently Michael was angry at him. Aaron had loaned him some games and wanted them returned, but Michael lost the games, so Aaron asked him to replace them. This had caused a problem between them, so Michael began talking about him behind his back.

Claytor eyed him steadily as he spoke.

"So I told him to stop," Aaron said. "And he stopped for a while, but then he started doing it again. At this point he was calling me names like 'fucker' and 'asshole.' So after school one day, I said, 'So when can I expect my money? Or do you want me to just call your parents?' And he said, 'I'll talk to them myself, but you aren't getting your goddamn games and you aren't getting any money either. I'm going to replace the games.' Besides that, he never got physical. Whenever he was angry at a person he would just curse them under his breath a lot of the time."

He told how Michael once became jealous over a girl Aaron liked, and the crush continued into ninth grade. There was another boy who liked the same girl and Michael had said he would like to kill "the little fuck." He also said Michael would talk about arguing with Stephanie. "It was nothing big, just sibling rivalry," Aaron said.

Sibling rivalry? Sweet words to Claytor, though he didn't show much of a response. Sibling rivalry made sense as a motive for murder. Nevertheless, Aaron admitted he'd never seen Michael argue with his sisters.

The subject of Aaron's sword collection then came up. Aaron gladly expounded on his collection, taking the opportunity to show off his knowledge of swords and similar weapons. This conversation easily flowed into Aaron's missing knife: *the suspected murder weapon.* Aaron explained that his mother was the one who discovered it was missing. And this conversation led to the subject of the missing forty dollars.

"For my birthday," Aaron said, "I was given some money and left some of it lying around in my room. Michael came over and gave me a birthday card with twenty dollars in it. Later that day I could not find the money from Michael that was in his card, and another twenty was missing."

"What about the knife?"

"I think I might have misplaced it, but I usually keep my knives all in one drawer. I don't like to just leave them lying around. Well, my mom brought up the subject, asked if I had checked my knives, so I checked the area where I usually keep 'em, and I checked the rest of the areas where it might be, but I didn't find it."

Claytor's expertise with interrogation was clear throughout this interview. He was not the tough cop who had interrogated Michael, or the hardass who would be interrogating Joshua later that day. With Aaron he was less serious, but serious enough to affirm his authority as a police officer. He even laughed a couple of times during the questioning.

So Aaron, although naturally nervous, felt no real threat.

That was exactly how Claytor wanted it. There would be plenty of time to set this kid on his ass—but not yet. There were a couple of tense moments before the questioning ended, however. Claytor became quite grim, and he told Aaron he'd heard that he'd asked Michael, "Have you killed them yet?" and he wanted an explanation for this.

Aaron showed a flash of resentment, or fear. "Can you tell me where it was heard, who said that?"

Claytor pretended not to remember.

Aaron half denied ever saying it, but then he admitted it. But he said it was only for a laugh; it was a kind of standing joke. Mostly it was about Michael's supposed "hit list" that had always given them laughs.

Claytor seemed to accept the idea that the comment had been made "for a laugh," and then only wanted to know when Aaron last spoke to Michael. Aaron told him it was on the telephone. He thought it was January 14.

The interview with Aaron seemed to be over. Before it ended, however, Claytor asked if Aaron would mind if the police searched his room. "Maybe we can find the missing money," he suggested with a smile. Aaron didn't mind.

In fact, he offered to show the detectives where he kept his swords, his games and his knives.

It didn't matter what Aaron or his parents thought about the police searching the Houser home. The search warrant had already been issued, and when Aaron and his mother arrived home, the police were already there, waiting. Six officers were on scene to conduct the search: Claytor, Sweeny, Wrisley, Lanigan, Han and Anderson. Several items were photographed and some things were removed from Aaron's room, taken to the police headquarters and given over to Detective George Durgin, who headed up the department's crime lab. The following items were impounded: a hunting knife with a five-inch blade; a green pillowcase; black plastic nunchakus; a Normark knife sharpener; five other smaller knives; a hatchet with its sheath, and a cutlery catalog. From a locked gun cabinet in the master bedroom, they took another hatchet and five other knives.

The fact that this family was so into knives seemed to intrigue the police—understandably.

After the police left, Aaron and his mother sat bewildered, talking over the ordeals of their day. Mrs. Houser glanced at the receipt for the items taken. *Well, the police have to be very thorough in cases like this,* she rationalized. She reminded Aaron what the police had told them: he was not, under any circumstances, to communicate with Michael or Joshua. She was convinced this was not about Aaron, this was about the other boys, and she did not want her son being involved any more than he already was.

Aaron was more relaxed by then. He had not been put under much strain. He'd not even been read his rights, so he didn't think it could be all that serious. In fact, he had found the experience interesting, something to remember. He wondered if Joshua had gone through the same thing.

12

• PRETEXT CALL •

Day Eight: Escondido, California
January 28, 1998
Midday

Joshua slept soundly. The sleep had been a welcome escape from the long, harsh hours as an accused accessory in the murder of Stephanie Crowe. There would be no real escape, however, for the police were working around the clock to bring an end to the case. As far as they were concerned, they had all the pieces of the puzzle. All they needed was a little more time. Time to get the three boys to provide them with what they needed.

It was only a matter of time before these three "little geniuses" would be where they belonged.

What amazed the investigators most was how these kids were so well prepared, as they saw it: that they had actually managed not to leave a speck of evidence behind.

Well, except for one thing: They had found the words "Kill Kill" written on Stephanie's windowsill. The handwriting analysis had shown, inconclusively, that the writing could have been Michael's.

The words "Kill, Kill" scratched into the windowsill in Stephanie Crowe's bedroom.

Anyway, writing "Kill Kill" on someone's windowsill did not make a murder case. What was needed was direct evidence. Or confessions. They had two

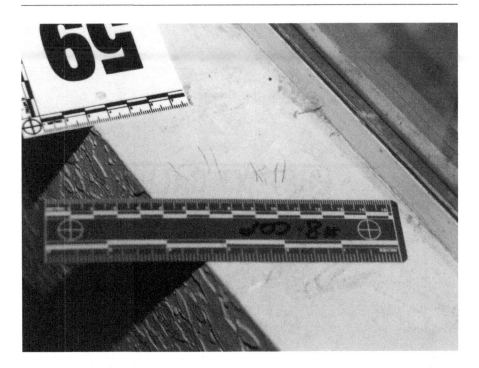

confessions: Michael's and Joshua's. But neither was as firm as they desired. What they wanted, and were determined to get, were "iron-clad" confessions.

But the police remained baffled about how the three boys could have covered their tracks so well.

• • •

Joshua was still sleepy when Claytor came to the Treadway house on the pretense of needing Joshua's help. Mr. Treadway was still convinced they were not after his son. After all, his son had merely hidden a knife, so those other kids had "used" Joshua without Joshua knowing it. He did not want his son protecting anyone who could have killed a little girl. So Treadway was more than pleased to provide help to the police.

Claytor was friendly. He greeted Mr. and Mrs. Treadway like friends. He made it clear again that Joshua was a "good boy," a kid who was simply a puppet of the "bad boys." Any sincere parent would swallow this, and Claytor knew it. In effect, he had the Treadways where he wanted them—on his side.

Claytor wanted Joshua to call Aaron and talk to him about the murder. And he wanted to record the conversation. Joshua felt pressured. He knew he had to do this; not just because the police were asking him to, but because his parents also wanted him to. Nevertheless, he could feel his heart pumping rapidly as he picked up the phone. He had nothing against Aaron. Aaron was his friend. Perhaps not his closest friend, maybe not even a good buddy, but a friend all the same. It made him queasy with guilt. *If only he had not told them Aaron had given him the knife to hide. If only he'd denied it, then none of this would be happening.*

He dialed the number.

Aaron's mother answered the telephone and would not allow Aaron to take the call. *Whoops.* Claytor had given strict orders that Aaron was not supposed to have contact with Michael or Joshua. *So now what?*

Joshua was quietly relieved, feeling he'd been let off the hook, until a moment later.

Claytor told Mr. Treadway to call Aaron's mother back and give her some story about it being okay if Aaron and Joshua talked. The ploy worked.

"Is this Josh?" Aaron asked.

Josh had been well primed for this by Claytor. "Yeah. Can you talk?" he asked.

"I'm in my room, alone."

"Full privacy? There's no one listening?"

"No."

"All right. I'm really scared." Joshua's sweaty hands clutched the phone in a death grip.

"About what?" Aaron wanted Joshua to get to the point.

"The police took me to the station last night. Did you know about that?"

"I'm not surprised."

"And they took the knife." Joshua glanced at Claytor, who gave him an approving eye—*You're doing just fine. Keep talking.*

"Okay Josh, listen up. Right now they probably think this is separate from what was going on with Mike. It sounds like if this had been caught [he was referring to his mother discovering the missing knife, calling the police

Aaron Houser

and reporting a theft], you could be charged with a misdemeanor. Minor, right? So they won't do much to you, okay? Where are you right now?"

"I'm at my house."

"Will you be at school tomorrow?"

"I don't know. They were asking me about blood on the knife. Are you sure it was cleaned off?" This was a "gonna-get-ya" question given to Joshua by Claytor.

"Why would it be cleaned? I don't need to clean it, do I?"

"I didn't know what to say to them."

"Josh, you've had this knife for what? About two weeks, correct?"

"No."

"How long?"

"Since Sunday."

"Sunday. Okay, for some reason I was thinking two weeks. You mean you came over with . . . Dr. Decker." Dr. Peggy Decker was the school psychologist.

"Uh-huh."

"You took it then?"

Claytor signaled, and Joshua responded, "I was given it then."

"Given it? Wait a minute. What do you mean you were given my knife, Josh?" Aaron's voice screamed alarm. "Exactly how did you get my knife?"

"Is that what you want me to tell them?"

"No, tell me. How did you get my knife?"

"You gave it to me on Sunday."

"On Sunday? You came over to my house with Dr. Decker. You came with your mom, and Dr. Decker came too. Right before she came, we played some *Twisted Metal 2*. We talked to Peggy, and then you left with your mom. At no point did I hand my knife over to you, correct?"

"No, I don't believe so."

"What do you believe happened?"

"I don't understand what's goin' on here. I'm asking for your help." This question was initiated by Claytor. If Aaron didn't readily admit giving Joshua the knife, he might offer some other self-incriminating statement.

"Josh," Aaron demanded, "tell me what you believe happened." Aaron was unnerved by what Joshua had said and couldn't figure out what this odd conversation was all about. "No one else is listening?" he asked Joshua suspiciously.

"No. What are we gonna do?"

"Josh, tell me what you believe happened. Tell me the truth."

"You gave me the knife on Sunday. And you gave me instructions to get rid of it."

"I *what?*" Aaron was incredulous; he now realized there was more to this phone call than a friendly report from Josh. He could sense big trouble; he felt it in the pit of his stomach and wanted an end to it. "Did you say I gave you the knife on Sunday, with instructions to get rid of it?"

"I did," Joshua said, his voice shrill, his nerves dancing on a thin wire.

"Tell me, Josh, why would I do that?" Aaron correctly suspected there were more ears on the phone than just Joshua's.

"I don't know."

"When did I give you the knife, the exact time?"

"Sunday."

"Time, not day. Time," Aaron demanded.

"I don't know, around twelve-forty-five."

"Before or after we spoke to Peggy?"

"Before." Joshua glanced at his father, then at Claytor, who had prepared the question. "I see what you're doing, just . . . just give me some help here. I mean come on, Aaron."

"What do you mean, you see what I'm doing?" Aaron snapped.

"I don't know. Maybe you're upset because someone else is listening there, but . . ."

"No one here is listening, Josh. No one in this house is listening."

"Look, I'm really sorry they found the knife. I mean . . . do we need a plan?"

"Why would we need a plan, Josh?"

"That's what I called you for. I'm really scared. I don't know what to do right now."

"First, I want you to take a really deep breath and . . . and breathe out slowly. Okay, listen: Michael's sister was killed with some kind of sharp object, correct?"

"Uh-huh."

"He also took a couple of hatchets, okay. Now, when do you think was the last time Michael was over at my house?" Aaron didn't know exactly where this conversation was leading, but he wouldn't be led. "It was around my birthday, in October, right?"

"I don't know what schedule you and Michael had together."

"It was in October, on my birthday. A long time ago, okay. Because Michael and I, as you recall, were not good friends lately."

"Aaron, I can't handle this."

"Calm down, Josh."

"I'm thinking of telling them everything."

"About what? Everything being what?"

Joshua looked at Claytor again. The detective prompted him, "Everything you told me on Sunday."

"What did I tell you, Josh?"

"You gave me the knife. Told me it was the knife Michael used to kill Stephanie, and told me to get rid of it."

"I never said that, Josh. Never at any point did I say that. I had nothing to do with Michael Crowe."

"Aaron . . . I had to take a lie detector test."

"Listen to me, Josh. Listen to me, okay. You know Michael and I hated each other, right? You were planning your birthday party this Friday, and we were, we had agreed not to talk to each other, right?"

"Uh-huh."

"You know Michael was insulting me, and stuff. I—"

"Except for the fact that it wasn't this Friday. It was—"

"Last Friday, but you bumped it up, right?"

"Uh-huh."

"So if I hated Michael so much . . . I mean, I guess hate's a pretty strong word. I didn't like him, you know, I just wanted to get my games back from him, right? Now why would I take the knife? And Josh, when would Michael come into possession of that knife? I would never help kill someone, would I? I mean, if Michael has killed his sister, if that really happened, which there's no proof of, and personally I can't imagine Michael killing anyone. Can you?"

Joshua had been paying more attention to Claytor than to Aaron. "Aaron, how am I gonna get by this test if they force it?" he asked.

"Josh, all that happened on Sunday was you came over and we played some *Twisted Metal 2*. You remember how you said, 'Oh yeah, this is a big relief,' ya know, finally playing something for fun. I didn't give you my knife, Josh," he insisted.

"I can't handle this, Aaron."

"Josh, right now they think, and I think, you just saw my knife and took it because . . . you liked my sword, do you remember, Josh?"

"Yes."

"Breathe in deeply. I want you to breathe in with your stomach, then your chest. As big a breath as you can take, and then hold it for a moment. Do it right now. You doing it?"

"Uh-huh."

"Now do it again. Breathe in some more. Calm down, okay. Now, I did not help Michael kill Stephanie. That knife was not used to kill Stephanie to my knowledge, okay?"

"Aaron . . ."

"Hold on, hold on. I will admit I don't really keep close track of my knives, okay. I mean I never really have. Because, well, I consider my swords a lot more important. I usually just keep my knives in that drawer. Now, on Sunday, I don't think you had a chance to steal my knife. I don't think you were really out of my sight for that long. As far as I can recall, you were in my room . . . that was when we were playing *Twisted Metal.* The rest of the time you were in the living room."

"Aaron, they said Michael said some things. I really need some help. I mean, we need a plan."

"Josh, we don't need a plan. We didn't do anything wrong. I didn't give you that knife. I haven't done anything wrong. Nothing at all. I didn't help Michael. Even if Michael did it, I wasn't involved. The police checked my house and they know I wasn't involved."

Joshua, at Claytor's prompting, continued to insist that Aaron had given him the knife to hide. Aaron repeated his denials, and, frustrated, eventually cut Joshua off and hung up.

Joshua was trembling, feeling faint. Claytor assured him he'd done just fine, but beneath the surface the investigator was wrestling with his own thoughts. *This kid Aaron was not only smart, he was smooth.*

• • •

By the time Joshua had completed that manipulated phone call, a lot had happened. On the previous day, January 27, the day Aaron and Joshua were interrogated, Stephanie's funeral was held. The Crowes were still being denied access to their house and, adding to the grief of burying their daughter, they suffered the pain of knowing their son was in Juvenile Hall, accused of the crime. They remained convinced of Michael's innocence, but their feelings had no impact on the police.

Finally, three days after the funeral—January 30—the Crowes were allowed to return to their home. Home? The very environment of a home changes when a loved one has been brutally slaughtered inside the family sanctuary. The house is reduced to a place of horrifying mental images. Thus, the emptiness that people feel when they lose a beloved child is intensified by the dire circumstance of how the loss occurred.

As the Crowes approached their house, their apprehension intensified. *Do we really want to see this house again? To walk in and look down that empty hallway, with its memories and the vision of Stephanie lying there on the floor?* Who would want to relive the horror? Yet they had to.

They parked in the driveway and slowly got out of the car. The exterior of the house looked ominous. Lifeless. They had to force themselves to go inside, to walk through the same door that, not three weeks before, had welcomed them into its safe bosom. Now everything had changed; this was a strange place and they were strangers at its doorway. This was no longer their home. And no one had had the courtesy to prepare them for what they were coming "home" to.

When they entered, they were shocked to discover their house in havoc, literally torn apart.

The police had not bothered to warn them how they had left the place. Its condition was shocking.

Their beloved home was utterly destroyed. Nearly every inch of wall, carpet, and furniture had been shattered, ruined or removed.

It reminded Steve Crowe of TV news footage from Florida after a hurricane.

In the bathrooms, everything had been torn apart by the investigators. Cheryl Crowe sobbed as Steve surveyed the house in a daze.

The more they walked about the house, the more upsetting their discoveries. The wall cabinets, planters, even stereo speakers had been pulled apart and left behind. Outside they discovered things from their master bedroom at the bottom of the pool. *How in God's name did those things get from the bedroom into the pool? Who had thrown them there as if they were worthless?*

But the most heart-wrenching disaster had been what was left of Stephanie's room. Or rather, what was not left of her room.

Nearly everything belonging to Stephanie had been removed: her stuffed animals, her toys, her clothing, her precious telephone—they had all been taken. *Even the carpet and wall panels in Stephanie's room had been removed.* It looked like a bomb had exploded, leaving only an empty shell. The happy childhood bedroom of the beloved daughter they had just buried was, like Stephanie herself, now just a distant memory.

And the devastating loss of their daughter was being compounded daily by the devastating actions of the police department against this heartbroken family.

Terrified, young Shannon reached for her mother's hand.

In a few short weeks, the little girl had witnessed more horrifying events than most adults do in a lifetime.

• • •

The following days were a nightmare for the Treadways, too.

Joshua had become a nervous wreck. He'd been forced to change schools, primarily to comply with the police order for him not to see or communicate with Aaron Houser. It was also thought that a change might be better for him. Peggy Decker, the school psychologist, had been informed Joshua might become suicidal.

Joshua was certainly carrying a lot of emotional baggage. For one thing, he found it extremely difficult to live with what he had done to Aaron over the phone. No one likes to think of themselves as a person who would betray a friend, but Joshua felt he was such a betrayer.

In the quiet hours, when Joshua was alone, his vivid imagination worked against him. Every sound of a car driving past, every distant siren made him seize up with apprehension. *Was it the police coming back to arrest him and take him away?* He would not leave the house. The world, except for school or church, had become intimidating and foreboding. There were dangers outside—a world filled with cops and courts and jails—and any second he might become subject to them, their victim. He fell deeper into depression every day, lower into the depths of despair and fear; with every passing day his apprehension intensified until it threatened to suffocate him. He was living his entire life just waiting for the ax to fall.

13

• HE GAVE ME THE KNIFE •

Day Twenty: Escondido, California
February 9, 1998

Between January 21—when Stephanie Crowe's body was discovered—and February 9, the investigation had been as intense as any in Escondido's history. Forensic tests had been applied and police dogs had been involved in the search for evidence. Many hours of detective work had been invested and still no evidence had been found. What the police concluded was that this was a well-planned murder, carried out with precision. Aaron Houser had the kind of mental ability it would take to think through and execute such a plan, leaving no clues behind. The police were convinced, mostly based on hunches, he was the principal, the one who had worked out the details and instructed the others in their roles.

Michael Crowe had confessed to the crime, but he had stayed with his story of not remembering it.

Like Aaron, Michael was also intellectual and, according to the police, was far less emotional than he pretended to be. They labeled him a "weird kid," and all the information gathered about him seemed to substantiate this. If one can honestly label someone who is shy, quiet, and contemplative as "weird," then the police definition of Michael was appropriate.

Then there was Joshua. Joshua was obviously more emotional than the other two and far more volatile. He was less ponderous than Michael or

Aaron and he wore his feelings on his sleeve. Any rookie cop could see that this boy was terrified at the thought of going to jail, and such a fear always makes police work easier, especially the task of squeezing out a confession.

Even locker-room gossip at the police station was focused on the easiest way to break this case: break down Joshua Treadway.

In time, he would finger the other two conclusively and even offer how the evidence was covered up.

That was the police assumption.

So Joshua remained the focus, and on February 10, he was returned to Escondido's interrogation room under the pretense of wanting to clear up "a couple of questions."

Joshua was anxious, praying this session would not turn out to be as long as the last one. It didn't seem to be starting out very intense. Claytor stayed just a few seconds and then McDonough entered.

He greeted Joshua with a broad smile. "Hey, Josh."

"Hey, Chris." Joshua managed to smile back.

"How are you? Got a haircut, huh?"

"Yeah."

"Hey, I appreciate you coming down. Did Detective Claytor tell you what I wanted?" The tone McDonough used relaxed Joshua. He'd be in and out of there in no time, it seemed to indicate. But McDonough was merely priming the pump. "Things goin' good?" he asked. "Tell me about how you been. What's been goin' on?"

"I was taken out of Orange Glen and put into Charter High School."

"Really?" McDonough showed interest. "Have you had a chance to talk to Michael?"

"No. Mike's mom called one time. Talked to my dad. She said she wanted me to write to Michael, and my dad just said I wasn't there. You know, he hung up."

"Uh-huh."

"And I don't want to write him."

"Has he tried to call you from Juvenile Hall, or anything?"

"No."

"Not one time?" McDonough wanted to make absolutely sure they had not talked, had not had time to put their stories together. He asked how Joshua felt after the last time they had seen each other—after the last interrogation.

"Well, I felt kind of like, you know, like I got rid of a heavy load."

"Is there anything that came up after that, anything you thought was important?"

"Umm . . . Oh, there's one thing, I think. I don't know how important it is, it's just something, you know."

"Okay."

"When Mr. Claytor last came to my house—Thursday, I think it was—he was talking to my brother. And my brother told him, you know, that he'd seen the knife a long time ago, in October or so; yeah that's true. I had it, um . . . at my house, I borrowed it from Aaron. I actually asked him, and Aaron said it was okay. So I took it home and showed my brother Zach, because it resembled a knife in a movie we'd seen."

"So you actually had the knife before . . ."

"Uh-huh."

"Okay, see that's good information." McDonough reestablished that Aaron was really into knives.

He listened as Joshua told how finicky Aaron was about his swords, how upset he would become if someone touched them. Then he retold the story of going over to Aaron's house on Super Bowl Sunday, and how he and Aaron played a game, and how he noticed Aaron wasn't into the game very much. So they stopped playing and walked over to the shelf where Aaron kept his knives.

"And that's when he made the pass off. Remember, as I said before, that's when he told me it was the knife Michael had used to kill Stephanie."

"Then what happened?"

"And then . . . like less than a minute after that, he sort of put it in my hand. I was like, you know, shocked. 'Aaron, what are you doing?' I asked. Then Dr. Decker arrived and they called us into the living room. So I've got this thing in my hand as I'm walking down the hall. So I put it in my pocket real quick and we sat down on the couch. I don't even think I heard half the things Mrs. Decker said, I was just so shook up and nervous about everything. And so I just kind of sat there with a blank look on my face."

"Was that the moment all the stress really started?" McDonough asked.

"Oh, yeah. It was like, bam! It hit me like a huge stone just slammed down, and I was like, oh, man. So then, I mean, I was just like ten shades of worried, just shocked."

"I would've been too."

"Because until then I didn't think Michael had anything to do with it."

"Right."

"And I was really nervous, because, I mean, I didn't think my friend would do anything like that."

"Did you think at that point you might be involved in this?"

"Well, I figured they might want to talk to me some—me being his friend. But I never figured anyone would suspect I was involved because I didn't do anything in the whole deal. I didn't even know, I still don't even know how everything went down. I don't know if anyone knows. I mean . . . all I know is Aaron . . . I was given the knife by Aaron and I'm beginning to think Aaron may have had something to do with it."

"And why's that?"

"Because Aaron's the one who gave me the knife." Joshua didn't want to waste any more time. He wanted to answer the questions and leave.

His only goal was to get out of there.

"Any conversations with Aaron since we last spoke?"

"None that I started. Mr. Claytor wanted me to call him . . ."

"Okay. Outside of that, any conversations?"

"No."

"Okay. Since that time, have you had any contact with Aaron?"

"No."

They talked a little longer and McDonough reminded Joshua that he was a neutral player. "I'm here to make sure you're telling the truth, okay? I'm on . . . I'm down the middle, just seeking the truth, okay. But really, I want you to pass these exams."

McDonough kept returning to the subject of Aaron; he kept fishing for something that would thread together the conspiracy theory. This was touchy, since it was a subject that could not be directly addressed. If Joshua believed he was suspected of having more to do with the crime than merely hiding the knife, he might withdraw or change his story again. The trick was to make Joshua think he was safe from any serious trouble just as long as he played it straight with the cops.

It worked.

Joshua believed the price of his freedom was giving the police what they wanted.

Joshua told McDonough of a dream he'd had about Aaron. Aaron had come to his house, acting normally, and Joshua felt terrible because he thought "bad things" about Aaron. But then, during this visit, Aaron had freaked out, gone crazy, started ravaging the house.

Joshua said he woke up in a cold sweat, wondering what Aaron's part in the murder really was. "That's another thing," he told McDonough. "I don't know if he . . . if he's involved more than he let me know, or—"

"Do you think he is?" asked McDonough.

"My gut tells me he is." This was enough to stir McDonough's zeal, and he zeroed in on Aaron's involvement. His experience told him Joshua was on the verge of opening up, and he returned to the CVSA. He spent a lot of time pointing out where the machine had said Joshua lied. Because of the CVSA, McDonough said, he knew there was more to the story, things that Joshua was still hiding.

Finally he said, "There's no such thing as loyalty, okay? Because what it comes down to is looking out for number one, okay? Just look out for Josh, okay?"

Joshua could feel his heart beating fast. This was the same message his father had been drumming into him. "He told me . . ." Joshua swallowed, his anxiety level rising. "He was there, too."

"What'd he say?"

"When I asked him, you know, he said, 'I was there.' When I asked him how he knew Michael was the one who did it, he said, 'I was there. I helped him.'"

"What did he say he did?"

"He said he helped kill her. That's all he said. And at that point I didn't know what else to say. I didn't speak after that. My mouth went kind of dry."

McDonough was careful not to show any emotion, but this was a break-through—a moment of triumph. At last, the hunches were beginning to pay off.

"So who killed her?" McDonough asked.

"Both did it."

"Okay . . . why?"

"I have no idea why Aaron did it. I think Michael would have done it out of jealousy, or whatever. Just pure hatred towards his sister."

"Okay." McDonough then added a little spice to the speculation. "What if . . . How about if Aaron said, 'Josh did it. He was with Michael.'"

"Well then he'd take the test and the graph doesn't lie," Joshua said. He was wholly convinced the CVSA was the key to his survival.

"What if the graph doesn't lie and he passes?"

"Well, he won't." Joshua sounded firmly convinced.

"Okay, but I don't want any surprises."

"I'm not too worried about that happening."

As McDonough continued his questioning, Joshua embellished his story, believing that telling the police what they wanted to hear would exonerate him. His only role, he insisted, "was just getting rid of the knife."

He claimed that he wasn't at the crime scene, that Aaron had told him that Michael "kept her quiet and held her mouth," and Aaron "took care of the rest."

Joshua, by then, saw McDonough as a sympathetic advocate, someone who would tell the cold and brutal authorities how helpful he had been, how freely he admitted wrongdoing and how sorry he was.

McDonough fell silent a few moments. Then he did his best to cover himself. "Okay," he said, "you know what I'm gonna do? I'm gonna bring Detective Claytor in here, okay, because as you're laying this thing out he needs to be with me, okay? You feel comfortable with that? With me and him?"

There was good reason for this sudden contrivance. McDonough was well aware that he was not supposed to be involved in gaining the confession. His job was simply to give the ten-minute CVSA exam and leave. As stated in an earlier chapter, even if the suspect wishes to confess during the exam, the examiner must go and summon the interrogating officer. McDonough was not about to give this one up, though. He wanted the confession, but he had to at least appear as if he "tried" to follow the rules. To this point he'd been the only one interrogating Joshua and was out of line, the same way he had been during Michael's interrogation. The trick, of course, was to let Joshua make the call, and he knew that the boy was afraid of Ralph Claytor.

"Well, I guess," Joshua said, his reluctance showing.

McDonough was slightly bewildered. "If you don't . . . just say it, Josh. Say no, I don't mind, and I'll continue as I have been."

"Well, I'd like to finish talking to you first."

McDonough was well aware there was yet to be a shred of real evidence, so he asked Joshua about the bloody clothing Michael and Aaron had on after killing Stephanie. He insisted that Joshua must know where it had been hidden.

Joshua denied having any knowledge of the clothing and volunteered to "take the lie detector test" again. He said he didn't know anything about the murder "until a few days later."

The interrogation continued, and McDonough used Claytor's name again to keep reminding Joshua that he'd better keep giving answers. Claytor did not appear for a long time, however, and might not even have been in the building. After a while, Detective McDonough excused himself, saying he'd be right back. He left Joshua sitting for eighteen minutes.

Joshua had, at that point, been under interrogation for more than two hours. But this was only the beginning.

• • •

After McDonough returned to the interview room, the questions targeted Michael for a while. Joshua told the detective Michael liked to read about medieval torture and was into O.J. Simpson. He said Michael had a kind of fixation with death and he read books with titles such as *Man, Myth and Magic.*

"He loved reading about weird things, you know. Some of the stuff in them was just wrong. I mean it's like, you know . . . Have you seen the gothic Catholic torture deal?"

"No. It sounds bizarre."

Moments later McDonough was, again, trying his utmost to place Joshua at the scene of the crime. But he knew there was the risk of sending Joshua into some deep corner of his mind, where he might stop talking all together. It was a delicate balancing act.

"I believe you brought the knife," the detective said, but with his next breath he added that he was unsure about whether Joshua had participated in the plan. He told Joshua he must keep weighing the consequences before saying something, and that could become a problem for him.

"You don't want any surprises, do you? Like the DA saying, hypothetically, 'We'll just charge them all with murder.'"

Joshua paled at the thought.

But as always, McDonough came to the rescue. "I'm going to prevent that, okay. That's my job, and my commitment to you, okay? I'm not in the business of doing that to people, and you're not in the business of making that happen in your life are you?"

Joshua shook his head. He was deeply alarmed by this line of talk.

"Okay, now you're scared because that's a big word I laid on you, right?" McDonough was making a strong point. He explained to Joshua that he didn't want any surprises because Joshua was afraid to say something. "Michael's going to say one thing and Aaron another, Josh. The crime scene is going to say another thing, and the evidence is going to say another. You follow?"

"Uh-huh." Joshua had become distant. He was dwelling on what McDonough had said about the DA, and the thought of being included in the murder charge.

"And all these factors," McDonough continued, "have to be put together, Josh. They all have to fit, okay? If they don't fit, then our responsibility is to ask, 'Why don't they fit?' and usually it's because people are lying. And then you can just figure out what the lies are and use them against a person. Did you know that?"

"Uh-huh."

"Yeah, you can use them to get at the person, okay? Because if a person lies, and then they get on the stand and testify under oath and tell a different story, then you can use their own statements against them, okay. Potentially, one day, you could be put on the stand and somebody would ask if you had not told the truth initially. And you're going to say, 'Yes,' okay, because you're telling the truth."

"If I didn't come clean initially?" asked Joshua.

"You didn't, and that's exactly what you have to tell them, because that's the truth, okay. So okay, Detective Claytor will be sitting there. No big deal, okay? And the jury will sit there and . . ." he continued with a convoluted story about how the jury would judge him if he said one thing and the evidence said something else. When he was finished with this subtle and confusing warning, he directly returned to being Joshua's ally.

"I want you to slide through that system, okay, Josh. I want to be able to say, 'Okay, Josh came through 100 percent, put it all on the table,' okay?"

"I have to tell you, the whole idea of going into court scares me."

"Scares me, too."

"Because I've seen it on TV."

"Dude, it scares me too, okay. It does."

The questioning went on for another half hour as they went over much of the same ground.

When did Joshua first hear about the murder plot? When did he first get the knife? Had he cleaned the knife? Did he know anything else?

At long last, McDonough decided to give Joshua the CVSA exam. Joshua asked if he could go to the bathroom, and another detective escorted him out and back. McDonough also left and was gone for fifteen minutes. When he returned, he prompted Joshua on the rules for taking the CVSA again. While he was putting the graph paper into the machine, the detective told Joshua that everyone was pleased with him."

"Pleased?" Joshua seemed pleasantly surprised. He knew, or at least assumed, that McDonough and Claytor had been talking. But with this comment, McDonough was using a ploy to relax Joshua, to loosen him up.

McDonough administered the test again, one of the questions being: "Were you present when Stephanie was killed?"

To which Joshua answered, "No."

They took a few moments to make sure Josh was relaxed, then McDonough repeated the test. After another short rest, he did the whole thing over for a third time. The stress grew in Joshua's face, but he answered all the questions each time in the same way.

Finally, after a pause, McDonough asked Joshua if he wanted to hear the results. Joshua said he did, of course, but the detective asked another question: "Did you talk to Aaron?"

When Joshua denied it, the detective told him to stop lying. He gave Joshua a long lecture on telling the truth, and with each word Joshua seemed to become more and more upset. But then McDonough hit him where he was most vulnerable.

"Maybe you were involved with it, but who got you involved?" he asked. "And why should you suffer for things they got you involved in? Did you make a poor choice? Sure you did, okay? You owe it to yourself to put the truth out on the table. Who cares about them? You think Michael or Aaron cares about you right now? No! So let it go."

Suddenly this was too much, and Joshua lost control. He began sobbing—nearly in hysterics. There was good reason, a specific trigger for this response. He had been told he'd lied in the CVSA exam.

When Joshua finally settled down, McDonough said, "Tell me what happened, huh? Tell me what happened,"

"I'm upset right now."

"I know. But were you present when they did it?"

McDonough did not waste a second, knowing this was the perfect time to press. The kid had broken down, and when a person breaks down he is the most vulnerable, most likely to tell the truth, even bring out his darkest secrets.

He asked Joshua if he had cleaned the knife, and Joshua admitted he had, saying that he didn't mention cleaning the knife before because he was afraid the detective would get mad at him.

Joshua broke into tears again and soon admitted that he had spoken to Aaron once. Once again he couldn't stop the tears. "He said if I talk to anybody about this he'd come after me and kill me too."

McDonough could not wait to get out of the room to report this new development. "Let me get you some water," he said. "I'll be right back."

Joshua, left alone, cried again. It was as if there were no way out for him. No matter what he said, it was never enough. He was never believed because they just wanted more and more information. He felt completely trapped. Suddenly he started praying: "Please don't let Aaron come and kill me. Please, God. Please."

McDonough came back and offered to take Joshua to get a drink. They left the room together and then, moments later when they returned, the detective wanted to know more about Aaron's warning.

"He told me on Super Bowl Sunday, 'Don't tell anybody anything, or I'll kill you, just like I did Stef.' And then, when he called, I don't remember the date but it was after the controlled call with Detective Claytor. He said that if I told anybody anything he would kill me, and my whole family too. I was scared Aaron might follow me, planning to kill me."

McDonough returned to questions about the knife and what else Joshua knew about the murder, but Josh kept returning to his fear of Aaron.

Another twenty minutes passed, McDonough pressing Joshua about telling the truth. And the "truth" Joshua had been telling since his first interrogation, on January 27 and 28, had changed. He was saying Aaron had given him the knife, as opposed to his original claim that he stole the knife. He also claimed that he'd cleaned the knife, and that he heard bits and pieces about the planning of the murder prior to the actual killing. All this added up to exactly what McDonough and the other detectives believed even before Joshua returned to the station for his second go-around in the interview room. All along they had been convinced that these three boys, Michael, Aaron and Joshua, had planned the murder together and executed the murder together.

The problem was that there was still no evidence, and Michael still had not said anything to entangle either Joshua or Aaron in the crime.

All they needed was to work Joshua long enough to make him bend and come clean. When this happened—and the police were sure it would—all the missing pieces of the puzzle would emerge.

McDonough's major goal was to get Joshua to confess that he was actually at the crime scene. He had subtly been working toward this end since the beginning. He suggested to Joshua that he was at least a "lookout" for the other two boys.

Joshua acknowledged that, but claimed he "never entered the house." He had remained outside, in the driveway, after joining Aaron at his house, then together going to the Crowe house, arriving "around ten-thirty, eleven or so."

He went on to describe how Michael and Aaron had committed the crime.

McDonough was especially interested in the clothing Joshua and Aaron wore that night. There had to be blood on that clothing, and those blood-covered clothes had not been found.

Joshua kept reminding McDonough that he had not been much more than a mere puppet during the crime. "I didn't want to do any of this," he said. "And Aaron told me if I didn't help him out with it I wouldn't be a true friend. He said if I didn't help him out he'd kill me."

He went on to say that, "Aaron, he . . . he told me on Super Bowl Sunday that, you know, this whole thing was just flawless. There was nothing wrong with it, you know. This was going to get by if I just did as I was told."

Within the next ten minutes McDonough exited again and fifteen more minutes passed.

Joshua's nemesis then entered.

As always, Claytor was all business. There was an air of inflexibility about him.

They talked about what Joshua had told McDonough and then Claytor asked about Aaron. Joshua again explained that Aaron told him that as long as he stuck to their plan everything would be okay. Claytor was curious about what "sticking to the plan" meant.

"Well, he . . . his plan was, I get rid of the knife and not say anything to anyone."

Claytor, staying consistent, showed no reaction. He continued questioning Joshua and said they had a big puzzle to put together. He said Joshua had given him only six or seven pieces, so he had to fill in the gaps. He wanted to know how far Joshua went into the house.

Joshua, by this time, had gone from admitting to stealing Aaron's knife, and having it under his bed at the time of the murder, to being given Aaron's knife after the murder to being a lookout at the time of the crime. Now he was being pushed to admit that he had entered the Crowe house.

And, surprisingly, he did admit to this.

He entered the house, he said, because he was cold and shaky.

"I just went to the kitchen area and stayed there." Aaron and Michael at that point "were down the hall."

"Now see, here's the problem," Claytor said. "You need to really understand this, and I kind of think you do, but when we come in to talk to you like this, *you never know what we know.*"

Joshua was totally thrown by the statement. His mouth barely managed its reply. "You're right, I don't."

"And you don't know what other people have told us, or what evidence we have. Your case is not gonna stick, okay. There's a lot in it. There's that much paper in it." He held his hands a foot apart.

"Was anything said about what if Mom woke up, or Dad?" Claytor asked. "What was going to happen? Was there any discussion about how to get away with this, and what happens after?"

"No. Just the fact that we needed to dispose of the knife."

Regardless of what they were telling Joshua, twenty days after Stephanie's murder, the police still had no evidence against Michael, Joshua, or Aaron. Joshua had become an unexpectedly easy target for their coercion, though, and the department's scuttlebutt, that this kid Joshua was a "talker," had proven correct.

"Just that I needed to get rid of the knife, later. He didn't give it to me right then."

"Why do you think he didn't give it to you right then?"

"I have no idea. He gave it to me on Super Bowl Sunday. I took a lie detector test questioning that."

"I know you did, Joshua, and you know you didn't do well on several questions. In fact, you did pretty lousy; obviously it wasn't the truth."

Claytor then told Joshua that he had to tell the truth; otherwise, his status would not change. The long, one-sided talk with Joshua was a show of exquisite police strategy. Joshua could clam up or open up, cry, laugh, plead, or bargain, and nothing would help or hurt him. He was, as Claytor said, in this thing as deep as he could be. In some way this gave Joshua an enormous feeling of relief. After all, things couldn't get worse.

At that moment, the big question became: *Would he give them the additional information they wanted?*

• • •

Joshua had been under interrogation for nine grueling hours by this time, so, in the face of being told that nothing was going to change and that he was in as much trouble as he could ever be in, he was relieved.

He was totally exhausted, but he found the energy to add some parts to his story. He said Michael came to the kitchen and rinsed the knife in the sink.

Claytor wondered why Aaron, who lived about a mile from Michael, didn't just chuck the knife in an orange grove or the flood control channel on the way home. Joshua didn't know why. He asked to see his father, and Claytor left the room, saying he would have somebody take him to the bathroom, and he'd get him something to eat.

Looking toward the closed door of the interview room, Joshua wondered what would happen next.

Meanwhile, Claytor and McDonough talked about Joshua's confession, summing up their conclusions. They didn't know where the deception was, but as far as Joshua being afraid for his life, they saw it as pure bullshit.

No, this kid was dumb like a fox. His entire confession was all about saving his own rear end and laying blame on his two comrades.

These were not the only cards stacked heavily against Joshua. As it turned out, the only fingerprints found on the knife were Joshua's. But the mystery of the clothing still remained. *How had these three boys gotten rid of the blood-splattered clothes they were wearing?*

And, why would the two plotters need to include Joshua? The lookout story was weak, at best. *Why would Joshua be told to stand outside, when the crime was occurring inside Michael's home?* It never occurred to the police that the lie told by Josh was that he knew anything at all.

If the story Joshua had slowly concocted were true, would he be no less a murderer than Aaron or Michael? In spite of how Joshua had laid out his virtual innocence in the entire ordeal, in spite of his insistence that he played a mere peripheral role in the killing, Claytor and McDonough still thought him guilty of murder.

If Joshua was this frail, frightened and emotional personality that he showed himself to be during both of his interrogations, why, then, had he not just run away? The question that followed was how, after being at the murder scene, after knowing he had been involved in a heinous crime, after knowing that while he stood in the kitchen his two friends maliciously stabbed Stephanie Crowe to death, he could be calm and collected enough to celebrate his birthday on the very day of the girl's funeral?

But this, instead of being incongruent to the police, was seen by them as evidence that Joshua was as cold blooded as the other two. What mattered most to the police, of course, was that Joshua had confessed, had told enough to start the process of wrapping up this murder case. There was only one problem.

While the police had all this on videotape, they had failed to properly read Joshua his *Miranda* rights.

Claytor and McDonough wanted to avoid the risk of going back in and giving Joshua his rights after all they had put him through. What if

Joshua rethought everything and recanted? What would they do if Joshua said, 'Sorry. I made a mistake. I lied. I was scared of you guys and I want to change my story'? It could happen, and the seriousness of the *Miranda* warning could trigger it, so why risk it? If Joshua was smart enough to use his so-called fear of Aaron in hope of getting himself out of trouble, what if he turned that around and used his fear of the police as an excuse for not giving up his *Miranda* rights. Then what?

They'd be back to square one, that's what.

14

· YOU'RE UNDER ARREST ·

Day Twenty: Escondido, California
February 9, 1998
7:25 p.m.

Detectives Claytor and McDonough returned to the interview room and Joshua looked up, wide-eyed. "Is my dad still here?" he asked.

"I think so," Claytor said absently. "I understand you're concerned, Josh, about what's gonna happen to you, right? We're being up front with you. As of now, it's 7:25 in the evening—"

Joshua was so focused on the possibility of seeing his father after so many grueling hours of hell, that he barely comprehended what Claytor said next:

"—and you're under arrest for your involvement in Stephanie's murder, okay?"

Joshua felt all the air get sucked out of his lungs.

"Nothing's going to happen right away," Claytor continued. "We've got some food coming, okay? Just hang tight. Remember what I said about these problems; they're not insurmountable. We can deal with this, okay? I'm gonna go talk to your dad."

"C-can I see him?" Joshua wailed fearfully.

"Probably not tonight."

"Can't he just come and visit with me alone?" Panic-stricken, his face blanched.

"No. What you need to understand, Josh, is you're under arrest, okay."

Joshua still had not been read his *Miranda* rights, so now, after all this time, Claytor decided he would bring Wrisley in to read the boy his rights and then get Joshua to restate his confession.

But Wrisley was off work that day, so there was a long delay. And with each tick of the clock, Joshua felt his world spinning slowly to a halt.

• • •

Wrisley was called at home and told to come in. When he finally showed up, he was given an update on all that had happened and told to finish off the confession. Wrisley had played the "nice guy" throughout this investigation, starting with Michael, and so he was seen as the best candidate to work with Joshua.

Anyway, Claytor and McDonough had been at this thing all day.

Wrisley greeted Joshua in a friendly manner. By then Joshua was so worn out, words no longer had meaning.

"Just so I'm clear on what happened, I want to ask you some things and, you know, maybe you can clear up some of the questions I have. But before I do that, I gotta read you your rights. You know, like on TV."

"Yeah," Joshua choked. He had no idea that he had a last chance to proclaim his innocence.

"So I'm gonna read these through, okay, and I want to make sure that you understand them, so listen to me carefully, Josh. You have the right to remain silent. If you give up the right to remain silent, anything you do say can and will be used in court against you. You have the right to speak to an attorney of your choice before questioning, and to have the attorney present during questioning. If you cannot afford an attorney, one will be appointed for you by the court, if you so desire. The attorney will not cost a thing; the services are free. Do you understand each of these rights I have explained to you?"

If he'd been clear-headed, if he hadn't been trapped in their web of deceit, he might have comprehended the words *you have the right to speak to an attorney of your choice before questioning.* His sluggish mind couldn't reason with the duplicity that they'd questioned him for more than eighteen hours without telling him that he could speak to a lawyer *before being interrogated.*

The detective asked again, "Josh? Do you understand each of these rights I have explained to you?" Joshua shook his head—perhaps an attempt to clear it.

"Is that a yes or no?"

"T-that's a y-yes," the boy stuttered.

"Okay, having in mind and understanding your rights, are you willing to talk to me?"

"Yeah." He fought to keep from passing out cold on the floor.

Wrisley explained that at Juvenile Hall his parents could visit him, and they would be in the same room, together.

"So we can have physical contact?" Sadly, this was his only glimmer of hope in all this madness.

"Yeah, it's not like one of those things where you have the glass partition."

What Joshua didn't know was that his father had been sent home. He asked a lot of questions about going to jail, whether he would be in a cell by himself or with others.

Wrisley said he didn't know, but he assured Joshua that "all the people down there will make sure you're okay."

When the actual questioning began, Joshua returned to his fear of Aaron. He added that he hadn't realized Aaron was so weird. But he had worried about him going through with the murder.

The questions went on and on, repeating all of what Joshua had already told McDonough and Claytor. It was a repeat of the confession he had made prior to hearing his *Miranda* rights.

As the session was coming to an end, Wrisley asked Joshua, "So when you left the house that night, did you know what had occurred—that Stephanie was dead? You're telling me now that you didn't go into her room and see with your own eyes?"

"No, I didn't see it with my own eyes. I think it would have been too much for me to take. I think I would have yelled, or something. I don't know."

"And all the evidence we've collected is gonna prove you weren't there?"

"Yeah."

"You're sure of that?"

"Uh-huh." The stress the boy had endured was fully in evidence. Zombie-like, he seemed to be nearly catatonic.

"And you know we've collected a ton of stuff." Wrisley repeated the same old lie.

"Yeah, I know. I'm confident it'll show I was not in the room."

They talked a little more, and Joshua finally asked when he'd be able to get some sleep. It was then ten forty-three. Joshua had been subjected to thirteen solid hours of constant pressure. Wrisley knew this, and he had all the needed elements of the confession recorded on video, more than once. He asked Joshua what he thought ought to happen to him.

"Is it okay if I don't answer that question? I don't know what should happen to me."

"Are you worried about it?"

"Yeah, kind of. Because Mr. Claytor said—I don't remember the word he used—but he said there were a lot of problems for me, you know. That scared me. It scared me a lot, you know. To think that . . . I don't know what should be done. I don't know. Well, it's not for me to decide. I don't know. I didn't really ever think about it."

"So while all this planning was going on, you never kind of projected into the future . . . like, what if we get caught?"

"No, because I never was a part of the planning. I was just sort of there, you know. And I never thought anything would actually come down."

"Okay."

"I never wanted anything to come down. I always thought it was just talk between Mike and Aaron and hoped it would stay that way."

"Do you think you were purposely excluded from a lot of their planning, or do you think it just happened that way?"

"I don't know. I think maybe I was purposely excluded. I don't know why, for what reason, but I think a lot of things Mike and Aaron did for their own reasons. They would know why, but I didn't."

"I guess if you had it to do over again, you'd make some different choices."

"Yeah."

"Okay, I guess we can get out of here and go see what happens next, okay?"

"Okay. Do you want me to get up and follow you out?"

"Yes."

They rose to leave. As the interview room door closed behind him, Joshua asked, "Do they take everything away from you?"

The detective didn't answer.

Joshua's legs could barely carry him as the full horror of his eleven-hour ordeal slammed home:

He was on his way to the dreaded Juvenile Hall.

15

• HOW TO KILL •

Day 22: Escondido, California
February 11, 1998
Mid-morning

I f Aaron Houser was worried, only his mother knew. He went to school that morning, just as he always did. Little did he know that Joshua Treadway had implicated him in the murder of Stephanie Crowe. Little did he know that the police had determined he was the brains behind the plot to kill Stephanie.

The police had Michael's and Joshua's "confessions," so now they wanted to nail the third. They talked about Aaron and agreed that he was a cool customer, a cold fish, quite the reverse of the vulnerable and impulsive Joshua and the introverted, twisted Michael. There was a kind of arrogance in Aaron, a self-assuredness, so breaking down this cocky little bastard would be a pleasure.

Not long after Aaron entered school that day, he was called to the principal's office and arrested. He was taken directly to police headquarters, where Detective Sweeney, who had been working on the case since it began, started Aaron's "interview." There was not an air of either accusation or intimidation, initially, and Aaron didn't seem to mind sharing his expertise with the detective. They talked a little about cars and school, and then, after nearly half an hour, Sweeney left the room and Detective Wrisley entered.

Wrisley, as always, was smooth and friendly. They talked mostly about swords. Wrisley told Aaron his family was Scottish, and they talked about getting an authentic Scottish claymore made. Aaron suggested a professional blacksmith could make such a sword historically authentic.

Chris McDonough then entered and introduced himself, telling Aaron it was a pleasure to meet him.

Aaron barely acknowledged the comment, so McDonough quickly got down to business.

"I don't know you and you don't know me, Aaron, but I'm with the Oceanside Police Department. I'm what they call a Computer Voice Stress Analyzer. It's my responsibility to make sure people are telling the truth. For those who aren't telling the truth, I say, 'Hey, you're putting a square peg in a round hole, okay.' It doesn't fit whenever a person is not being honest, understand?"

Aaron hardly responded again. He was being whitewashed and he knew it. He knew what a lie detection system was all about, no matter what they called it.

McDonough continued, undeterred: "And, you know what, Aaron? In police work there's always room for tools and . . . uh . . . gifts, for lack of a better term, to get to the truth of the matter. I'm not on their side, okay. I'm down the middle, okay. I'm the . . . the instrument that becomes your advocate, okay? Do you understand what I mean by that?"

"Yeah." Aaron sounded bored. He wasn't; he was nervous, but he didn't show it.

McDonough explained that he didn't want Aaron to stress out, because it was necessary for him to be calm. He explained the CVSA, as he had for the other boys, and he then turned to the subject of music for a while, then to sports—soccer especially. Finally he returned to swords. He told Aaron he had been to Japan and found the Japanese culture fascinating. "Their ninjas, with their swords and all that stuff . . ."

Before long, the subject of games came up, and a book called *Witch's Brew* entered the conversation. The reason all this seemingly pointless banter went on for so long was probably the fact that Aaron's father, Gregg

Houser, had learned his son had been arrested and had called the station and told them not to interrogate him before he could get there. Gregg Houser and Aaron's mother were divorced; he was driving frantically from Rancho Peñasquitos, where he lived.

In any event, McDonough elected to compliment Aaron, saying, "I can say something to you, right off. I see a fascinating, intelligent young man here, okay? And this is interesting. You know, I think you're gonna be okay. And in terms of . . . as we go through this process here . . . I didn't mean to interrupt okay . . . I didn't mean to cut you off in mid-sentence, okay. And you're lookin' at me kind of like, *Wait a minute, why'd this guy just cut me off?* And I . . . I apologize, but—"

"It's okay."

"I say this to you because, you know, this instrument is, you know, it will verify the things you're going to say, okay? Oh, I just thought of something," McDonough paused, realizing he needed to engage Aaron more in the conversation before getting to the meat of the interrogation. The police were obviously acting in accordance with their own theory of the crime and in deference to the intelligence of the fifteen-year-old Aaron Houser. As a result, they were walking on eggs with him; being careful to ease him into the interrogation. They were concerned about his high intellect and were seemingly afraid to upset the apple cart. They didn't want to do anything that would turn Aaron hostile.

"I . . . we have a . . . I wanna talk to you about a lot of things, okay?" McDonough was thinking hard. "And I need to get to know you," he added. "But as I was sitting here, I was thinking, you know, I have a form that talks about . . . er . . . me, because I work with another agency. You can understand that."

McDonough continued to patronize him. "I'm not sitting here and hitting you with a rubber hose, you know, holding a big light over you, saying, you're, you know, you need to do this, you need to do that. I mean, I want you to feel comfortable and relaxed with the process as we go through it, so that, you know, er . . . you're doing this because you want to, okay? Not because I want you to, not because the other . . . uh . . ."

"Detectives?" Aaron said, helping him out.

"Yeah." McDonough nodded. "They want you to do it, of course, but it must be because you wanna do it, and . . . er . . . what I want you to do is . . . and the only reason I interrupted you is so I can get this out of the way, and I can go on and listen to you, okay? More and more without having to think, 'Hey, did I forget something?' Me, not you, okay? To keep my boss off my butt, for lack of a better term, you know, keep him away from me in the long run. He, you know, I have to show you this. If you would read it, okay? You have questions, let's talk about it, okay? It's not a problem. You . . . you follow me? Is that a yea or a nay?"

"Yeah," Aaron agreed, even though he couldn't possibly have made much sense out of the garbled explanation by McDonough.

"How do you spell your last name?"

"H-O-U-S-E-R."

"See now, that's what I mean." McDonough volunteered lie number one. "I didn't even know your last name, okay?"

Aaron glanced at the paper McDonough had handed him.

"Aaron's a good Irish-Scottish . . . er . . . a little connecting thing, huh?"

"I have a lot of German blood in me."

"That's where the Houser comes from?"

"And I have some Cherokee blood, too."

"Oh really?" McDonough showed fake admiration. "So you're a . . . an Indian?"

"My grandma."

"Are you into . . . er . . . South America and all the Mayan and Inca and all the pyramids and stuff like that down there?"

Aaron looked puzzled. "No," he said.

"Okay, I'm a history buff, too, and I love that kind of stuff, but it's more . . . it's not the middle ages, ah . . . it's more, you know, the Middle East. How did civilizations get . . . how did the pyramids . . . go ahead."

"When I think about the Incas, it always reminds me of the Egyptians."

"And that's . . . that's what I'm into," McDonough smiled—*just two chums jawing about their mutual interest in history.*

McDonough continued his incoherent rambling. "I'm more into, y'know, more of the myth and magic as to what was going on. You know, why they were on the stone temples down there, and why there's pictures of horses? Wait a minute, though. The Spaniards brought the horses over. Why were the Egyptians carving, you know, that's the kind of stuff? I'm getting sidetracked here . . . Hello!" He snapped his fingers. He had lost Aaron's attention.

Inwardly, Aaron thought *what a moron.* Outwardly, he offered, "One of the things I really enjoy is Greek mythology." Aaron stifled a yawn.

"Okay."

"I also dig Norse mythology."

"Okay!"

"As in, like, Thor . . . or Loki," Aaron flaunted his knowledge. "Thor was the Norse god of war. Loki was a mischievous Machiavellian type—an evil god, really, a devil. I need to brush up more on it some because we're doing it at school, it's called NCAL: N-C-A-L."

"What's that?"

"It's the . . . um . . . academic competition. Each school year the academic students challenge each other to a *Jeopardy*-type match."

"Cool."

"Really enjoyable."

"Yeah, well, you get into . . . It's intellectually stimulating, right? Are you into that? I mean, I'm into that too, I cannot . . . you know, I'm not the smartest person in the world. No question about it, okay? But I'm not the dumbest either, you know. And it just drives me nuts to not have an intelligent conversation with somebody. You sit there and you go, 'Did you even understand what I said?' Now I don't expect them to comprehend everything I said, but let's start with, 'Did you understand me? Let's start there.' Does that drive you crazy, too?"

Aaron replied: "We're speaking the same language."

McDonough changed the subject. "What I want you to do, Aaron, I want you take your time, okay. Read this. If you've got questions or whatever, let me know. If you agree with it, sign it. I'll add the date and your address and all that stuff later, okay?"

"Okay." Aaron took a moment to read the form, and then he looked up. "The only thing I need to do before I sign this is talk to my dad."

"Okay, you want to talk to your father? Sure."

"Yeah, because he told me I was not to talk about the incident under any circumstances unless he or his attorney was present."

"I'll be a couple of minutes," McDonough said. "I'll go tell them what we've talked about here."

"Okay." Aaron seemed relaxed.

"And we'll see if we can make that contact, okay?"

"Okay."

"All right. Be just a second."

The document McDonough wanted Aaron to sign is duplicated below:

I _____ do hereby submit to a Voice Stress Analyzer Exam. Having said technique explained to my satisfaction, I hereby release the Oceanside Police Department and the interviewer and examiner administering this examination from all claims resulting from, or arising out of this examination, and do further authorize the release of the said examination results and the information obtained to those parties having an interest in same.

I also understand that I have the right to remain silent and that anything I say may be used against me in a court of law. I understand that I have the right to a lawyer and have him present while I am being questioned. If I cannot afford an attorney, one will be appointed to represent me free of charge before any questioning. The services are free.

I was advised that I could not be forced to take this examination by anyone. To the best of my knowledge at this time, I have no physical or mental conditions which would prevent me from taking this examination.

I have read the above admonition and hereby understand all of my rights to voluntarily, without duress, coercion, promise, reward or immunity, submit to examination by the voice stress analysis truth verification technique.

Just how intimidated by this fifteen-year-old boy and his high IQ were the police? Aaron had been at the police station for at least an hour and thus far had been more pleasantly indulged than anyone else. Why? The ploy was simply to get Aaron to sign the release form that would allow for the CVSA exam to proceed, and it appeared evident that the police were extremely cautious in presenting him with the option. No one knew how Aaron might respond. But this form was not the usual form used; the blatant skullduggery lay in the second paragraph. The police had slipped in the *Miranda* rights clause in hopes that he would sign them away, either without noticing or by thinking this was ordinary procedure. They did not want to confront Aaron orally, being afraid he might refuse to submit to interrogation until an attorney was present—and they wanted their third confession. This was not only deceptive, but in the long run it proved to be damn stupid, a key factor in the unraveling of their case.

When McDonough returned to the room, he told Aaron they were trying to contact his father. In the meantime, he'd take down some informal data, such as where Aaron was born, his height, weight and so forth. Aaron was asked about his parents. Mr. Houser had been a career man in the Navy and retired as a Master Chief. Aaron said he had considered a military career himself, but had changed his mind recently.

Mr. Houser finally arrived and said to Aaron, "Okay, let me explain to you what the attorney told me. He said to tell you what they're doing is very accurate, not Hollywood stuff. You don't fool with this, in other words. If you're innocent, it's in your best interest to do the test. If you're on the periphery . . ."

"What does that mean?"

"On the outside edge . . . like the guy who drove the car but didn't go into the bank, that routine. If so, he says it's still in your best interest. So you got my blessing. Go for it, because I believe you're innocent 100 percent. I've spoken with the guy who . . . the guy who'll be doing the test. What do you think of him?"

"He seems pretty nice."

"How do you feel about the whole deal?"

"I'd rather be in school."

"I don't blame you." Houser then asked Aaron if he wanted to take the exam. Aaron admitted being "as nervous as hell" and his father said that was to be expected. "McDonough is going to take that into account, son. Hell, I'm nervous too." They talked for a few brief moments, and then Houser called out to McDonough, "Hey, we're all done and set up . . . ready to roll in here . . . rock and roll."

"Okay," McDonough said as he entered.

As soon as Mr. Houser left the room, McDonough asked Aaron to explain what the form meant, confirming his understanding.

"Basically, it says I understand I'm taking this test. I'm not going to sue you for taking this test, and if I say something wrong . . . If I say something that ends up incriminating me, it can be used against me in a court of law."

"Okay," McDonough said, seeming pleased. "And it also says down here that you've read the admonition. You understand all these rights and you voluntarily, without duress, coercion, promise of reward or immunity, submit to the examination by a voice stress analysis, a truth verification technique, okay? You understand all of that?"

"Yes."

As before, McDonough began by telling Aaron how he could understand why people were nervous and he said this was called "situational" stress. He also added that it was essential for them to feel comfortable with each other, so the test could get 100 percent results.

It was important for any suspect to believe that this machine *could not be fooled.*

The conversation resumed with the simple questions McDonough had asked before: date of birth, nationality, zip code. They talked a little about books again. Aaron had been reading a series of twenty-one books and McDonough was impressed. They talked a little about sports again, and then games. Games were the big issue here, since the police believed boys who delved constantly into violent games might well take that violence into their own real world. Aaron was obviously good at such games, and McDonough wanted to know if he was analytical.

"Define analytical," Aaron said.

"Okay. Would you . . . do you perceive a situation, think through the situation and then create the decision, or do you see the situation and make the decision more spontaneously?"

"I would say I'm not too spontaneous. I like to formulate the mental picture of everything. I think about it, usually."

"I'm exactly the same way. That's a sign of . . . uh . . . intelligence, okay?"

"Of course it is." Aaron's eyes sparked with a touch of humor.

"Yeah. Okay . . . er . . . and that's a gift."

"Great minds think alike, right?" Aaron said, actually seeming to be toying a little. While there is no doubt this boy was feeling anxious, he was not blatantly nervous in the same way Joshua had been. Nor was he emotional and confused, as Michael had been during his interrogation.

McDonough and Aaron talked for a while about games, and then about school again.

The dialog and game playing had been pleasant, perhaps even fun, and a certain rapport had been established. If one doubted McDonough's skills, that doubt was washed away by this handling of Aaron, who had previously been seen as a hard nut to crack. Throughout the first couple of hours, Aaron was treated respectfully and in a friendly, courteous manner. Viewing the videotapes, one would get the impression that McDonough was a good cop, doing a good job, being unbiased and neutral. He had been open with Aaron, receptive, and even flattering.

But all of this fraternizing had been a mere ploy, a tactical maneuver designed to bring down Aaron's intellectual guard, penetrate his emotions and eventually dismantle his self-confidence. McDonough had told Aaron he didn't even know the boy's last name, but McDonough clearly knew far more than that. He knew every detail of this case, every suspect and every word of every lie told to the boys, including the claims about evidence. So all this rapport was draped with the cloth of a single goal: *to bury this kid along with the other two, and end the case with three slam-dunk convictions.*

McDonough began the process of digging into Aaron's mind. From this point forward he would seek keys, clues, signals, signs, any indication that Aaron was losing his self-assurance, his will to beat the system. The detective intended to accomplish this by using what can only be called interrogative psychology. But this was pseudo-psychology, really just game playing and manipulation, with the ultimate goal of matching wits with the suspect.

McDonough no doubt liked the challenge; it represented a chance for him to emerge as a super-cop, heroic among his peers at Oceanside and the Escondido Police Department. After all, when push came to shove, he was the one who had obtained all the confessions. He was the one who had used his experience and his own impressive mind to solve a case in which there was virtually no evidence. And what about his glorious machine, the CVSA? Hadn't this electronic marvel graphed out the truth and purged the lies from the homicidal boys? And who was the CVSA expert? Why, McDonough, of course. The one who was destined to be honored by his department for his work on the Crowe case.

The detective began his quest to break down Aaron by telling a tale he hoped would work on his young suspect's mind. "You know," he said, "one of the most interesting personalities I ever met was a man by the name of Westley Allan Dodd. He was a serial child killer in Washington. A fascinating, intelligent human being. Very cordial. Very matter-of-fact. He said, 'Sure, I'll tell you whatever you want to know. Whatever you need to hear.'

"But I walked away from that case with a new understanding of the human psyche. I remember talking to him about how he had gotten to that point. Could something have been done different, you know what I mean? In a situation like that you almost want to reach out and say, 'Hey, this persona you exemplify is false. Deep inside, you're still a human being. You know, you still have feelings.' I mean, society has said, 'Let's tear out that guy's heart because of what he did.' And the things he did were pretty horrendous, but they were horrendous to him, too. He didn't wake up one day and say, 'Okay, I think I'm going to start killing people.'"

"So it wasn't just a spontaneous decision?" Aaron asked. He seemed interested in McDonough's story. He hadn't caught on to the idea that the detective was comparing him to the serial killer.

"No, apparently it wasn't. It was a catacomb of events that thrust him to the point where he said, 'I have to do this.' And it took . . . it took the acts themselves, or their exposure to public scrutiny, for him to realize what had gotten him to that point.

"It's almost like the analogy to a bullet, McDonnough continued. "Once the bullet is fired, what mechanism does it take to pack the powder, to compress the powder, to put the primer in there, to make a shell casing? All those components of his life, okay, came to a head and, you know, he got to a crossroads, and BOOM! Anyway, the bullet exploded and he then started internalizing who he was, why he was the way he was. He was not the evil demon psychotic person everybody made him out to be. He was a human being. Yeah, Westley was fascinating to talk to. Did I agree with what he did? Of course not, but we made a connection, intellectually. . . .

"If we look for a pattern in life . . . if we look at his relationship with his father, for example . . ."

McDonough was working on the assumption that Aaron had some deeply rooted psychological problems and he was cleverly delivering this story of Dodd to induce Aaron to surface them. The detective continued with the father theme: "He had a volatile relationship with his father, okay? A tremendous resentment. His parents went through the divorce situation . . ."

McDonough compared it to a game, saying Dodd started fantasizing about games, then asked Aaron for his impression.

Aaron speculated that Dodd needed to release the stress building up inside, but "he made some mistakes, and that only made it worse." Aaron acknowledged that he had wondered what drove a person to kill others . . ."if they understood the consequences . . . why would they, if they were rational?"

McDonough then offered a theoretical scenario that he believed mirrored Aaron's: a young adult, in his mid-teens, his father and mother's relationship is dissolved, and he wants to connect with his mother emotionally.

"He gets to a point where he seems devoid of emotions," McDonough said. "Now that doesn't mean he *can't* feel . . ."

"It's just the outward appearance," Aaron said and shrugged.

"He's screaming out . . . 'I don't understand the pain; therefore nobody will understand it. I must suppress it.' . . . But in due time he realizes . . . what it was all about. And he goes through his adolescent years and molests over a couple hundred kids."

McDonough continued. "Eventually, he got to a point where he was molesting so many kids he realized he had crossed over the threshold."

Aaron nodded, completely drawn in.

McDonough thought himself very clever, using this anecdote about Westley Dodd to subconsciously "mirror" Aaron's own life. After all, they were both misunderstood intellectuals from broken homes, and he—McDonough—could understand, even appreciate, what had triggered them both to undertake their dark deeds as few others could. He asked Aaron why he thought the divorce of Dodd's parents would have affected him so much.

Aaron said Dodd probably felt abandoned. McDonough asked Aaron what Dodd had turned to, in seeking to be understood.

"Sex," he said.

And then McDonough asked, "Since Dodd did not understand his adolescence, who did he turn to, to validate his feelings?"

Again, Aaron came up with a thoughtful answer: "A child."

"Right again. Then he gets to a point where he takes somebody's life." McDonough was anxious to get to the subject of killing.

And once again Aaron showed understanding. "He wanted to understand death," he said. "Maybe he was thinking about himself, feeling suicidal."

No matter how McDonough had prejudged Aaron, he was obviously impressed by the boy at this point. Impressed with his capacity to think. But of course it was this capacity that made him the prime suspect for plotting Stephanie Crowe's murder. And so, throughout this long and convoluted exploration of the motives of Westley Dodd, McDonough kept repeating how the man was trying to reach out, to communicate with others; and how he was seeking help and understanding. What he had been trying to do was convey to Aaron, through metaphors and symbols, that help and understanding were waiting for him as well. Like Westley Dodd, Aaron had *buried his emotions*, but everyone knew that he had needs and feelings, that he too was a human being longing to be understood, even if he had killed someone.

Well, that was McDonough's assessment.

Actually, Aaron had not captured the message McDonough was trying to deliver. He was too caught up in the story itself, and too busy playing psychological sleuth to guess what games the detective was up to, or even to be concerned with it.

When the Dodd story ended, there was some talk about Aaron's school friends. Then what seemed to be a spontaneous question came up. McDonough suddenly, as though it had just dawned on him, asked Aaron why he thought Michael would kill his sister.

"I can't say." Aaron seemed puzzled. "From what I knew of him and his sister they got along okay. They did yell at each other now and then. Once I heard of him hitting her, and she was crying on the phone, but usually they got along. I heard them laughing and playing together. Whenever he would get mad at somebody he'd curse them under his breath. He wouldn't get into any confrontation, and he never got physical. Never."

McDonough could see, or thought he could see, the wheels turning in Aaron's head. He had been forewarned that Aaron could not be interviewed as a typical suspect, that he would have to be "handled" differently; worked from a special angle. He would have to be romanced, intellectually, coaxed, maneuvered and even humored. But as McDonough had so often said, he was patient, and it would only be a matter of time before Aaron was confessing and screaming for help and understanding. As soon as that happened, and McDonough was determined it would, the kid would be sent to Juvie, and then the courts would have him in their grip.

McDonough swung the conversation to the subject of swords and killing, and Aaron seemed anxious to share his knowledge about these interests. The detective asked about the effectiveness of a knife in a combat situation: "I mean, in utilizing a small unit like that," he said, "a small hand tool like that—a knife—what would be the vital striking points on a human body?"

"You would try probably for the neck. You could try slicing at the . . . at the stomach . . . or stabbing through the rib cage."

"So what's the purpose? What would be the effectiveness of that blow?"

Aaron took the bait and described how that would play out. He went into great detail about the effectiveness one approach to a stabbing versus an ineffective approach.

McDonough urged him on, and Aaron, unsuspectingly, continued to describe the most effective way to kill a person with a knife.

"I'd say the neck would be the prime one to go for. . . . The only problem with that is it might be difficult to get at the neck, because of the shoulders and the chin . . ." in which case he would "go for the chest region, or the back."

McDonough believed he was hitting the jackpot here. This kid had thought about killing, had studied it, and now was boasting about his knowledge. Aaron clearly wanted to impress McDonough and he certainly had made an impression.

"Let's go past all that. Tell me about Josh," the detective said.

"Josh? Josh always seemed like a person . . . he's always very timid, he wouldn't stand up for himself, and in a way I guess he wanted to be dominated."

Another jackpot. This was exactly in line with the police analysis. There was no incongruity here; this kid was cold and he was a killer. It was all falling into place.

"I think he always looked up to Michael and me," Aaron offered.

"That's interesting," McDonough said encouragingly.

"Listening to what we had to say about things, talking about things. He was always asking me to show him my swords, and, like, how they would be used to fight. He was definitely interested in the rapier, and I'd say, 'You don't want to fight with a rapier, Josh, because once you get within two feet of the person, the rapier's almost useless.' When he first met my mom— just as an example—he was like, 'Hi, Mrs. Houser,' or 'Oh, I'm sorry, I didn't mean to do that,' things like that. He always wanted to make a good impression."

"Very apologetic."

"Uh-huh," Aaron said, nodding.

"Easy to manipulate?"

"In some ways, yes."

"Tell me about Stephanie."

"Well, I only ever had one conversation with her and her mother, and that was about band. She was in the chorus, and I happened to be in the band. . . . I really didn't get to know her."

"What did she look like?"

"She looked like Michael, a little bit smaller, longer hair, maybe some makeup. She did definitely look like Michael."

"If Michael were to stab her, what area would he utilize, what targets?"

"I'd say probably the chest and neck, maybe the stomach."

"Why?"

"End the struggle, get it over with; do it quickly and effectively."

"No mistakes and there she goes . . ."

"I can't imagine Michael torturing anyone. He might, I guess, but I doubt it because it would be taking chances with her."

"Hmm?"

"It takes too long. And if he decided to torture her first, well, he'd have to make sure she couldn't scream."

"Hmm."

"He'd have to make sure she couldn't make any noise. Couldn't, in other words, alert anyone else. Make sure no one could find out. Make sure he was safe."

"Hmm." The detective nodded.

"At least that's what I would do; that's the only thing I can think of."

"Hmm."

"I think Michael would do the same because that's one of the things about us, we thought alike."

"How's that?" McDonough asked.

"Keep yourself safe. Not be self-destructive. Personally, I've never wanted to kill anyone," Aaron said. "I've hardly ever gotten into any fights. I think I got in one when I was in first grade, one a couple of years ago, maybe, with my brother, but nothing too serious."

"How about Josh? If Josh were to kill Stephanie, how would he do it?"

"That's a tough one. Josh was always a very peaceful person. He didn't really like to fight much and the only thing I enjoyed about fighting was the challenge of it. You know, it's kind of like a chess game. You need a strategy, anticipate what your opponent will do."

"Hmm."

"But I never wanted to seriously fight; I just enjoy sparring, maybe karate. Josh, he didn't enjoy any violence. He enjoyed the fighting a little bit, but not much. I don't know any way he would kill Stephanie. I don't know if he would think about such things. I just can't imagine Josh doing something like that."

"Okay . . . and anticipating my next question . . . how would you do it?"

"I don't know." Aaron paused to think. "If I were to go after Stephanie, first thing I'd do is put the knife so that it was not in my hand but in a place I could reach, like maybe back here, tucked in, so I could grab it when I needed it but she couldn't." Aaron indicated the back of his trousers, in his belt.

"Hmm."

"I would grab one of her arms and put it behind her back. Then, with the other hand I'd close her mouth and nose and pull her chin up. I'd pull her back, let go of the arm while it's behind, grab the knife and cut her throat. That would be the best way I could think of, if I was going to kill somebody."

"Okay."

Aaron then added another thought: "The only problem with that is that I'd get blood on myself probably. And then I'd have to make sure I was wearing sparse clothing so there was not much of a chance for blood to get on it . . . or so it would be easy to dispose of, and then I'd find a way to get out of there and clean myself off."

"What type of clothing would you wear?"

"I don't think I'd wear gloves, because gloves leave things behind, like hands do."

"Hmm."

"And clothes can be washed in some ways that hands can't. The only thing I'd be leaving fingerprints on is the knife. If I killed someone with a knife, I would take the knife and like fire it to try to destroy any chemical evidence on it."

McDonough remained composed, but now he felt sure he'd soon learn exactly how these three boys had done such a clever job of hiding the evidence.

He believed he was on the verge of finding out *exactly what happened the night of Stephanie Crowe's murder.*

McDonough listened intently as Aaron gave details of how he "would have" killed Stephanie. As a detective, he was interested in the way the boy was so careful, going over each detail, making sure his tracks were covered and he got away clean. There was no doubt in his mind that Aaron's ego was pushing him to show off his genius, how cleverly he had executed the perfect crime. *What a pompous kid. To sit here and think he can actually map out exactly what he had done and still get away with it.*

McDonough was doing his own thinking, making his own calculations. *Let him talk, let him think there's no contest, here. Then, when he least expects it . . . Checkmate!*

"How about gloves?" McDonough asked nonchalantly. "What kind of gloves would you choose?"

"Well I have some Isotoner at home, those are the only gloves I have."

"Are those band gloves?"

"No. Band gloves have holes under the fingers, so you can play the clarinet in them."

"They're black, right?"

"No, they're white. All white, with holes in the fingers. Not exactly ideal for killing someone."

"I agree. What time would you pick?"

"Two or three in the morning."

"Why?"

"Well, people stay up late—to eleven usually. Two or three is good because not many people are up at that time. And three would be cutting it pretty close for early risers. Everyone is asleep by two or three."

"How would you get in?"

"Through a small window, because doors have locks and can be noisy.

Large windows might have locks too, and can be noisy. A small window might be a little noisy but they . . . I don't think they usually have locks, and they're—like say a bathroom window—you ever seen those? It would be difficult, but I think I could fit through one of those."

"Okay. What's the advantage of having someone let you in?"

McDonough already had Joshua's confession, so he thought Aaron might be trying to throw him off at this point, talking about going through a window when Joshua had already told him Michael had let them in through the back door.

"It could be more silent, and you could work together to warn if anything happened. Like someone approaching."

"What's the advantage of that?"

"Well, let's say if I had Michael with me, and let's say, a hypothetical situation, that I killed Stephanie. If I had Mike let me in, and I was approaching her room, and someone was coming but I hadn't killed her yet, I would definitely like take off my gloves, put them in my pocket and create some reason I was there. Like, 'Gee, I forgot to give . . . ' Or better yet, I had a reason to get away from home, like my mom's mad, really, really mad at me. I'm worried."

"Hmm. So what about a third person?"

"You mean, in a hypothetical situation, besides Michael?"

"Yeah."

"Too many people. If you're going to kill someone you need to keep it a secret. When more than two people know, it's really not much of a secret anymore."

"If you went to her room and you saw her, how would you approach it?"

"Well, at this time she'd probably be sleeping. I'd probably just cut her throat as quickly as possible, without really waking her."

"So how would you do that?"

"If she was sleeping on her back I would . . . with my left hand I would hold my hand over her mouth until I was sure she was dead."

"And how would you know?"

"The tension of the muscles. If she were dead, they would relax. Pulse, breathing, eyes. If the eyes were wide, and had terror in them, she would probably be shivering. Something like that. The body would be completely still, relaxed."

"And how much time would that take?"

"I don't know. I really don't know how long it takes for a person to die from being cut in the throat. I know in the movies, like William Wallace, for example, *Braveheart*."

"Yeah, *Braveheart*."

"When his first love was killed, I didn't think it was quite that quick. But I don't know," Aaron added. "I don't have any experience."

It was not difficult to catch the shadow of doubt in McDonough's eyes when he said, "Would you take her out of the bed?"

"There's no reason to take her out of bed. It would just be a waste of energy. If I had killed her, I'd want to get away from it as quickly as possible."

"How would you get away?"

"Leave the house? Probably the same way that I came in."

"So Michael would let you out?"

"I guess he might. Yeah."

"Would Josh be outside, or in the kitchen?"

"Like I said, when you have a third person . . ."

"What if there *was* a third person?"

"Probably outside."

"Would you wash the knife?"

"Maybe."

"At the house?"

"No."

"How come?"

"Spending too much time at the scene of the crime. I'd want to get away quick and not leave evidence where I'd washed it."

"Then what would happen?"

"After I'd gotten away? Well, I'd try to make it seem like none of us were suspicious. I'd try to get Josh home, and me home. And Michael to act normal."

"And how would you do that?"

"I don't know. Well, Josh and I would have to leave. I don't know where Josh would go, but I could walk to my house from Michael's. Josh would take a lot longer because he lives a lot further away."

"Hmm."

"So I don't know what I would do with Josh, but I would walk back to my house and I'd probably . . . maybe pull out a screen on my window and climb through the window."

"Okay, and how would you control Josh?"

"Josh is a timid person. I don't know if he'd be able to handle it emotionally. Michael always suppressed his emotions a lot more."

"Okay, how would you handle Michael?"

"I don't know if there would be anything I could do with Michael. Josh, he kind of looks up to me, so I can kind of say, 'You should probably do this.' But Michael? He might try to blackmail me. I don't know."

"Betray you?"

"Perhaps. Michael wasn't always the person you could completely trust. I tried to trust him as much as possible but, later in our friendship, at my birthday party, I was missing forty dollars . . ." Aaron went on and told McDonough how he had been trying to get his CDs back from Michael and how, at one point, Michael had cussed him out.

McDonough was now willing to take a calculated risk: "Josh betrayed you too," he said, waiting for the reaction.

Aaron didn't show surprise. "He lies . . . if Michael told him to . . ."

"No, he did it on his own."

"He did?" Aaron was concerned. "How?"

"He told us what happened."

"How could he?" Aaron suddenly seemed to lose confidence. His face paled. "What did he tell you happened?"

"We've just gone through it," McDonough said.

"He told you that happened?" There was disbelief in his face and voice.

"We just went through it," McDonough repeated.

"Oh, shit, that sucks." Aaron was obviously shaken.

"It does suck. But you can get back. Time for revenge."

"Yeah, but . . . tell me what you think."

"I think it happened just as you said," McDonough said with an air of certainty.

Suddenly Aaron was on his feet. "*You think I helped kill her?*"

"Yes." McDonough said. "And now it's time for revenge, for lack of a better term. Give them a little bit of their own medicine. Tell me your side."

"You're going to have to stop this right now," Aaron said frantically. "I've got to go to the bathroom." The interrogation had been textbook, to this point, and now the detective had a new tool.

Aaron was frightened.

When someone has to go to the bathroom urgently it adds to their anxiety; it increases the likelihood they'll say something they otherwise would hold inside. So the police do not allow a suspect the release they need. They want him to sit, holding it, hoping he'll 'fess up. What matters to the cops is that he's restrained, trapped, and cannot obtain release and comfort until he's handed over whatever the cops need.

"If you've got to go to the bathroom, hold on for a bit," McDonough said. "I'll be right back." And he left Aaron alone in the room.

As soon as McDonough returned to the room he admitted to Aaron, calmly, that he'd been playing a game when he implied he had something to do with the murder. "I had to see where your stress level was going to go," he said.

Now his strategy was to relax Aaron again and get him ready for the CVSA exam. And so McDonough acted the good guy for a while and began telling Aaron how much he wanted him to pass the exam, come out with flying colors—to be proven innocent. He even had the gall to say to Aaron, as an old friend might say, "I'm going to help you get you through this, okay? You're going to pass."

Aaron nibbled at the bait in the trap. What else would he do? He needed a friend here, a cop on his side, a cop who wanted to see him get out of this potential mess. McDonough did most of the talking, telling the boy how crimes are often solved through DNA, through electronic dust collectors and other forensic science that give the police information. "Every time we step on the floor," he said, "the molecules dissipate." He wanted Aaron to be cognizant of the high-tech nature of his work, and how they could find a needle in the proverbial haystack. During all of this he kept calling Aaron "son," as he had done with Michael and with Joshua. He was projecting himself as the caring father figure, the concerned parent of a kid in trouble and in need of help to get out of whatever mess he was in.

"And let me remind you, son," he said, "your best friend right now is you, okay? It's a dog-eat-dog world, okay? Your best friend, Aaron, is your story. Michael is a fourteen-year-old recluse in his room all the time, and he comes from a dysfunctional family, like Westley Dodd. Inside, he's screaming for help, okay? He's jealous of his sister getting all the accolades. He gets grounded while she gets put on a pedestal. He has loyal friends, though, and he betrays the friendship by suggesting something. Now he takes it further by laying out what happened and then playing it like, 'I don't know what you're talking about.' So how do I know Michael was at the door to let you in? Hypothetically, let's play that, okay? How would I know the knife was washed in the Crowe house?"

"I don't know," Aaron said. He was not swallowing all the bait. Unlike Joshua, or even Michael in the early going, he was aware now that he was a serious suspect. And he was not buying the "I wanna help you" routine either.

"I'm thinking about it," he said. "There could have been blood traces, Stephanie's blood where it was washed. And there might be some traces of the knife in that blood?"

"Hmm."

"Like a certain kind of steel, or maybe how blood would react to that steel."

McDonough changed the subject for a moment, talking more about how police uncover evidence.

He flattered Aaron again: "You're very intelligent," he said. "I respect that, okay? I want you to pass, okay? Michael says you helped him," he blatantly lied. "Listen to me. He says you helped him, okay. I don't know if that's true or not, yet. I think he was trying to mitigate some of his involvement by throwing some of it on you. Josh did the same thing."

It's an old interrogation trick to convince any suspect that their cohorts in a crime have already confessed and pointed a finger of guilt elsewhere, but McDonough went further. He wanted Aaron to get angry with Joshua and Michael, angry enough to confess his own guilt. He'd rather spend his own life in jail than let his disloyal friends off the hook.

"Josh says he met you at your house," McDonough continued. "You two guys then went up there and Michael let you in. Josh came in later. They laid it all out, how it happened, why it happened, where it happened. But I think you're smart enough to say, 'Well, I'm gonna tell you what they did too, because I don't think it's fair that you get a one-sided story.' Know what I mean?"

Aaron said something in a whisper. He was clearly devastated, appalled. McDonough could see the boy's discomfort and continued to push. "Yeah, and all the evidence starts pointing at you. . . . They're laughing at you in this situation, Aaron. I used the word betrayal because I think it's appropriate. Loyalty is important in friendships, okay? But think about it, the picture they're painting is, 'He planned it. He got into the house and stabbed her. But we only did this and this.' See where the scale is? I don't think it's fair. That's betrayal. That's why you should turn the tide. You tell me your side of the story, son, so I can present them with the truth.

"Why would I kill her?" Aaron asked. A logical question, whether he was guilty or innocent.

"I don't think you wanted to kill her. Michael said it was his idea."

"But I didn't even know her."

"That makes it easier."

"I can't say I didn't know her, but I barely knew her."

"Okay, you can call that disassociation. That's okay."

"I wasn't friendly with Michael. The only reason I was still talking to him was to get my games back."

McDonough spent more time setting up Aaron for answering questions, vital questions. In one breath he was telling Aaron he didn't think he was involved, in the next he was telling Aaron he believed he was guilty. It was unclear at this point what McDonough really thought, and this was exactly the way he wanted it. Pointing the finger of guilt at Aaron, he said, "Let's deal with Michael. Let's start at the scene, okay. He let you into the house, right? What was he wearing?"

"I didn't have anything to do with it."

"Listen to me for a second and I'll listen to you, okay. You have to understand something, all right? I want you to pass the exam, okay?" From this point on McDonough worked on relaxing Aaron again, getting him ready for the test, which finally began.

"Is your name Aaron Houser?"

"Yes."

"Is the wall white?"

"No." The same rules prevailed.

"Are you sitting down?"

"Yes."

"Do you know who killed Stephanie?"

"No."

"Is today Wednesday?"

"Yes."

"Did you kill Stephanie?"

"No."

Aaron was smart, but apparently not smart enough or in control enough to beat the incredible electronics of the machine, at least according to McDonough.

"Look at question five," McDonough said. "Do you know who killed Stephanie? You answered, no, but there's deception indicated; you're not telling the truth."

If the police lie to a suspect about who committed a crime and claim they have "evidence" to prove it, surely they must realize the suspect will then be in conflict if they ask if he knows who is involved. The suspect may "know" nothing, and say so, but his inner responses are now in conflict because he's been told who did it, and his "lie" is revealed.

As a defense attorney, I'm well aware that such trickery, deliberately contrived, has been declared legal by the courts, but it is anything but fair. Aaron was expected to hold out, but in the end the cops thought he would confess. It never occurred to them that their theory of this crime was completely false.

Aaron responded to McDonough's assertion of deception with "I'm being screwed over!"

"You blow a gasket?" McDonough inquired. "I think maybe that's what happened. Maybe it wasn't? Am I wrong?"

"I already told you, you're wrong."

"Then why would Josh and Michael lie? What's their motive?"

"I don't know. How many different ways can you say, I don't know?"

"I don't know," McDonough stated sarcastically.

"Good answer," Aaron replied.

Aaron was scared, very scared, and yet he had the wit and the spunk not to collapse under the pressure he was enduring. There was also anger simmering in his voice.

"You're welcome," McDonough responded pompously.

"How many more times do you want me to say, I don't know?"

"I don't know. Now ask me how many times I've heard people say, 'I don't know.'"

"Probably a whole lot."

"A million. Now ask me how many times in that million have they done something."

"Probably a lot."

"Now ask me, when they finally told me, 'I did know,' was I surprised?"

"Probably not."

"No. I certainly didn't think I had 'stupid' tattooed on my forehead, nor is it on yours."

Aaron, after four and a half hours of grilling, lost this ill-founded battle of wits with the detective. He was formally arrested for the murder of Stephanie Crowe and taken to Juvenile Hall.

But McDonough lost, too. Despite the detective's best efforts to coerce Aaron into a confession, none came. This was a defeat for McDonough, but what the hell? Aaron was going down anyway. In the eyes of the police, it was a job well done. Case closed.

PART THREE

An Alternative Theory

16

• IS TRACY THERE? •

Day 27, San Diego, California
February 16, 1998

After reviewing the seemingly endless hours of video recordings of the police interrogations of not only my client, Aaron Houser, but those of Michael Crowe and Joshua Treadway, I became more convinced than ever of their innocence.

Both Paul Blake and Mary Ellen Attridge, attorneys for Michael and Joshua, reached the same conclusion: These boys did not commit the crime. But if they didn't do it, who did?

We soon discovered that there had been another suspect in the murder of Stephanie Crowe, albeit briefly. The police picked him up on the day of the murder but they quickly dismissed his involvement in the crime.

Who was this man? Why had he been picked up and why so quickly rejected as a suspect? As it turned out, this man changed the course of the case against Aaron, Michael and Joshua.

Richard Raymond Tuite (pronounced "to-it"), also known as Richard Ray Myers, had been in trouble off and on since he was fourteen years old. Born in 1969 in Escondido, California, by his twenty-first birthday Richard had been arrested a number of times for drug abuse and theft. His parents were divorced when he was thirteen, and his mother disappeared after the breakup. He had lived with his dad until he was out of school, and he

Richard Raymond Tuite

claimed he had a good childhood. He had to repeat seventh grade, however, and would often leave the school grounds and go to the beach, where he would laze away his days. His troubles with the police started early. In the beginning, it was just petty trouble.

But in 1990, Tuite was arrested for car theft, evading officers, and reckless driving. Getting him to confess was no challenge; he had been caught red-handed and there were witnesses. While incarcerated, Tuite kept drifting in and out of reality and demonstrating mood changes. He would often be quite coherent, but at other times it was apparent he was hallucinating. A psychological evaluation conducted on Tuite by Dr. Richard Murphy concluded there was significant evidence of psychosis. Another evaluation of Tuite, by a Dr. Judith Vukov, states: "He presented himself in an unusual, distracted and sometimes bizarre fashion. He shows evidence of hallucination." At the end of the doctor's report, it said, "Mr. Tuite's overall emotional functioning is highly problematic. There is no doubt that this man is psychotic and has been for a number of years." It was strongly recommended that Tuite be given treatment in residence at a locked and secure facility. Later, he was diagnosed as a chronic schizophrenic but not a danger to others.

He was, however, definitely in the neighborhood the night of Stephanie Crowe's murder.

On the morning of Stephanie's death, a small group of neighbors gathered outside the Crowe house, the sirens of the police cars and ambulance having stirred people's curiosity. Word spread rapidly about the tragedy, and a number of neighbors told police about a "strange-looking man," with long dirty blond hair and a beard, roaming about the neighborhood the night before. The police quickly matched the description to Tuite, a well-known transient.

The twenty-eight-year-old Tuite's hair and beard were constantly dirty and unkempt, his clothing soiled and baggy. He looked frightening to most people as he drifted, sleeping here and there and finding ways to eat and subsist. He had a history of drug abuse and lived in a world of illusions most of the time, hearing voices in his head and sometimes proclaiming "They" were out to get him.

Tuite, despite his paranoia and other problems, seemed to be aware of the difference between right and wrong. Once, when a policeman asked him if he knew why he had been arrested, he answered that it was because he had done something that he wasn't supposed to do. No one could explain the workings of this man's mind, or how he comprehended good and evil. He committed crimes and got arrested, that much we knew.

• • •

On February 12, 1998, the day after Aaron was arrested, Tuite had sat on bus number 320 headed toward a section of San Diego called Hillcrest. The bus stopped to pick up passengers and Tuite watched a woman and man climb aboard with the woman's daughter, twelve-year-old Karen, and her friend, thirteen-year-old Somer. Both these girls noticed Tuite's ragged appearance as he looked back at them and began circling his lips with his tongue in a vulgar way, taunting them. This frightened the girls and they told Karen's mother. The woman told the girls not to pay any attention, but Tuite continued to leer at them. To escape his gaze, the girls put their jackets over their heads.

The girls, Karen's mother, and Karen's mother's friend Hector, were grateful when it was time to get off the bus and transfer to one that would take them to Escondido. But Tuite followed them, this time sitting even closer to the girls, and repeating the lewd act with his tongue. When Hector, Karen, her mother, and Somer finally reached their destination, Richard Tuite followed them off the bus again.

Karen's mother and Hector walked the girls to their gated apartment complex and, seeing the girls safely inside, they walked across the street to a small market to get something cold to drink. But Tuite had followed them to the apartments and had somehow managed to get through the gates, following the young girls into the complex. The girls were alarmed to make this discovery and even more frightened when Tuite began calling out "Tracy" and saying he wanted to have sex with them. He became quite angry when the girls did not respond favorably.

The girls ran to Karen's mother, who was returning from the store, and the woman immediately called the police from inside the apartment. The police arrived and found Tuite at a nearby Taco Bell restaurant.

They arrested him for "annoying a child."

Remember that on the night of the Stephanie Crowe murder, Richard Tuite was in the Crowe neighborhood looking for someone by the name of Tracy. Since Tuite was our one shot at an alternative theory of the murder, and we saw him as the potential perpetrator in the Stephanie Crowe case, it's appropriate here to delve a little deeper into this man's history, exposing his apparent fixation on the mysterious young woman named Tracy.

Tracy was not a figment of Tuite's imagination, or some drug-induced apparition. She had lived in the vicinity of the Crowe house two or three years before the tragedy. She was a few years younger than Tuite and at one time shared Tuite's enthusiasm for methamphetamine, probably as part of a small circle of other drug abusers. Nevertheless, it seems Tracy ultimately made up her mind to overcome her habit and she moved away, to a rehab center in Orange County, two hours away. By all accounts, Tuite never accepted the reality of Tracy's departure. He also began a precipitous decline at that time, a decline into a dreadfully unkempt, incoherent and confused mental state.

• • •

At around 8:00 p.m. on the night Stephanie was stabbed, Sheldon Homa was relaxing in his home, across the street and down the hill from the Crowe residence. Sheldon was startled to see a bearded face peering at him through a window. He quickly went outside to confront the individual. Tuite stood calmly before him and said he was looking for a girl by the name of Tracy, who he claimed lived in the neighborhood. Sheldon said he didn't know anyone by that name, and he called 911 to report the incident.

About a half hour later, Sheldon Homa's son was walking along the road with his girlfriend. They both saw Tuite and were alarmed. They stopped by a church and warned the youth leaders there that a stranger was lurking nearby. By this time, Tuite was knocking on Danette Mogelinski's door, and she broke the common sense rule by inviting Tuite inside. Tuite had told her he was looking for a person named Tracy. Mogelinski said that she didn't know anyone by that name, so Tuite left, but moments later he walked back into the house, unannounced, and repeated the questions about Tracy.

At around 9:20 p.m., Tuite crossed the hill toward the Crowes' side of the street and knocked on the door of a trailer house occupied by Patrick and Misty Green. Tuite asked if Tracy lived there and was told she didn't. They closed the door, but Tuite suddenly opened it and stepped inside. Patrick was alarmed and ordered Tuite outside. Tuite left as ordered and went to the main house on that same property, where the Reverend Gary West lived. Reverend West was the Crowes' immediate neighbor to the west. The reverend told Tuite he did not know a Tracy and sent him on his way. Reverend West also called 911 and reported the intrusion.

A police car was sent to the area, but the officer had gotten lost and had to call dispatch for directions. When he finally did arrive, the transient was nowhere in sight. The cop actually drove up the eastern leg of the shared driveway leading to the Crowe home and he noticed the back door next to the garage closing, as if someone had entered. But he drove away to continue his fruitless search.

The evening of January 22, Tuite was spotted inside an Escondido laundry by a patrolman and was taken in for questioning. Detective Barry Sweeney, who had been involved from the start of the Crowe murder case, told Tuite a murder had occurred in the west end of Escondido and wanted to know if Tuite had contacted anyone there. Tuite's memory seemed okay, since he admitted talking to several people in the area, but he insisted he'd not gone inside any house. The police took fingernail scrapings and clippings and examined his hands and arms. They discovered a one-and-a-half-inch cut on his right palm. They also took Tuite's clothing—black jeans, black Nike shoes, a white T-shirt and a turtleneck sweatshirt—and replaced them with sweat clothes and released him after he was photographed. But they forgot to fingerprint him.

A patrolman was sent out to bring in Tuite again the next day. This time his fingerprints were taken, and again Tuite was released. Three days later, however, on Super Bowl Sunday, the police were called to a Best Western motel, where a transient was reported looking into car windows. Sure enough, it was Tuite.

When the officer asked Tuite why he was there, he said he was looking for the family of the little girl who got killed. The cop searched Tuite and, finding no weapons or drugs on him, let him go on his way.

This motel was the same place the Crowes had stayed following the murder of Stephanie.

Tuite should have been a serious suspect in Stephanie Crowe's murder. The police, however, had not even bothered to videotape their brief interrogation of him. As I pondered the details of this man's past, and his activities on the night of the murder, I found it difficult to believe he had not been checked out more thoroughly. One would not have to be an attorney, a police officer, or a psychologist to determine that Tuite had a profile that would suggest the possibility he could have been the deadly prowler that night. The big problem—the very absurdity of the police attitude—was that by then, they were convinced Michael Crowe was guilty. This fourteen-year-old boy was their "bird in the hand," and Joshua Treadway, along with Aaron Houser, were their "two in the bush."

Okay, so I had an early theory. Tuite could have been the killer. But there was a fly in the ointment. George Durgin, who manages the police crime lab in Escondido, had helped collect and analyze what little evidence there was in the Crowe case. This included Tuite's clothing. Durgin's report showed there was no blood found on the transient's clothes, nor was there any match of his fingerprints at the house.

Ironically, two weeks after Stephanie's murder, Tuite was arrested for a burglary attempt. He had tried to pick a lock with a black plastic fish. He was sentenced to three years in state prison for the offense.

However, there wasn't anything to connect Tuite to the murder, so I was back to square one: Those damn confessions!

17

• DOLLAR CRUNCHES •

Day 34: San Diego, California
February 23, 1998

I began seeing Aaron once a week. Above all else, I wanted to gain his trust. I had to feel confident he was telling me everything, not holding back on even the slightest involvement he might have had with the murder.

Unlike most juveniles his age, Aaron was composed. I could sense he was terribly upset, yet he was not the type to allow others to see his anxiety. It was difficult to draw him out. Aaron possessed a strong, determined character, and he had intellectualized his situation; he had reckoned with his own feelings. In ordinary circumstances this would be admirable, but I was also greatly concerned about what a judge or a jury would read into this apparent calm. Here was an accused murderer of a twelve-year-old girl, his friend's sister, not screaming his innocence, not crumbling in hysterics. Instead, he was facing it all with a firm and dispassionate denial of involvement. In this case, such maturity would not be of help to him. His straight-faced aplomb could be read as callousness or a lack of emotion. Surely the prosecution would use this against him. He could end up as his own worst witness; especially since he had already been deemed a sociopath by Dr. Lawrence Blum. But that assessment had been based exclusively on watching Aaron's videotaped interrogation. My only hope was that the biblical axiom would prove true and the truth would set him free.

During March, I had several conversations with Gary Hoover, the initial prosecutor in this case. I told him Aaron might be interested in talking with the police, maybe even taking a lie detection test, but not if he was confined. They had no evidence against Aaron, nothing tying him to the murder other than Joshua's so-called confession, so Hoover agreed, tentatively. Aaron would be sent home under house arrest if I made that petition in the hearing.

On the day of the hearing, however, I made the mistake of telling Mary Ellen Attridge of my minor victory for Aaron, and she immediately asked the court to allow Joshua to be released under the same conditions. Her petition was refused, of course, because it was not supported by the prosecutor, but the little game played by Attridge had ruined my chances for getting Aaron released. I was angry as hell at Attridge, but I also knew her client held the key to Aaron's future, so I had to sit tight and wait.

I cannot describe the feeling in the pit of my stomach as I left Aaron in his cell that day. The prospect of release—and then the court's denial—was too much for the young man. He became very depressed. I was worried about him. I knew his depression was likely to deepen. I told the supervisor at Juvenile Hall of my concerns. Perhaps I was overreacting, but I was not willing to take any chances. I had dealt with depressed young people before, and I knew Aaron had confronted a significant setback, one that could erupt in any number of ways—including suicide. Later that day, Aaron was stripped, put in a room where he could do no harm to himself, and placed under watch.

As soon as the psychologist released Aaron from observation, saying he thought Aaron was not suicidal, I immediately went to see him again. He was close to tears as he told me he wasn't doing very well, that he had pains in his stomach and was having problems sleeping. I told him he had to be tough. "The best way to be tough," I said, "is to keep your body active." I showed him how to do sit-ups and I told him I would give him a dollar for every one he did over fifty. He lit up, a big smile on his face.

"I know you're going to take me for a lot of money, but the challenge is on, right?"

Donald E. McInnis, defense attorney
for Aaron Houser.

"I'll do it," he answered.

I told him every time he felt lonely or depressed, or if he felt like he wanted to cry, he should lie down on the floor and do crunches. He followed my advice and came out of his depression. It cost me seventy dollars, but I felt it was a good investment.

If Aaron and I had previously had a barrier between us, that barrier disappeared. The much-needed trust between client and attorney developed, and I was thankful for that. But we still had a long road ahead.

The first issue I had to address was the cause of Aaron's depression. I decided to allow Aaron to have a roommate. He needed more contact with his own age group. I believed Aaron could avoid being tricked into making incriminating statements.

18

• JUVENILE HEARING 707 •

Day 156: San Diego, California
June 25, 1990

The prosecutor and defense attorneys had an informal discussion in chambers with Judge Laura P. Hammes, the jurist assigned to determine fitness of the boys for trial as juveniles under California Welfare & Institutions Code section 707. Where the boys would be tried was of paramount importance. If they were tried as adults, and convicted, they could be sentenced to life without parole. If they were tried in juvenile court, however, they would be released at age 25, even if found guilty. So the Fitness Hearing was a major first hurdle.

The CBS television documentary series *48 Hours* had asked to cover the hearing live. The three defense attorneys and the families of the boys had no objection, but Judge Hammes denied it, being concerned about a national "circus." Attridge even wanted to release the interrogation tapes to *48 Hours*, but that was not allowed either. Reporters and a sketch artist were allowed into the court though, as is customary.

The hearing began thirteen days later, on July 7, 1998, more than five months since Stephanie Crowe's death. I encouraged Aaron's army of fifty supporters to show up for the hearing, and a similar group representing Josh and Michael also came. They were all ushered into the court along with the press and the ever-present "curiosity-seekers" as we prepared to enter and make our cases.

Media representatives questioned us outside the court, and we happily responded. The more TV and newspaper coverage we got, the better. Attridge, especially, seemed to revel and excel in these outside the courtroom opportunities. We had several of them.

After everyone was seated, Judge Hammes asked the immediate family members of the three boys to identify themselves and announce their kinship. They had been directed to sit in the jury box, there being no jury for this hearing. Deputy DA Gary Hoover had been relieved of his assignment as prosecutor and replaced by Summer Stephan, a deputy DA with nine years of experience. The problem was, as with most prosecutors, her diligence was in seeking the bits and pieces that would strengthen her case. She didn't want to hear about possible innocence; she wanted to win her case at any cost. Summer Stephan is, in my view, something of a self-appointed Joan of Arc. She spends time with the victims of her cases, and she sees herself as a crusader in the arena of crime. She would even talk to the parents and relatives of defendants, asking for their cooperation, telling them they were not betraying their loved one. Now, what did she mean by that show of concern? Was this an attempt to win their support, so they would help her get "justice?" In this case, she even had the audacity to telephone the Crowes and tell them she thought Michael should admit to the murder. Steve and Cheryl Crowe wanted nothing to do with the prosecutor, however. To them she was the bitter enemy, the vulture circling, trying to take their son away forever.

Wasn't it enough to have lost a daughter?

What was most in our favor was having Judge Hammes on the bench. In spite of the confessions, Hammes would not allow herself to be swayed by anything but facts. She would give both the prosecution and the defense all the room they needed to make their case before the court.

I had gone over the confessions a number of times and was sure Michael's, in particular, would not hold up in court. The interrogation and coercion, to the defense, were positive factors. Most importantly, both Michael and Joshua were now denying the crime altogether. As for Joshua's confession, during his interrogation, the police had kept him from eating, from going to the bathroom, even from sleeping very much. And for most of his

Summer Stephan

interrogation, Joshua had not been Mirandized. Further, the lies told to Michael and Josh by police—and the promises made by them to "go easy" on them—I saw as coercion.

While the prosecutor felt secure with the evidence, all three defense attorneys felt we had more than a fighting chance.

Judge Hammes made herself clear at the very start of the next phase of the hearing. "We're here because a twelve-year-old girl was brutally murdered in her bedroom," she declared, her own feelings now in evidence. "And three young boys have been charged with that murder. That's enough to send chills through the heart of everyone in this courtroom."

This was a straightforward declaration, and it placed the defense—me and my client, my colleagues and their clients—at the bottom of an awesome uphill climb.

The prosecutor called her first witness, Barry Sweeney.

"How are you employed?" Stephan began.

"I'm a police officer for the City of Escondido."

Sweeney had been a police officer for twenty-four years and assigned to

the investigative division for nearly twenty years, working undercover nar-
cotics for ten years. He said he had been involved in homicide investigation
between fifty and one hundred times. There were questions about the morning the detective entered the crime scene, routine things, and then he was
asked about a paramedic who had been first at the Crowe house. His name
was Steve Mandich.

"Is he a paramedic you are familiar with?" Stephan asked.

"Yes, he is."

"Are you familiar with how long he's been a paramedic?"

"It would be my guess, but between—"

"Objection," Attridge interjected. "Calls for speculation."

"Lack of foundation," I added.

"Sustained," Judge Hammes answered. "Lack of foundation sustained."

Stephan changed her question: "Have you worked with Steve Mandich
or seen him on other homicide scenes?"

"Yes, I have."

"Do you remember how many?"

"At least two or three cases."

"So what you were told by Mr. Mandich was that Stephanie Crowe was
dead, correct?"

"Yes."

"With respect to her location, could you be specific as to what the paramedic told you about how he found the body of Stephanie?"

"He told me that she was partially in a bedroom doorway and partially in
a hallway of the residence."

"At that point did you view Stephanie's body yourself?"

"Yes, I did."

"And could you describe what you saw?"

"There were two doors in that part of the hallway, one on each side,
and two doors further down the hallway approximately another five feet.
The doorway to my immediate left was the bedroom later identified as
Stephanie's. The body of Stephanie was lying on the floor with her head almost into the hallway area. The remainder of the body was lying on its side,

going diagonally into the bedroom. The bedroom door was fully open. She was lying on her side, with the right side of her head to the floor. One hand was over her, in a position like this." He demonstrated and continued, "The other was out front, pretty much like this. She was . . . there was a pool of blood in the left ear. There was dried blood on her cheek. There was blood on her neck. Her upper clothing was blood soaked, and there was blood on the carpet."

Stephan obviously had a goal in mind. She wanted to be able to establish that Stephanie was lying in Michael Crowe's line of sight when he passed that bedroom doorway, two hours before Stephanie's body was discovered by her grandmother. He either lied about getting up and walking to the kitchen, or he lied about not seeing his sister sprawled out on the floor in her bedroom doorway. She wanted the court to accept that no one could have passed Stephanie without seeing her.

Stephan established that the body displayed rigor mortis—it was stiff to the detective's touch. This would be useful in establishing the time of death. She continued on to the subject of how secure the house was from an outside intruder.

"Did you check for evidence of forced entry to the house?"

"Yes, I did." Detective Sweeney explained the locations of the entrance doors and said that the sliders had been closed. And while he waited for other units to arrive, he went outside and noted that there were no windows broken or open. Stephan asked about the formal double entry doors on the side of the house.

"They are on the east side of the house," Sweeney said, "and Judith Kennedy, who is the grandmother, said that nobody ever used those doors."

"Is that the door that displayed evidence of not being used, with cobwebs attached to the door itself?"

"Yes, it is," the detective said and nodded.

Stephan wanted to establish early that Michael Crowe had fabricated part or all of his story about going to the kitchen at around 4:30 A.M., and that there was no way someone had entered the house during the night. In short, she wanted to substantiate that the homicide had been committed by someone already in the house. That someone was Michael, who had opened the door and let his two conspirators in. All this was consistent with the conclusion of the police and stayed within the boundaries of the actual confessions. The only variation was that Michael had not implicated either Aaron or Joshua, but Joshua had said all three had been in the house that night; all three had been involved with the killing of Stephanie.

After a short recess, Stephan set up a diagram showing the layout of the house, intending to continue questioning Sweeney. Judge Hammes said, "Let me indicate, before we go forward, that I'm not sitting as a normal court, because I've had the advantage of reading all the reports in the case, so I'm light-years ahead of where the normal fact finder would be. When you are dealing with photographs and these things, you can screen through that. I've already got a picture of this house in my head and I'm aware of where you are going, so just make it quick."

Judge Hammes was aware of what Stephan was trying to establish, and she was telling Stephan to "cut to the chase." Stephan reestablished where the outside doors were and where Stephanie's body had been discovered.

"Now detective, you were involved in the search of Joshua Treadway's home, right?"

"Yes."

"I'm going to show you what has been marked People's Exhibit 3, a photograph of a knife; is that right?"

"A knife and a knife sheath."

"And the knife has written on it, 'The Best Defense,' is that right?"

"Yes."

"And could you tell the court where the 'Best Defense' knife was located?"

Sweeney explained that this knife and another, a compass knife, were found exactly where Joshua said they would be found, under his bed. Stephan then pointed out that there were other items in the house that were dangerous.

I objected: "The fact that other knives or implements that could be used to harm or injure were found at the house is irrelevant to this proceeding unless a foundation is laid as to whether or not those particular implements or weapons caused the injury."

Judge Hammes surprised me: "Overruled," she said.

Stephan then referred to photographs of Aaron's sword collection and other knives in the Houser house. This was followed by a presentation of pictures of Aaron's room.

"And what are those things up in the corner?" Stephan asked Sweeney.

"Those are medieval-type castles, dragons and such, displayed on a shelf. On the desk was a pair of black leather gloves. Next to the gloves was a bottle of hydrogen peroxide."

"Okay. What else is on the desk, there? Kind of peeping through?"

"I believe it's a newspaper article on the investigation of Stephanie's murder."

"Okay. And what's displayed here?" Stephan pointed.

"Most of them are medieval times books and games, and some videos."

"And the names are just visible. *Wizard's First Rule, Stone of Tears, Blood of the Fold, Temple of the Winds,* so on and so forth, is that right?" Stephan was no slouch when it came to courtroom drama. It was not difficult to put the "gore" in the sound of these titles. Her line of questioning continued and focused on the contents of Aaron's locker.

"Detective, you also searched Aaron Houser's school locker, is that right?"

"I served a search warrant on his school locker, his music room and his PE lockers."

"Okay, and looking at People's Exhibit 15, what does that picture show?"

"It's a locker in the music room. It has Sergeant Anderson pointing to the locker. Inside those papers and documents, I found a piece of paper that was, in essence, about DNA testing. It had Aaron Houser's name on the top."

"Okay . . . involving DNA testing?"

"Yes."

"No further questions," Summer Stephan said confidently.

19

• BEDROOM DOOR •

Day 168: San Diego, California
July 7, 1998

I had been watching the three boys during the prosecutor's questioning of Detective Sweeney.

They showed grave concern on their young faces. I believe Joshua managed a slight smile when Attridge stood up to question the detective. The first thing she did was establish that five police officers and/or paramedics had arrived at the Crowe house before he had.

"And do you have personal knowledge as to whether or not any of those persons had contact with the body prior to your arrival?"

"Mandich told me he touched the body. Everybody else said they had not."

"You were informed that family had touched the body, isn't that correct?"

"Yes."

"And so you have no personal knowledge as to exactly where that body was located when the family found it, isn't that true?"

"I believe it was right where I found it."

"You believe that, but you have no knowledge, because you weren't there when they got up at 6:30 in the morning and found the body, true or false?"

Judge Hammes intervened, again surprising me. "We can cut out the argumentative questions. I got that. Don't answer," she told Sweeney.

Mary Ellen Attridge

Attridge changed her line of questioning, pointing to another photograph. "I'm showing you what's been marked as Defendants' A; it reflects the position of Stephanie Crowe's body. Is that correct?"

"Yes," Sweeney acknowledged.

"Is that the position you saw the body in when you arrived at the house?"

"Yes."

"The position of Stephanie Crowe's body is not directly in the hallway leading to the other bedrooms, isn't that correct? Because there's an alcove, true or false?"

"It's in the alcove."

"Okay, so her head is in the alcove, right, not the hallway?"

"Yes."

"Not in the hallway directly accessing the other bedrooms, true or false?"

"That's correct. It was in that alcove."

Attridge, of course, wanted to turn the detective's previous testimony around. What he had just admitted was different from what he'd first said, and this meant there was a possibility Michael could have left his bedroom and gone into the kitchen and returned without seeing his sister's body. Later testimony would establish that the door alcove was two-and-a-half feet deep.

What followed were questions about the entrances to the house. Sweeney had reported seeing cobwebs on a door, and then Attridge pointed out that cobwebs were not visible in the photographs. She also pointed out that while Sweeney had mentioned all of Aaron's books, with all the gory titles, he had failed to mention that *The Hobbit* was also among this collection. It was a subtle point, showing that Aaron read things beyond the gore. But Sweeney had been on the witness stand countless times. A seasoned cop, he was not about to soften any evidence against the boys if he could help it. Attridge knew this and kept at him. She wanted his testimony weakened by information he himself would deliver.

"Your interview with Mrs. Kennedy was on January 21 at approximately nine p.m.?"

The detective nodded.

"She told you that the evening before the homicide, before Stephanie said 'Goodnight, Granny, I'm going to bed,' Stephanie and Michael were in the living room watching *Home Improvement* on television, is that right?"

"Yes."

"And at that time they were tickling each other, and Stephanie was laughing?"

"Yes."

"Further, she told you Michael loved Stephanie and was very protective of her, true?"

"Yes, she told me that," Sweeney admitted. That was what Attridge wanted everyone to hear, and she strategically moved on to another subject.

Since it was known that Sweeney had been in the monitoring room, watching and listening to Joshua's interrogation, she wanted to know if Joshua had been fed.

Sweeney said he had been fed, at least once.

"And you were actually seated in the room with him?"

"Yes, I was," Sweeney answered. "I think for a while he was laying on the floor."

"Sleeping?"

"I think he was eating."

"He was laying on the floor, eating?"

"Sitting on the floor and at times he'd lay down on the floor, and was also eating while on the floor."

"And did Joshua, when he lay on the floor on February 10, close his eyes?"

"I'm not sure." Sweeney knew exactly what counsel was getting at. She wanted to establish how exhausted Joshua had been.

"Did he appear to be tired?" she asked.

"Not really."

"I'm sorry?" Attridge responded in a tone of disbelief.

"Not really. We were talking." Sweeney stuck to his guns.

"So you saw no evidence of fatigue?"

"I didn't see any, no." Sweeney reaffirmed his answer. Attridge knew that Judge Hammes had seen the tapes for herself.

Attridge glanced up at the judge and said she had no other questions.

Paul Blake followed and opened by asking Sweeney about the diagram of the house. Blake pointed out that the diagram was not to scale. Sweeney agreed that it wasn't.

"Now, referring to your interview with Mrs. Kennedy," Blake said, "we know that her room and Shannon's is down here. Is that correct?" he pointed to the diagram.

"Yes."

"All right. If she were to step . . . if she were to open her door and step into the hallway, there's no . . ." He paused for a moment, to hand the detective a pointer. "If I could just have you sort of indicate with the pointer, draw a line there, between Stephanie's room and the doorway. That doesn't really look to be a line-of-sight view. Is that correct?"

"From Shannon's room, I would say that's right," Sweeney said and shrugged. He knew this was leading directly to the question of how Michael could have walked past Stephanie's doorway without seeing the body.

"So someone would physically . . . if they were going to see the position you have indicated for Stephanie's body, they would have to literally walk down the hallway at least until they turned the corner there, is that correct?"

"No. The light switch is right there, and standing there, turning on the light switch you could see Stephanie's body."

"Did you note in your report where the light switch was?"

"No, but I recall the light switch."

"You recall the light switch. You didn't put that in your report at the time, the location of the light switch?"

Paul Blake

"No."

"When you arrived, the house was dark?"

"No."

"It was fully lit on that January morning?"

"There was light coming through the sliders, light coming through the living room window. It was not dark."

"But from 6:30 to 7:00 there's considerable difference in the lighting. By the time you arrived there's more light, right?"

"Probably." Sweeney wasn't about to commit to anything that he didn't have to.

"Were any lights on when you arrived?"

"I believe there was one in the foyer, which would be right by the inside doors. I believe that was the only one."

Blake had a way of being quietly aggressive. He was just the opposite of Attridge, but no less effective. "Detective Sweeney," he said, "isn't it more correct that when you were interviewing Mrs. Kennedy, she told you she had to go physically into Stephanie's room to find her, and that she was fully inside the doorway to her room?"

Sweeney did not like this. "Absolutely not," he answered.

"And didn't she also tell you that the door was partially closed, maybe just about that much of it open?" He demonstrated with his hands.

"Absolutely not," Sweeney said, shifting in his seat, his mouth drawn tight.

"Six inches?"

"It couldn't have been, and she did not say that."

"But if Stephanie's body was inside, fully inside her room when the door was shut, no more than six inches open, she would not be visible directly across from Michael's room, isn't that correct, judging from the layout of the house?"

Sweeney's voice thickened. "If she was inside she would not be visible," he answered. "However, she wasn't inside. She was right there, and the blood was matted to the carpet, so I don't believe she'd been moved."

"If your recollection is correct, and I'm assuming we'll see later, but if that's correct, the large bloodstain on the floor directly inside the doorway of the bedroom, just what I'm referring to . . . that particular bloodstain might indicate that her body had been shifted, perhaps by the family that morning."

"No," Sweeney answered flatly. He meant to sound final. He was not going to let any doubt in his testimony reach the judge's ears.

"You believe you saw dried blood in her ear, is that correct?"

"Yes."

"But you didn't find bloodstains where her head was, correct? Or other large stains where you have her physically laying, is that correct?"

"Well, there was blood all over her head. There was blood on the carpet below her, and there were blood smears at the base of the doorway."

"Which could have happened when the family walked in and attempted to either revive or assist her?"

"No, it could not," Sweeney insisted.

"But you have no independent knowledge of what transpired until you arrived there, isn't that correct?"

"Until I arrived? Well, I can tell you by some evidence I observed that some things . . . things that happened that night."

"Sir, that is not the question. You weren't physically present at the time the body was discovered, isn't that correct?"

"That's correct." Sweeney had no choice but to concede.

My colleagues had certainly not lost any ground for the defense. In this part of the hearing, the invincible foe was not looking so invincible anymore.

However, just because a few battles go well doesn't mean the war is won, and Summer Stephan had been chomping at the bit to put her talents to work.

I wondered if she had even a slight doubt that perhaps the boys were innocent. Prosecutors get tunnel vision. It's their job. She was there to see these villains behind bars. We were anxious to prove they were not villains at all.

I began my cross-examination with questions about the security of the Crowe house. "Isn't it true one of the reasons Michael was interrogated, and stands accused of killing Stephanie, was because you felt the murder had to be from within the residence?"

"I believe the murder had to be . . . must have been done from within the residence."

"Because you found no point where a person broke in from outside, correct?"

"Correct."

"You saw all the windows locked, correct?"

"I saw them all in closed positions."

"In regard to the doors, you felt the murder had to be within the residence because all the doors were secure, correct?"

"It was a combination of two things. One is from statements by people on how the doors and windows were, but also from Michael's own statements. He came out of the bedroom at 4:30 in the morning with the light glowing from his TV and specifically said that all four doors . . . or all the doors in the hallway were closed, and I know that couldn't happen." Sweeney kept his cool. He knew what the defense was searching for and was not about to say anything that would cast doubt on the boys' guilt or on the police methods. I asked him about the family and their demeanor the morning the body had been found.

"Well, if I could explain it this way. Steve, Cheryl and Shannon were sitting on the couch and they all appeared to be very distraught."

"How old is Shannon?"

"I believe she's ten."

"Okay. And Michael?"

"Michael did not appear to be distraught, he showed no emotion."

"And that was important to you?" I was baiting him.

"Not at the time," he said, not taking the bait.

"Why wasn't it important to you at the time?"

"I was thinking of other things and I don't recall what those things were, but Michael was sitting in that chair and he did not appear to be in the same condition as Cheryl and Steve. Even though Cheryl . . . I believe Cheryl asked Michael to come over with the rest of the family, and he said no."

I asked about Stephanie's body being touched. We knew that both Steve and Cheryl had touched—held—the body. "When Stephanie's father tried to lift her up, did he say he had moved the child, or what he did with her?"

"He told me he couldn't move her because she was stiff."

"When did you first form the idea that someone in the residence had to have committed the crime?"

"After talking with Judith Kennedy. The grandmother."

"What time was that?"

"That would be at nine o'clock at night."

"And who did you tell?"

"I have no idea."

"You did tell someone though, didn't you?"

"I'm sure I did."

"Who was in charge that you would report to?"

"At that time . . . I'm not sure."

I returned to the subject of the house, the alleged cobwebs on the doors and so forth. What was vital to we three defense attorneys was to somehow prove, or open the possibility, that the house had not been secure, all the doors not being locked. Even proving this would not make our case, but it would allow for the possibility that someone from outside could have entered. Once that possibility was established, we had the opportunity to build from there. That the house was not tightly secure was indeed established as the hearing proceeded.

There was a recess at this point, and I took the opportunity to reflect on Sweeney's testimony. He had made it a point to mention that a paper on DNA testing had been found in Aaron Houser's school locker. We were all aware that my client, Aaron, was the one accused of masterminding the homicide, the one accused of actually murdering Stephanie while Michael "kept her quiet." Aaron had also been labeled "a Charlie Manson with a high IQ, a sociopath," by the Orange County psychologist, Lawrence Blum. Sweeney's implication was that Aaron Houser—known to be bright, stoic, intellectual—had studied DNA testing while plotting the murder. Because Aaron had above-average intelligence, anyone who believed he was involved with the killing would readily believe he might be smart enough to explore DNA testing while plotting the perfect crime, perhaps just for the challenge of it. This speculation had to be discredited, so I planned to get back to this point as soon as we returned to court.

"Detective Sweeney, when you looked in Aaron's room you found band equipment there, did you not? Musical instruments, a clarinet, other instruments?"

"I don't recall any."

"You don't recall any musical instruments?"

"No,"

"Did you find any band-cleaning materials, other than the hydrogen peroxide?"

"I don't recall anything to do with the band. I know out in the hallway there was a picture of him in a band uniform, but I don't recall anything in the room."

"Did you know he was in the band?"

"Yeah, I found out later. Yes, sir."

"And you made some reference to medieval items on a shelf, is that correct?"

"Yes."

"Did you check them closely?"

"I remember looking at them."

"Did you know that Aaron was studying DNA in biology at school?"

"No, I didn't."

"Did you make an effort to check the notes you found on DNA to see if they were or weren't in the school's curriculum?"

"I did not check the school's curriculum at all."

While I do not know for certain, I feel confident that the police had a field day with the supposition that this bright kid had studied DNA testing while plotting his homicide. Sweeney had been quite good at getting that into his testimony. Well, that piece of speculation had now been eliminated, and we had made another small but positive step forward.

Summer Stephan returned for redirect examination. Her quest was simply to reestablish that Stephanie's body had not been moved on the morning of the homicide. Sweeney reaffirmed this for her. Since the prosecution had no solid evidence, the point that Michael said he'd left the room and walked down the hallway without seeing the body became significant to their case. What Stephan was actually doing was making sure the court was reminded of this. This, after all, would cast a dark shadow over Michael if it could be established that he could not have gone into the kitchen without seeing Stephanie's body. As far as Stephan was concerned, this was soundly established.

Stephan called Linda Davidson, the boys' probation officer, to the stand and asked about Joshua Treadway's friendship with Michael Crowe. "Would you tell me what he told you about his relationship with Michael Crowe?"

I boiled. The Fifth Amendment is nothing but propaganda for the masses, and the authorities routinely find a way around it. Davidson's interview took place prior to any of the boys having an attorney or getting legal advice.

"He described Michael as his best friend."

"And what did he say about Michael's role in this murder?"

"He stated that he couldn't imagine how or why Michael would have done it. That if he did it, he didn't do it alone."

"That's something Joshua came up with? If he did it, he didn't do it alone?"

"Yes."

"What did he tell you about Michael's relationship with Stephanie?"

"He said sometimes Michael was angry with his sister, and she was considered perfect in the home and got lots of extra attention, and he wished she would go away."

This testimony was important to the prosecution, of course, and Stephan knew it directly reflected what Joshua had stated in his confession. As I have said before, the confessions were the strongest and only evidence the prosecution had, and this was Stephan's earliest attempt to nail down their validity.

Mary Ellen Attridge followed Stephan for cross-examination. "When you saw Joshua, he had been unable to sleep overnight, is that correct?"

"To the best of my knowledge."

"And when you wanted to talk about the offense itself, he told you he wanted to speak to his parents, or a lawyer, is that right?"

"Correct."

"He told you he had spent many hours with the police, is that right?"

"Correct."

"He told you the police had frightened him quite a bit, is that correct?"

"I don't recall if he used the word frightened. He said they talked for many hours."

"In your report, on page 7, paragraph 3, it states, 'The minor stated he had spent many hours with the police, and they had frightened him.' Is that correct?" She was triumphant at the witness's error.

"Yes."

"And he also told you he was very tired when he spoke to the police?"

"Correct."

"He told you the police had him place a telephone call to Aaron, correct?"

"Correct."

"And the police had written the text of that telephone conversation out for Joshua?"

"Correct."

"He told you he did not believe Michael could have done the murder, correct?"

"That's correct."

"He further requested that you bring him a Bible?"

"Or that he be given one, yes."

"He requested to see his youth minister?"

"Correct."

"And he told you, and I believe it is in quotes, 'I just pray for God's help. I know He knows the truth and He will not forsake me.' Is that what he told you?"

"Yes, it is."

"I have no further questions, Your Honor." Attridge returned to her seat.

"Mr. Blake?" Judge Hammes offered Blake the opportunity to cross-examine.

"No questions," Blake said.

I was then given the same opportunity, and I too declined.

20

• KILL KILL •

Days 168-170: San Diego, California
July 7–9, 1998

W hat we thought would be a one- or two-day hearing began to stretch out as more details emerged and more witnesses were called.

Aaron had admitted that he and Michael had not been getting along well for some time prior to the murder. It was a crucial issue since it weakened the accusation that the two of them had plotted the murder together. True, if the boys were indeed guilty this might have been a clever ploy, pretending enmity. On the other hand, if they were actually in a serious dispute, it would be difficult to imagine the two boys sitting around plotting a violent criminal act which would require a high level of trust between them. All this would wait, however. The next witness called was Joseph Carruesco, another San Diego County probation officer.

"What did you ask Michael?" Stephan asked.

"Towards the end of the interview I asked him . . . Well, actually I told him the police believed he was involved in the death of his sister. . . . That's when he made the statement that's quoted in the probation officer's report."

"And could you tell us what's in the statement?"

"He said, quote: 'There's a chance I didn't do this, but it is possible I did, I guess. I'm almost sure I didn't do it. Almost 100 percent sure.' End quote."

I suppose with some twist of logic this could place greater suspicion on

Michael. If the assumption was that he'd been covering up his guilt in the pretense of a lost memory, well then . . . But I was pleased that Stephan had brought this quote to light from her side of the table, and I assumed so were Attridge and Blake.

Since I was convinced of Michael's innocence by this time, I thought, *What a horror story.* Here was a kid, unsure about killing his own sister because the police had used psychological coercion on him, made him believe he was possessed by a demon he had within him. They assured him when he was totally exhausted and emotionally drained, an unconscious monster who hated enough to brutally murder his own sister.

And all this without access to parents or an attorney.

I glanced toward Michael's parents and those of the other defendants and wondered what they might be thinking at that moment, what they might be feeling. The three boys, Michael, Joshua and Aaron, could not be read; they looked wide-eyed and numb, perhaps contemplating an empty future. Aaron had told me, earlier in his cell, the worst part was thinking that this was going to be for the rest of his life.

Paul Blake started the cross-examination. "Mr. Carruesco," he began, "when you interviewed my client, he was still in Juvenile Hall, correct?"

"That's correct."

"And you had not reviewed any reports in this case at that time, is that correct?"

"That's correct."

"Police reports?"

"I had at that time—before I interviewed him—a declaration in determination; which is basically a probable cause form the police need to get a kid into Juvenile Hall."

"And that was based on some information from the police, is that correct?"

"Correct."

"You did, for example, view the videotapes of Michael's lengthy interrogation prior to him coming to the hall, is that correct?"

"That's correct."

"So you have no way of knowing whether or not he was not still under the influence of the incredible coercion, the deception . . ."

Stephan interrupted, objecting, and Blake rephrased the question; but his point had been made.

The next witness was Portia Nowak, an evidence technician with the Escondido Police Department for nine years, who worked on crime reports and crime scene investigations. She had been called to the Crowe residence during the investigation.

"And what did you do there?" Stephan asked.

"I was called to collect evidence."

"Did you also photograph many items at the residence?"

"Yes, I did."

"What time did you arrive at the Crowe residence?"

"About 8:40 A.M. on the day the body was discovered."

"Ms. Nowak, there's a couple of photographs I'd like you to take a look at and tell me if you took them. Specifically People's Exhibit 25."

"That's my evidence item number 59; it's handwriting on the windowsill in Stephanie's room. It reads, 'Kill Kill.'"

Stephan was leading up to the point where she could attribute those words to Michael Crowe, but she didn't accomplish her goal. Attridge, Blake and I objected. We questioned Nowak's qualifications in handwriting analysis. Stephan acknowledged that the witness had no qualifications but said she had an expert coming in for that purpose.

While Stephan still had Nowak on the stand, however, she brought out two issues that could strengthen her case. The first was the food plates found in Michael's room, dirty dishes. She would try to establish that Michael's home life was less than it should have been. There was also a stack of tabloid magazines in the room. Stephan placed emphasis on the fact that the thirteen magazines had a common theme.

I objected to the witness making comment on the tabloids because it called for speculation. Attridge joined me in the argument, adding that Nowak was not a psychologist or social scientist. But we were both overruled, and Nowak was directed to answer the question.

"The common theme was that every one of them had stories of the O.J. Simpson murder trial." (O.J. Simpson, for anyone who might not know, is the famous football star and TV personality who was accused of murdering his wife and her male friend. Nearly all the evidence pointed to his guilt, but he was found not guilty.) While the entire country had followed the O.J. Simpson trial, and certainly the news of it sold countless tabloids and other publications, the point here was that Michael was interested in murder, in murder trials and, if nothing else, in a blood-and-guts crime.

• • •

William Leaver was called to the stand; he was a forensic document examiner with the Forensic Science Laboratories in San Diego. He was Stephan's expert, the one who would connect Michael's handwriting to the words "Kill Kill" on Stephanie's windowsill. It soon became apparent that Leaver liked hearing himself talk. I don't say this to be cruel, or humorous, but the man tended to expand on his testimony endlessly. He went on and on about how he had matched the letters from something Michael had written in his room, and the words "Kill Kill" written on the windowsill. It sounded like he was saying the handwriting on the windowsill and Michael's handwriting were carbon copies.

But Attridge zeroed in on the truth of the matter. "You are testifying that Michael could be the writer. But he might not be, right?"

"He could be the author, yes," Leaver said.

"And he might not be?"

"There's a possibility he might not be."

"No further questions, Your Honor."

"Next witness," Judge Hammes ordered.

Brian Blackbourne, a physician and forensic pathologist for the county medical examiner's office, had been at the murder scene and later performed the autopsy.

Stephan began, "Dr. Blackbourne, did you perform an autopsy on Stephanie Crowe?"

"Yes."

"And did you reach a conclusion as to the cause of death?"

"Yes. Homicide by multiple stab wounds."

"And the multiple stab wounds, how did they result in her death?"

"From internal and external bleeding."

"So she bled to death?"

"Yes."

"Doctor, you viewed the room of Stephanie Crowe, is that right?"

"Yes."

"You viewed the bedroom and her bed, is that right?"

"Yes."

"Could you tell where Stephanie was when she was stabbed?"

Both Attridge and I objected, claiming speculation, but the judge allowed it.

"I believe some of the stab wounds were inflicted on her bed."

"And could you tell from the location of the stab wounds while she was on the bed what position she would have been in. Sitting up? On her side? On her back?"

"From the location of the wounds, I believe she was lying face down on the bed. At least when some of the stab wounds were inflicted."

"Lying face down on the bed?"

"Yes."

Judge Hammes turned toward Cheryl Crowe, having noticed her discomfort. "Would you like to leave for a few minutes, Mrs. Crowe? It's up to you. You can stay if you wish."

Cheryl elected to leave, and after her exit, Stephan prepared to show graphic photos of Stephanie and the wounds she had endured. Paul Blake interrupted, saying that Michael requested to leave the courtroom during this testimony.

A recess was called.

• • •

Michael, Aaron and Joshua were all allowed to leave during the testimony showing photographs of Stephanie's wounds. Judge Hammes offered to allow Judith Kennedy, the grandmother, to leave also, but she wanted to stay. After viewing the pictures of the wounds and hearing Dr. Blackbourne's explanation of them, Stephan turned to the suspected murder weapon. Aaron's Best Defense knife. "So, Dr. Blackbourne, is this knife consistent with the wounds on Stephanie's body?"

"Objection," Attridge said, "Leading."

But the objection was overruled. The witness went on to say that the deepest wounds were consistent with the "Best Defense" knife, but he stated that more than one knife could have been used. The two-knife theory was highly speculative, however, and not given much consideration. The prosecution had but one knife, anyway. The other knife they had examined (the hunting knife with a compass in the handle) did not match the deep wounds in Stephanie's neck and shoulder.

What came out of the testimony from Dr. Blackbourne was the question of how much "thrashing around" Stephanie had done while being stabbed. This was important since it would have to do with how fast rigor mortis set in, and this would indicate a time of death.

"Rigor mortis can come on more quickly if it follows a violent struggle," Dr. Blackbourne stated. "Such movement can cause rigor mortis to accelerate."

Based on the undigested fragments of carrot and lettuce in Stephanie's stomach, along with the data on how long it takes for rigor mortis, Stephanie died no later than 12:30 A.M., but she could have died as early as 9:30 p.m. This turned out to be of vital importance as the hearing unfolded.

So far, the hearing had gone well, I thought. Just as the confessions were our biggest obstacle, the lack of hard evidence was the prosecution's major hurdle.

That, however, did not seem to deter Stephan. She did not have to prove the boys guilty to have them sent to adult court. This was a hearing, not a trial, though trial tactics were being used by both sides in the arguments. In layman's terms, all the prosecution had to do was create a strong enough case against the accused to persuade the judge to have them stand trial as adults. I knew, as did my colleagues, that if the boys went to adult court the chances of saving them would be greatly reduced. I have said this a few times, I know, but this was the thought that kept churning through our minds, and we lived with this thought day after day.

But as our conviction that the boys were innocent became stronger and stronger, we became more and more determined to not let these innocents be lost. Unless we could put a lot of missing pieces together, however, we were bucking the odds. What we would eventually have to do is pull some reluctant rabbit out of the hat, but we were attorneys, not magicians. Illusions would not work in the courtroom, where we had to deliver solid arguments if we had any chance at all.

As a result, Richard Tuite became our best shot.

21

• THIRD-PARTY EVIDENCE—TUITE •

Day 171: San Diego, California
July 10, 1998

We were all back in court the next morning and Paul Blake's cross-examination of Dr. Blackbourne commenced; it did not take long. He simply established that there was a possibility that Stephanie had been moved from the bed by someone. Dr. Blackbourne readily agreed with the possibility.

During my cross-examination, I asked Dr. Blackbourne if he had been shown any other knife, or types of other knives, to determine whether they could have been used in the stabbing. He said he'd seen one other knife during the time he had been involved in the case. I was seeking data that would disqualify Aaron's knife as the murder weapon, or at least raise doubt. I was grasping at straws, really, since it had already been established that if it wasn't Aaron's knife, it was a knife quite similar. So it was a standoff.

The prosecution couldn't prove Aaron's knife was the weapon, but I couldn't disprove it.

"In regard to the collarbone and the transverse cervical vertebra," I said, "you indicate they were cut by the knife itself, Dr. Blackbourne."

"Yes."

"Can you determine how much strength it would take to penetrate and cause a cutting action into the collar- or clavicle bone?"

"It would take a degree of force, depending on the sharpness of the knife."

"Given the knife in evidence, it would require considerable strength, would it not, to cut through the bone?"

"It's hard to say with certainty, but yes, it would take some force to cut into the bone. Not super-human strength, by any means, but it would take some strength, yes."

"Are you capable, in your expertise as a coroner, to determine whether a child or an adult could have caused that wound, or is it just indeterminable?"

"I guess one would have to define the age of the child."

"Can you help us?"

Attridge objected. "Your Honor, this is vague." Judge Hammes overruled the objection.

"My answer would be . . ." Dr. Blackbourne paused. "Anyone of normal muscle mass, weighing, you know, 130 pounds or more, could do that."

"That would include male and female?"

"Yes."

Michael was five feet, two inches tall and weighed a mere 100 pounds, so I had heard what I wanted from this witness.

Stephan began redirect with questions about the bloodstains again. Then she offered a supposition: "If you were given the hypothetical notion that no one heard Stephanie scream, is that consistent with her head being covered with a comforter, muffling her sounds as she was getting stabbed, her head down on the pillow as we see in this picture? Is it consistent?"

Attridge objected, saying that it was outside Dr. Blackbourne's expertise to answer. I also objected, but we were overruled.

"Yes," Blackbourne said, "that would be consistent with noises being muffled, either by the comforter or by a pillow."

Stephan proceeded to reestablish that Stephanie had died at least six hours before her body was discovered, and that she had lived at least ten minutes after the stabbing. Then Stephan presented another question: "In a hypothetical, there's evidence presented that if it was her bloody hand pulling that door open, and then dying at the doorway there, obviously, she would have had to do that while she was alive, right?"

We all objected to this as clearly hypothetical, and no evidence had been entered that had anything to do with this speculation by the prosecutor. Again our objection was overruled.

"Yes," Dr. Blackbourne answered.

"Okay. So based on what is reasonable, and of medical certainty, if Stephanie's body was found in full rigor at 6:30 A.M. . . . would you expect that at 4:30 in the morning she would have been in the same position, assuming no one moved her?"

"Yes, yes I would."

Stephan knew that as long as the prosecution could maintain even reasonable doubt that Michael could not have passed Stephanie's bedroom door without seeing the body, her case would quickly mature into an easy victory. This was such a crucial piece of evidence for both defense and prosecution, so strong, that it would play heavily on the court's final decisions.

Attridge followed Stephan for reexamination. She established through the testimony that it was not possible to determine if all the wounds had been inflicted while Stephanie was on the bed.

She then returned to the subject of the time of death: "With respect to the time of death, is it your medical opinion the latest the time of death was approximately 12:30 A.M.?"

"Yes."

"And because she had undigested salad materials in her stomach, is it your medical opinion the time of death was, in fact, somewhere between 9:30 p.m. and 12:30 A.M.?"

"Yes."

Stephan objected. "That misstates the testimony," she said.

Attridge was quick on her feet. "Your Honor, he just agreed with it. It obviously does not misstate the testimony."

Stephan's objection was overruled.

"And with respect to the knife," Attridge continued, "and the redirect on that issue, the bottom line is this: There are literally thousands of knives in San Diego that could have inflicted those wounds, is that correct?"

"There are many, I presume, yes."

"So it is impossible for you to say that this knife is the one used to kill Stephanie Crowe?"

"That's correct," Dr. Blackbourne concurred.

The court excused Dr. Blackbourne, and Johnny Jay Martin was called to the stand. He had been the police officer who stayed with the family at the Crowe house on the morning of the homicide. Aaron, Joshua and Michael returned to the courtroom at this point. They had not been in court during the testimony of Dr. Blackbourne because of the graphic pictures and conversations about Stephanie's death. Detective Claytor was asked to leave, so that he would not be privy to the testimony of a fellow police officer.

Martin, a policeman with sixteen years' experience, arrived at the Crowe house ten minutes after the 911 call.

Stephan's major goal was to use this man's testimony to discredit Michael's story of walking past his sister's body, as he claimed. "What did you overhear Michael tell his family?" she asked.

"That he got up about 4:30 in the morning, turned on the television for light and went to the kitchen to get a glass of milk. He said he didn't see his sister in the hallway."

"And this statement was made to his family, not in response to any question by you."

"That's correct."

"As you looked down the hallway, the body of Stephanie was not visible, correct?"

"I don't recall looking down the hallway, I walked directly to her."

"I'm sorry?"

"I walked directly to her and stood above her."

"She was in an alcove that leads to the bedroom. Is that correct?"

"A doorway, a doorjamb area, right."

"And so it was not out in the hallway proper, which is depicted as a further distance from the body, as shown in Exhibit A., is that right?"

"I guess you would call it like an entryway to the bedroom."

"So it wasn't like if you were walking straight down that hallway, her body would have been in the recessed area in her room, is that right?"

"That's correct."

Blake's turn came to cross-examine. "Officer Martin, I'm showing you what's been marked as defense item D, and it appears to be a photocopy of an Escondido Police Department document. Do you recognize it?"

"Yes, I do."

"Do you recognize the handwriting in that document?"

"I do. It's mine."

"And on that document you note various people were distressed, is that correct?"

"Yes."

"It says 'the fourteen-year-old son was crying,' I believe, or words to that effect, right?"

"Yes."

"He was upset and crying?"

"Yes."

"Thank you."

This was important. The police had said one reason they suspected Michael was that he did not respond to his sister's death adequately. Stephan knew this officer had diluted this opinion, so she returned for redirect.

She showed the diagram of the Crowe house and asked, "Have you seen this layout of the home before?"

"Yes."

"And are you familiar with the layout—the rooms and so forth?"

"Yes."

"That's because your own home is similar, is that right?"

"Almost exactly," Martin answered.

"And where's the room directly across from Stephanie's room?"

I objected. I knew where she was going.

Stephan continued, "Looking at the location of Stephanie's body, when you saw it—"

I objected again, but to no avail.

Stephan continued, "Could you see Stephanie's body?"

Attridge objected: "Vague. We don't know under what circumstances," she said.

Judge Hammes responded, "Sustained as to circumstance. If you can put it in another way, counselor."

Stephan added circumstances. "If a TV light was on in the one room . . ." she said, creating the circumstances to match those Michael had described, "the one across from Stephanie's, when you walked out of that room, could you see the body?"

I objected again, and so did Attridge. "Incomplete and hypothetical," she argued.

"I'm going to let this go forward," the judge ruled. "You may add what you wish."

"Yes. I would see the body."

There was a brief morning recess, and when we returned, Detective James Lanigan was sworn in. The day after the murder, Lanigan had interviewed friends and others who knew Stephanie, including Joshua, who said he was "a close friend of Michael, but a mere acquaintance of Stephanie." Stephan wanted to know if the officer had seen anything of interest at Joshua's home.

"As I walked into the living room I saw a knife on the couch, and I mentioned it to Josh." (He was referring to the knife with the compass in its handle, not Aaron's "Best Defense" knife.)

Stephan asked Lanigan to tell the court how Joshua described his friendship with Michael, what games they played, and their mutual interests. She also resurfaced the phone call Michael made to Josh from the police station. Lanigan had written in his report that Michael said he'd found Stephanie's body.

Then the subject moved to Aaron.

"Do you see this person in the courtroom?" Stephan asked.

"He's sitting to the right of defense counsel, with the red tie, a white shirt, dark hair, glasses. He has a pencil in his left hand." The officer identified Aaron. He also stated he had interviewed Aaron.

Most of Lanigan's testimony was a rehash of what was in the reports. Aaron and Michael were friends, but not close buddies. Aaron had a knife collection. No, Aaron had never loaned Michael a knife. He'd mentioned lending Michael some compact discs and computer games and Michael had lost them, so he would not think about lending him anything valuable, like a knife or sword. When he made his report to the lead investigator, Ralph Claytor, Lanigan mentioned the knives. Lanigan stated that Claytor wanted to talk with Aaron in a more "formal" atmosphere, at the police department.

Stephan wanted to renew the point of Aaron's apparent intellectual prowess. "Did you note something about Aaron's level of sophistication, or was it the way he talked that you relayed to Detective Claytor?"

I objected. "Calls for speculation, Your Honor." Attridge objected too, but we were overruled.

"Yes, I mentioned to Ralph Claytor that Aaron, a fifteen-year-old, spoke in very measured tones, like somebody much older, somebody very experienced. And I told Claytor that when I asked questions, Aaron would give me the answer but wouldn't give me anything else. Some people will expound on things. Aaron just answered my questions and that was it."

I don't know if I thought about it at that moment, but I remember visualizing the portraits the police had so persistently painted of their three "killer" kids: Here was Aaron, *the brain*. He was studious, unemotional, with the kind of intellect storytellers give mad scientists and murderers. Then there was Michael; he was smart too, but buried deep within him was this evil monster that takes over the boy's psyche and turns the good Michael into the *evil Michael*. Joshua, the artistic type, *the gullible one* of the trio; he simply goes along with the murder because he's told to by the others. I could not help but think this sounded like cheap pulp fiction.

But the police had sold this story to themselves and then to others. Now, three young boys who had never been in trouble, who were good students, who had never even had a serious date, were standing accused of a vicious crime.

Detective Mark Wrisley was next on the witness stand.

Stephan established that Wrisley had held the final "interview" with Joshua before his arrest. Also established was that Joshua had shown a lot of anxiety during the interrogation. *And who wouldn't?*

"Prior to my interview with Joshua, prior to me Mirandizing him," Wrisley said, "I had spoken with him about . . . he had concerns about Juvenile Hall, and what might happen to him down there, and he showed a lot of anxiety, which was very understandable, given the circumstances. For several minutes, he and I conversed about procedural things at Juvenile Hall. I was trying to lower his anxiety. So it was very clear to me he understood, at the end of that evening, he was not going home. He was going to Juvenile Hall."

This was really in our favor because we wanted to show that Joshua had confessed under duress. But Attridge objected anyway.

"Move to strike," she said. "Based on speculation. The witness is not a clairvoyant." Judge Hammes overruled the objection.

Stephan continued. "How long was this interview?"

"One hour and fifty-three minutes."

"And during this one hour and fifty-three minutes, detective, could you describe the tone? Did you ask a lot of questions and did he give you short answers, or just talk freely?"

Attridge and I objected vehemently. Judge Hammes ended up dismissing Wrisley until 1:30 that afternoon because she wanted to have a discussion with all the attorneys—prosecution and defense—about procedure. She told us the videotapes were statement enough on how the interrogations were handled by the police. She also said she had taken Attridge's assertions that juvenile confessions had to be proven beyond a reasonable doubt, and she had been reading the appropriate law ever since the reference had been made. She made it clear she was researching it, even though there seemed to be no case law truly definitive on the issue. Another matter Stephan brought to the table was that Wrisley's time was limited, and she was trying to expedite things because of this. I thought this bizarre. Attridge joined me and we saw no reason to move too rapidly.

We took a lunch break, and court resumed thereafter.

Soon after the cross-examination commenced, Stephan asked Detective Wrisley about Michael. "Tell the court about your interview with Michael, what you discussed."

"That interview took place in our children's interview room at Escondido PD. Only Michael and myself were present at the time." Wrisley was speaking of what is called an informal interview covering what occurred when Michael and his family were first brought to the police station.

"Essentially," Wrisley continued, "I had Michael recall for me the events of the morning of the 21st, when Stephanie's body was discovered. I then had him retrace for me the events of the day of January 20—the family's comings and goings and their activities of that day."

"And what did Michael tell you took place on the evening of January 20th?"

Michael had eaten breakfast cereal for dinner and the family had eaten separately. He had watched television for a while and then returned to his room, where he fell asleep around 10:00 p.m. "He told me that sometime after midnight he was awakened by the sound of pounding, which he estimated lasted just a few seconds. He indicated that the pounding came from the door adjacent to the garage. He did not get up to investigate, and he didn't recall hearing the sound of any family members up and about. Eventually he fell back to sleep, after the sound stopped."

"Did he indicate whether the family dog barked in response to this noise?"

"Michael said he heard no dog barking," Wrisley answered, and he continued his testimony, taking every opportunity to subtly support the prosecution on every issue. When it came to the moment of Michael's arrest, he said: "Michael and I were seated in separate overstuffed chairs. Detective Claytor approached Michael and told him he was under arrest. Michael said something like, 'I knew this was going to happen. I didn't like her anyway.'"

Stephan ended her examination by bringing Aaron into greater focus. "And also, detective, when he was describing Aaron to you did Michael indicate Aaron might be his . . . somebody he'd want to kill also?"

"That's true."

"Nothing further, Your Honor." Stephan was satisfied for the moment. Actually, her last question could not have been better for my own purposes, defending Aaron. If Aaron was someone Michael would have liked to kill, how farfetched was it that these two kids had collaborated in the murder as allies? So many things simply didn't make sense, but of course we weren't dealing with common sense here, we were dealing with the complexity of the judicial mentality, where irrationality surfaces every day. It was surely possible these three kids had committed homicide just for the pure thrill of it. And so, even if Aaron and Michael weren't best of pals, they could have done this horrible thing on something as stupid as a dare. I didn't believe this, nor did my colleagues, but the prosecution did, and the prosecution's case was not weak. *If two of the three defendants said they did it, well then, they did it, right?*

Attridge questioned Wrisley next. Her major interest was Joshua, her client. She wanted what we all wanted: *to show why the boys said they did this crime.*

"Do you recall Detective Claytor telling Joshua, 'I think what you need to do is go the route that's going to cause you the least problems.' Do you recall him saying that to Joshua, or something to that effect?"

"I believe he said something like that," Wrisley said.

"Do you remember Detective Claytor telling Joshua, essentially, that he—Detective Claytor—had the knife that was used in the homicide, and that Joshua better explain how it got from underneath his bed?"

"I remember Detective Claytor asking for an explanation, yes."

"Okay. Now, isn't it a fact that there were no forensics or other testing of that knife at the time of the 27th, when Claytor asked the question, to tie that knife to the homicide?"

"I'm not aware of any forensics being done on the knife at that point."

"Are you aware that Joshua Treadway was kept at the police station that night from approximately 7:00 p.m. until 8:30 the next morning?"

Stephan objected strongly, saying the detective had already said he didn't spend the entire night at the station during the "interview" in question.

Attridge kept pounding away at Wrisley, wanting to establish the true nature of the interrogations. "Do you recall Joshua telling his father he'd told Detective Claytor he had received the knife from Aaron because Detective Claytor told him, quote, 'You could be charged as an adult'?"

"I remember Joshua making a statement that he had received the knife from Aaron. I don't know if it was in connection with him being afraid of something Detective Claytor said."

"But Mr. Treadway told you his son falsely confessed to Detective Claytor because Detective Claytor told the boy he could be tried as an adult and go to prison forever."

"I recall Joshua making the statement that he'd essentially lied to Detective Clayton."

"And, in fact, he told you the reason he lied is because Detective Claytor told him he could go to prison forever, right?"

"I don't recall Detective Claytor saying that."

Judge Hammes called for a recess, and when the hearing resumed, Attridge kept Wrisley on the stand. She dwelled on the interrogation of Joshua: the long hours of questioning by Claytor, by Sweeney and by himself; the lack of food; the lack of sleep; and the high anxiety; and she made inquiries about Joshua's *Miranda* rights. She pointed out that after Claytor had been "interviewing" Joshua, Wrisley replaced Claytor and had asked Joshua to repeat what he'd told Detective Claytor. She sharply reminded Wrisley that he had done this because Joshua's statement, on February 10, was not made under the protection of *Miranda*.

Wrisley admitted this, and also admitted that *after* Joshua's confession, he had to give him his *Miranda* rights because they intended to arrest him as a murder suspect.

Paul Blake began his cross-examination, going back to January 21 and the murder scene. At an appropriate time, he made his point by asking, "Do you recall if it was Detective Claytor or yourself who elected to further investigate Michael simply because you didn't believe his reaction to his sister's death was 'normal?'"

Wrisley skirted the issue. "I was taking direction from Detective Claytor," he said. It didn't matter. Blake had reestablished what first had brought attention to Michael as a possible suspect. Judge Hammes would know this was a textbook observation; she would also know that all of us, but especially a young teen, might well conceal his feelings in such circumstances. And anyway, many people repress their feelings for hours, days, sometimes even longer. So Blake wanted this brought to the surface. He followed by asking Detective Wrisley if he had Mirandized Michael the next morning at the Polinsky Childrens Center, the morning after the murder. Wrisley said he had.

"Do you do that to all witnesses?" Blake asked. "Every single witness you've ever interviewed, you always read them their rights?"

"No."

"So you simply Mirandized him, what, out of an abundance of caution? What was the reason for it? I'm talking about the first interview."

"I Mirandized Michael because he was in a home in which a person had been the victim of a homicide. I did not know at that particular time what role he may or may not have had. I felt it was important if I was to receive any statements, admissions, or even confessions. Important that I did it under the cover of *Miranda*."

"And your interview at Polinsky, on January 22nd, what time did that interview begin?"

"It was morning. Possibly 9:00 or 9:30. I didn't want to get down there right at the breakfast hour. I wanted to be sure the children had been fed. I know the routine there."

"Let's back up just a minute. Where is Polinsky Childrens Center?"

"It's in the Clairemont Mesa area of San Diego, right behind the county annex building, just off . . . immediately west of Interstate 15."

"If I understand correctly, on January 21st—prior to taking either Shannon or Michael to Polinsky—you elected to Mirandize Michael, is that correct? And take his statement?"

"That's correct."

"Moving back to the interview at Polinsky, was that interview recorded?"

"It was."

"And with perhaps the exception of a detail or two, he told you the same story as the day before. Isn't that correct?"

"That's correct."

"During the course of your interview I believe you indicated that Michael's family was in a hotel, is that right?"

"I didn't make that statement to him. I didn't talk about where his family was."

"You don't recall him asking when he could see his family?"

"I don't recall him asking that. I mean, he may have. I just don't recall."

"And if we saw the transcript, the audio tape, that would be the best evidence of what transpired?"

"That would be accurate."

"And if it shows that he made a request to see his family, that would be correct, right?"

"That would be correct. I just don't recall him saying that."

"And if you made a response indicating you couldn't make that decision to allow him to see his family, that would be correct also?"

"That would be accurate. It's not up to me." Wrisley shrugged.

Blake zeroed in. "Yet you were involved in the decision to place him at Polinsky; is that not correct?"

"That's correct."

"Well, Detective Wrisley, if it was not up to you, who could allow him to see his family?"

"It was up to . . . he was a ward of the county at that point. It was up to the supervisory administrative personnel at Polinsky."

"But you'd already made the determination Michael was a suspect, no?"

"He was a potential suspect," Wrisley countered.

"If he was a suspect, and you—and when I say 'you' I mean your police department—you made the decision to place him at Polinsky, then was he not under your control at that point?"

"I don't know if he was," Wrisley answered. "Michael and Shannon, his sister, were under protective custody."

This was a cat and mouse game, of course. What had been established, however, was that Michael was more than a possible suspect, at least from the time the detectives all gathered to talk over the case, prior to Michael being sent to Polinsky for protective custody. Michael was in custody, and that was a vital point to make as clear and as early in the proceedings as possible. Blake had done his job well on this, but it was only a small link in the chain of events and testimony that would have to unfold if we had a chance of saving the boys from adult court, or saving them altogether.

"On the evening of the 22nd, was there a psychologist named Dr. Blum present?"

"Yes."

"Do you have a recollection of what you were told by him?"

Wrisley said he was only instructed to redirect the conversation with Michael to some particular subject that needed clarification.

He was not about to admit anything that would establish a strategy to entice, coerce or create a confession from Michael. But the truth was Dr. Blum was the source of the notion that Michael would respond to the idea of having an "inner demon," some repressed being deep in his subconscious, a demon who hated his sister, wanted to kill his sister. But Wrisley would not volunteer this truth, and Blake could not ask for an off-the-record account. He knew Stephan would object.

It didn't matter; Judge Hammes had seen the tapes, and she knew.

I glanced over at Michael during the time Blake was questioning Wrisley. I could not help but think about the cruel psychological coercion they had used on a boy under the stress of tragedy, on the very day of the murder of his sister; telling him that a wicked, hateful killer lurked inside him. I wanted to shout, *This boy should not be tried in a court of law. Why don't we merely have him exorcised?* I wondered what his parents were thinking, what the parents of all three boys were thinking. They had become as convinced as we attorneys were that their sons didn't do it.

"Did Dr. Blum participate in the interrogation of my client?" Blake continued.

"Do you mean actually asking him questions?"

"No, no. Was he either monitoring, or was he there during the interrogations?"

"He was monitoring," Wrisley said, "and providing support, direction and advice to the investigations. He was never in the room with Michael."

Blake seemed pleased. "Thank you, detective. I have nothing further."

• • •

My cross-examination followed Blake's, and my first objective was to establish that the boys—Michael, Joshua and Aaron, my client—had not only been interviewed before the hidden video camera, but also off camera in the detectives' offices at different times. This was no small point. When Wrisley told Michael his parents believed he was guilty and that they did not want to see him again, it was off camera. The idea, of course—the major obstacle we all had to deal with—was to discredit the confessions themselves. If we failed to do that, then no matter how many battles we might win over the course of the hearing, the war would be lost.

"Why was not the children's interview room used? These are children," I asked, my pugnacity evident in my voice.

Stephan quickly objected. "Your Honor, I object to that characterization. It's opinion, I think, as to whether or not they are children."

Stephan's attitude had not escaped Judge Hammes. "There's an undercurrent in the courtroom I want to temper," she said. "I can feel the vibrations. I want the witnesses to be able to talk. I want the truth to come out in a conducive atmosphere. So I'll tell everyone to keep the vibes down, and let's continue. Mr. McInnis, rephrase and continue," she added.

I rephrased my question and went on to the point that had already been established by the police: that Michael was the prime suspect prior to being sent to Polinsky Childrens Center. Wrisley denied this, so I made the inference stronger.

"Were you aware, on the evening of the 21st, that one of the officers stated that he felt Michael was not grieving sufficiently, and therefore abnormal; appeared to be a possible suspect of higher importance than the other members of the family?"

"Someone may have made that observation."

I left the subject of Michael and turned to Aaron's interrogation. Wrisley had not been very involved in questioning Aaron, not as much as he had been during the interrogation of Michael and Joshua. I asked him why he had been sent in to speak with Aaron during a break that occurred during the long "interview."

"There was a point in the interview where it was decided to take a break, which is typical in any lengthy interview, and I just went in to kind of fill some time. Aaron and I chatted about a variety of things: history and some of his other interests. But I didn't ask him any specific questions related to the case."

"Isn't it true, detective, that you were sent in there to do that so as to maintain a rapport with him; keep a good working relationship with him, not just because you had spare time to go chit-chat?"

"I don't know if that was the intent, but that's a pretty good idea." Wrisley no doubt thought his answer was cute, that he had turned the rabbit into the fox.

"Wasn't this discussed before you went in?"

"I was asked to go in and talk with Aaron, put him at ease, let him relax a bit."

"And the purpose for that was to get him into a more cooperative mood, correct?"

"I believe he was already cooperative." Wrisley was smooth. I asked why he watched the interrogation on the monitor if he wasn't involved. He said he didn't actually monitor the entire interview. An evasive response.

"But when you were there, watching, correct?"

"Yes."

"Were you not counseling with the interrogators, off camera, discussing what should be done next, along with Dr. Blum?"

"On occasion, yes."

"Did you observe Dr. Blum making notes as he listened to the interrogations?"

"I'm going to say no, because it was being videotaped."

The court was adjourned for the weekend, and the hearing recommenced on the following Monday. Michael's mother and grandmother sat in the jury box, as did Aaron's grandparents, Mr. and Mrs. Higgins. Aaron's mother and Joshua's mother, father and brother were also there. As anticipated, they all looked weary and worried. They too, in a way, were on trial, subjugated in a painful and unreal experience beyond their control and comprehension. Their future, uncertain and potentially bleak, was tied to the outcome of this hearing, as was that of the three boys.

Joshua, the artist, continued to draw portraits of the witnesses and others. They were quite excellent, really—some of them comical, rather like caricatures. Joshua didn't mind adding horns and other denigrating characteristics to the prosecutor's witnesses, and he had a nice time drawing the prosecutor herself.

Before the hearing began, Mary Ellen Attridge addressed Judge Hammes, asking her to consider two cases she had discovered that involved juveniles making coerced statements without being Mirandized. She also announced that she had subpoenaed Deputy District Attorney Gary Hoover. Judge Hammes was not pleased that Attridge had subpoenaed an attorney in a death penalty case. She said to Attridge that it wasn't clear that Gary Hoover's presence would be needed. Attridge insisted, however, because Hoover had been witness to parts of the interrogation, and he would therefore be able to shed light on the circumstances of the interrogations. Finally she said, "I'm not telling the court he is a necessary witness. I am saying, however, that if it does come to light he was at the Escondido Police Department, giving legal advice to the detectives taking the statements, he, in my opinion, is going to be relevant."

I spoke up, defending Attridge's position: "Your Honor, I would join in that and emphasize also that Mr. Hoover should have some notes from what he saw."

I had a very early contact with him in Paul Pfingst's office. As a consequence, I thought it important for him to produce those notes and tell what he saw on a discovery issue. So I added a request that he produce all the discovery he had.

Judge Hammes was composed, but impatience showed in her eyes. "This is an off-the-cuff discovery motion, and I'm not inclined to entertain it," she said firmly. She did agree to reserve her ruling, though, saying, "I'm not ruling on anything right now because I don't think it's ripe for a ruling, or even a discussion."

We won and lost on that issue.

Attorney Attridge then asked for the opportunity to introduce evidence that another person killed Stephanie: the transient, Richard Tuite.

22

• IT'S ALL IN! •

Day 171: San Diego, California
July 10, 1998

Prosecutor Stephan objected to any evidence coming out about Richard Tuite. Her mind had been running a mile a minute as she waited for her chance at rebuttal. She was livid, and she started a tirade of statements that she said proved the boys were the guilty parties. She first addressed having the videotapes played in the courtroom, an earlier issue, and then she added that she thought all the recorded tapes of Joshua should be seen openly in the court. But she hedged, saying she thought there should be a detective present, to explain and answer any questions the court might have. Obviously a detective would support the prosecution and would certainly want the confessions to hold up. Stephan also flatly disputed that there were evidentiary grounds to consider a third party as the possible perpetrator.

She followed this with a self-serving statement on how well she had prepared her case: "I have presented the details of the crime, a murder in the first or second degree of an innocent girl in the sanctity of her own home, at approximately midnight. She wasn't alive at 4:30 in the morning and she wasn't moved. The victim's brother, Michael Crowe, was very comfortable telling the police and his family that he got up at 4:30 in the morning and did not see anything, but he thought her door was closed because when they left her, they left her on the bed and thought she was dead. When Stephanie crawled out of her bed, dying—and this will be presented through fingerprint evidence—her own hands clawed that door open." Her voice cracked with emotion at this point. "Stephanie's body lay in that doorway, but Michael said he didn't see her at 4:30 in the morning because he knew, or thought he did, they had left her dead on the bed.

"I've presented a circumstantial case that in a locked house, inside this girl's room, someone wrote: 'Kill Kill.' I've presented papers by Michael where it says on it . . . has a picture of an angel on it, under a cross. We know that Stephanie was an angel. We know she attended church, which will be presented later. And it has on it 'Killed by an ally.'"

Attridge tried to interject, but Stephan continued: "And when you take that in conjunction with a handwriting analysis it tells you Michael is a suspect who should not be excluded.

"We look at not just that, but the fact that inside this house Michael played fantasy games such as Dungeons and Dragons. We have an expert coming who will tell the court the way these people score their points is by killing. And when there are two people in a room doing the killing, they each get a point. Therefore—"

Attridge lifted her voice, "Your Honor—this—"

Stephan tried to continue her tirade, but finally Judge Hammes spoke up; I hoped she would end this prejudicial rambling.

"I do not want interruption when one counsel is talking," Hammes said coldly.

At this point I pulled Attridge close to me and whispered for her to let the prosecutor rant on. She was helping us more than herself. I could tell from the look on Judge Hammes's face that she wasn't buying all this.

Stephan continued showering the court with her theory of the crime, and her case against the boys: "I've presented evidence that the knife found under Joshua's bed is, in fact, Aaron's knife. And it happens to be the knife consistent with the murder weapon in this case. The cut made by this knife was eerie." Stephan wanted mental pictures. "It is a mirror image, the way it narrows and the way it cuts into the bone. The depth, the shape, the curvature. It is the knife used in the murder, and I'm going to present the statement by

Joshua. We know that Josh had another knife that belonged to another kid, the compass knife. Scott Colegrove, who is here to testify this morning, Scott Colegrove will testify—"

"Excuse me," Judge Hammes interrupted, "is he sitting in the courtroom now?"

"No," Stephan answered. "He'll testify the only person who knew about this knife was Aaron, not Josh. Aaron knew about this knife and his knife disappeared and on January 27th, the day of the search warrant and after his house had been searched, Aaron called Scott Colegrove immediately and said, 'Guess what? The police just showed up at my house and I discovered that my knife was missing.' That morning, Susie Houser, Aaron's mother, called the police about this knife, so this is not just any old knife. This is a knife that was reported missing. People admitted stealing. And there just happens to be another knife, another killing weapon found under Josh's bed, because as the game expert will tell you, the master of the game designates and has weapons ready. Josh had two knives ready to commit this murder. I believe Scott Colegrove's knife was on him too, as he acted as a lookout, but Aaron's knife was used to stab Stephanie.

"There were two knives stolen shortly before this murder. One of the knives was used to cut into that little girl's body. I'm going to present the comforter and show the cuts in it. I'm going to present the expertise. I'm going to present Josh's statements . . ." and she continued on and on, ranting incoherently at times. The judge paid close attention, but I believe she showed her own disbelief.

As soon as Stephan ended her attempt to dissuade Judge Hammes from allowing Richard Tuite to become an issue in the hearing, Attridge moved in to take advantage of the shallowness of Stephan's remarks, and she drove home her own key points.

"I think," Attridge said, "that if I had twelve people sitting in that jury box right now, and I were a prosecutor, I'd get a guilty verdict on Mr. Tuite, the transient." This was a double-edged sword she had swung: one side to convince Judge Hammes of how vital Tuite was to the defense, and the other side to cut Stephan's rambling and highly questionable arguments down to size.

"And so," she added, "while this is a rather unusual time for us to be arguing our facts, what I'm asking the court to do is to sit back, look at the facts on both sides, and allow due process requirements of the U.S. Constitution to exonerate three innocent boys."

Who would not have applauded?

Judge Hammes wanted to know if there was anything further by Blake or me. I could not help but make an observation.

"Well, I'm just glad I didn't stay home in bed this morning, Your Honor," I said, in an effort to inject some humor. I was referring to my fever from a bout of influenza.

I believe the judge appreciated my comment, but she did not crack a smile. So we waited.

What she decided could dash our hopes of saving the defendants from going straight to adult court. There was nothing to do but listen to the judge's decision.

Judge Hammes paused for a while, thinking. Then she said, "One of the central tenets of the People's presentation is the argument that no one else could have come into the house, which is a key issue in this case. I tried in the beginning to limit the scope of this hearing, but now, er, hearing testimony, it is my opinion that I cannot limit any further presentation of evidence in this case. The statements by the minors are also problematic in their admissibility. So everything this court can get, to make the decision, I must have. I will permit third-party evidence at this time. The court will be making a ruling on the admissibility of the statements, based on the legal standards of *Miranda* and voluntariness, and so I invite counsel to open up the doors and bring in what you have."

Our hearts were pumping. Judge Hammes was not going to stop the flow of any evidence that would prove the boys' guilt or innocence. This was going to be a trial in the guise of a hearing. Both the prosecution and the defense were free to bring any reasonable witness, any expert or piece of evidence to the table.

This was truly a moment of glory for the American court system. No one was going to win or lose because the judge was more concerned with the load of criminal cases stacking up on her desk. No one was going to fall victim to the pressures of a system that cries about the cost of lengthy procedures. Laura P. Hammes was one of those judges you read about in law school and hope you run into. This was a judge who wanted justice. She knew that more was at stake than the loss of a young child and the lives of three young boys; thus she opened the door for the truth to emerge.

23

• AN ALIBI •

Day171: San Diego, California
July 10, 1998

Stephan next called fifteen-year-old Scott Colegrove. Scott knew Aaron, Michael and Joshua; he was the boy from whom Joshua had stolen the compass knife. That too weakened our case. Character counts, and Josh had stolen, no matter how much he swore his intention was to return the knife. Many kids go through a stage of taking things that don't belong to them. But in the eyes of the law, a thief is a thief, and guilt of theft makes for proof of a dishonest or weak character.

Attridge countered by establishing that Scott had *never* heard any of the three accused boys plot to kill anyone. Blake followed by establishing that Scott and Aaron had agreed Michael could never harm his sister.

Judge Hammes asked Scott about Michael and Aaron seeing each other after Christmas of 1998, and their dispute over the games Aaron had loaned Michael.

In my cross-examination of Scott, I established that Aaron was popular with the school's band members. This was important because the prosecution wanted very much to present Aaron as weird and withdrawn, a mad-dog killer in the guise of an excellent student—something out of a horror movie.

The rest of Scott's testimony was mostly about the books Aaron read and the computer games the boys all played. Stephan worked hard at presenting the video-game playing as a kind of ritualistic prelude to the actual murder of a young, innocent girl.

Much of the prosecution's case was based on the idea that the viciousness of the electronic games had stirred the three boys into taking their fantasies into real life. It was a common thought in the mid-to-late 1990s among many police officers, psychologists and even many conservative analysts that violent video games were corrupting the youth of the nation. This undoubtedly led to the police prejudice in the Crowe murder case. Nevertheless, young Scott Colegrove did not add much fuel to the prosecution's case, and he certainly didn't harm the defense. As a result, Stephan took a kind of vicious U-turn.

She suggested that Scott had been pressured by the boys' families to give positive testimony about their sons. "Didn't they call your parents and tell them you were likely to be arrested as part of the conspiracy, and things like that?" But Scott had been intensively interrogated by Detective Claytor, who failed to implicate this boy in the crime at all. Stephan missed the mark again.

The witness to follow Scott was none other than the heroic Detective Chris McDonough, who had a great courtroom presence. He was pleasant, open, unruffled and articulate. Stephan wanted to establish his credibility and so she asked about his experience.

"I've attended numerous post-academy courses," he said, "as well as Department of Justice courses on interviewing. I've also attended the National Institute of Truth Verification courses. I've been through Department of Justice classes and the Reid Technique of interviewing."

"Tell us about that technique."

"It is a different style of approaching an interview," McDonough said. "It's a more confrontational approach, versus allowing an interview to flow. I've also had lots of direct experience interviewing numerous individuals throughout the course of my career."

Ms. Stephen wanted McDonough to elaborate. His experience and expertise was vital to the building of her case. "The individuals you've interviewed, throughout your career, how do they vary—as far as being witnesses, suspects, murderers, petty thieves . . ."

"There's a wide range," McDonough said, following her lead, knowing what she wanted to hear. "Serial killers on death row, murderers, petty thieves, robbers and burglars; a variety of different personality types. I've had exposure to quite a range."

Stephan, obviously pleased, asked, "How many such interviews in your career?"

"Thousands."

"Including juveniles, teenagers?"

"Yes," McDonough answered quickly, adding, "In fact I interviewed a five-year-old." The mental picture this conjured flushed my face, and I looked away from the man, repulsed. But Stephan continued building the foundation of McDonough's skills as an interrogator.

"Okay, so you had prior experience interviewing teenagers?"

McDonough had just answered this question, but it was asked again. The idea, apparently, was to remove any shadow of the hard-nosed interrogator. This was a nice guy, doing a professional job. Certainly a man like this would not coerce a confession.

"Yes."

Stephan wanted more than credibility; she wanted respectability and competence. "And beyond what you've been taught in books, and your formal training and experience, do you know anything about boys aged fourteen to sixteen?"

"For the past seven years," McDonough needed no coaching, "I've taught a religious course in the morning—every single morning—through Carlsbad High School, dealing with freshmen. I've had seniors, too, and sophomores, juniors."

"You teach religious courses *every morning*—is that what you said?"

"Every morning, yes. Well, last year I had freshmen—fourteen- and fifteen-year-olds—and every morning I had twenty-three students."

Stephan's smile was barely concealed as she turned to another subject: the confessions. The video of Joshua's confession was the first shown to the court. Joshua was out of the courtroom during this time; he did not want to sit through the ordeal, watching himself being coerced into implicating Michael and Aaron. There was plenty of coercing apparent in these so-called interviews with Joshua, but the problem remained: *What had made him so compliant?*

The court interrupted proceedings to allow Joshua's father to testify. His statements, at least in part, explain what happened to Josh, and why he lied.

Mary Ellen Attridge began, in what became a pivotal point in the hearing: "Mr. Treadway, when you took Joshua to the police station on that first occasion, you told Detective Claytor you wanted to be in the room, right?"

"Absolutely. Yes, I did."

"And Detective Claytor told you they don't allow parents in the room?"

"Yes. If I could backtrack . . . why I made that request is that when they came over previously to talk to Josh—I believe it was the day after Stephanie's murder—two officers came to our house and waited. My wife doesn't work outside the home, but she volunteers in a class. Two minutes after she pulled out of the driveway, they knocked on the door. Call that great timing. But it seems to me they did that on purpose."

"So you suspect the police were trying to interview your son without a parent present?"

"Yes. I even made a call to the police department and told them I was not comfortable with the fact that they came to my house and talked to my son without a parent there. 'Is there a rule about that?' I asked them, and they said, no. It's normal procedure, they told me."

"Okay. So what did Claytor tell you about having a murder warrant hanging over Joshua's head?"

"When he came out and told me he was going to let Josh go, I said, 'Great!' And he left. He came back a few minutes later and said, 'Josh wants to take a lie detector test.' I said, 'I don't feel comfortable with that. I think I need an attorney.' Those were my exact words to him. He said, 'You don't need an attorney. All you need is to sign these release forms.' I said, 'I still don't feel comfortable with that.' And he said, 'Listen. The DA is here with a murder-one arrest warrant for Josh. We've got the murder weapon. His fingerprints are on it. He's going down for the murder of Stephanie Crowe. I don't believe he did it. But that is what we're going to do unless he takes the lie detector test.' And that's when I signed the release form."

"And did they ever admit that, in fact, there was no murder warrant on Josh?"

"No."

"So were you under the continuing understanding, after you left the police station on the 28th, that there actually was some sort of murder warrant with Josh's name on it?"

"Yes. I don't know how that works, so I figured if they say they have a warrant, they have a warrant. Whenever they want to serve it, they can serve it."

"Did Josh complain of any physical ailments, other than his stomach maladies?" Attridge asked.

"He mentioned his stomach and was holding it all the time, and his hands . . ."

"He was wringing his hands?"

"Yeah, it was one of the things I noticed. And he had headaches."

Next, Attridge asked about Joshua's sleep patterns, and none of us will ever forget the answer. It made obvious what kind of lifestyle and home life the Treadways experienced.

"I always used to tuck my kids in every night, no matter how big they got. I give them a kiss and I pray with them. But that wasn't an every-night thing any more. I do with my little boys, but the older ones I just reach in and say goodnight. Well, it was more of a 'Dad, come in and give me a kiss goodnight.' So I was being asked to do that, as opposed to just doing it on my own."

"And previous to his interrogation, on the 27th and 28th, he had basically expressed to you that he had outgrown the kiss goodnight situation?"

"Yes. 'Night Dad,' he'd say. That type of thing."

"Okay. Then, after he came back on the twenty-seventh and twenty-eighth, he would specifically ask you to come in and kiss him goodnight?"

"Yes."

Attridge returned to Joshua stealing Aaron's knife, which led to Joshua's actual arrest for Stephanie Crowe's murder. She asked Joshua's father to state what he remembered about the night of the homicide.

He was home, he said, and his wife Tammy was home too, as were Josh and the other boys, Zach, Mike and Alan. He remembered going to bed at 11:30 p.m. and told Josh and Zach to keep quiet because Josh had finals the next day. Earlier in the evening, Mr. Treadway had been helping Josh with his science homework. He said he remembered being awake at ten minutes after midnight. He heard Zach and Joshua's chatter in the next room, but then he'd gone back to sleep.

This, of course, gave Joshua an alibi because of the estimated time of Stephanie Crowe's death—between 9:00 p.m. and 12:30 A.M. He would have had to leave home at the very latest by 11:15 p.m., given that Michael lived approximately four miles away. Joshua would have gone to Aaron's house first, which was roughly half the distance to Michael's house.

While this is important—vital to the defense in fact—it is minimized because Treadway was Joshua's father. A loving father is likely to say anything to save his son. So did he really know what time it was when Josh went to bed? Did he truly remember looking at the clock at ten minutes after midnight? But character surely comes into play. Here we have a man who is community- and church-spirited, a responsible, loving family man who is supportive of the police. And so a judge might well consider his statement, but it would be minimized as substantial evidence. Nevertheless, it remained valuable testimony for the defense.

"You're a locksmith, right? Do you bring your work home sometimes?"

"Absolutely."

"Did you install the locks on your own front door?"

"Yes, I did."

"What kind of locks do you have?"

"I have a handle set and a double cylinder deadbolt."

"What?"

"It's locked inside and the out. You have to use a key to open it up from either side."

"Can you hear people coming in and out your front door when you're in bed?"

"Yes."

"How easy is it to hear?"

"Easy. From where I sleep to my front door is no more than a few feet." Attridge asked about the boys' room; Zach and Josh shared a room.

"They keep that door shut, but I need to work on it. It's hard to open, makes a lot of noise."

"Why is it hard to open?"

"The latch rubs against the strike. You have to give it a tug to get it open."

Would Judge Hammes buy this? If it came to a trial, would a jury buy such testimony from the father of the accused?

Attridge finished her cross-examination by asking Treadway to recount the phone calls Josh had received from Michael. The first was on the night before the murder, when they had talked about the next-day finals at school. The second was when Michael called from the police station, telling Joshua about the death of his sister, the morning after.

Paul Blake followed this line in his own cross-examination. "When Joshua got the phone call from Michael, about Stephanie's murder, did he indicate how Michael was doing?"

"Yeah. That was my first question, and he said he was really upset."

"When you were told Michael was a suspect, did you find that credible?"

"Not at all."

I followed Blake for my cross-examination of the witness, and then Stephan returned to redirect, hoping to discredit Treadway's testimony about what time he looked at the clock in his bedroom.

Finally, we took a lunch break, and that afternoon we watched more of the interrogation tapes.

24

• LIES & TRICKERY EXPOSED •

Day 181: San Diego, California
July 20, 1998

Scheduling conflicts stretched out the hearing even longer. The proceedings resumed with Mary Ellen Attridge on center stage again. She had seen a new report from the DA's office concerning the transient Richard Tuite, who had been serving time for a crime unrelated to the Crowe case. This transient was our only other hope, so Attridge was interested in what the DA had written about Tuite's prior arrest for stabbing a person. We all were.

Stephan, as always, became very defensive when it came to anything having to do with Tuite. *Why waste time on him when we are so busy convicting the boys?* She didn't say this, but it was reflected in her attitude.

"Your Honor, very briefly," she began, "I mentioned in chambers that I had some notes in my file that indicate this was not as it is being portrayed by the defense—that Tuite stabbed this person in the throat without reason."

The judge, however, was open to the idea that Richard Tuite was not above suspicion; after all, he had demonstrated being capable of using a knife on another human being, and he had been in the neighborhood on the night of the murder.

After the short excursion on the subject of Richard Tuite, and the subtle locking of horns between Stephan and Attridge, the court ordered Detective

Chris McDonough back to the stand for cross-examination. Attridge began by going over his training and experience. She snapped, "In your training, haven't you been told that it is improper to give promises of leniency to a defendant?"

Judge Hammes ruled the question irrelevant and Attridge was quite distraught, but she quickly rephrased her question. The point had been made. It was time to expose the role played by McDonough in coercing Michael's and Joshua's confessions. "Isn't it recommended by the Department of Justice that questioning a juvenile should never exceed six hours?"

"That's the guideline, but it's not concrete. It depends on the circumstances."

Attridge then went to questions directed at the CVSA—the Computer Voice Stress Analyzer that was used on the three boys. "Say you were to ask a suspect the following question: 'How did you come into possession of a knife?' The CVSA could not gauge a full-sentence response to that question, because it only gauges responses to yes and no, isn't that right?"

McDonough knew exactly where Attridge was heading, so he quickly began to hedge. "Well, based on the scenario you just presented, that's an improper way to conduct the exam. The formulation of that question is improper. It's the same with a polygraph."

"Okay. So the open-ended question, 'How did you come into possession of the knife?' is not something that can be tested by this alleged verification instrument, true?"

McDonough was no stranger to the witness box. "Well, the questions are formulated through the process of the exam with the examiner. The two of us sat down [he and Joshua] and we formulated the questions that he would—"

Attridge's interruption was exquisite. "Your Honor," she said as she turned from McDonough, "I'm going to object. A non-responsive witness at this point."

"Sustained," Judge Hammes said, directing McDonough to answer the question. "So the answer is, true?" Attridge said, turning back to McDonough.

"Yes," he said.

The cross-examination continued for a few minutes, but then Judge Hammes objected to Attridge's questions of McDonough's knowledge of the law, his training in the law and whatever advice he had been given by the DA's office on the law. Attridge was very insistent, however, wanting to keep to her line of questioning. So Judge Hammes allowed a ten-minute break to discuss it.

What Attridge was trying to bring to the surface was that McDonough knowingly violated his own training, breaking the rule that it is impermissible conduct for police officers to give suspects, particularly juveniles, promises of leniency, or to threaten them, deprive them of sleep, deny them the right to see a parent, deny them food and water, and so forth.

But Judge Hammes didn't budge from her decision after the recess.

Attridge wisely turned to the CVSA; her challenge was strong and tenacious. "Are you aware that the Department of Defense Polygraph Institute has taken the position that the CVSA is, in fact, an unreliable instrument in the area of truth verification?"

"The polygraphers organization has a report saying it's unreliable. Is that your question?"

Attridge turned again to Judge Hammes. "Your Honor, could I have that answer read back? I didn't understand."

McDonough's answer was read. It was clearly an evasive response.

"Listen to the question," Attridge said, now on a roll. "Are you aware that the Department of Defense Polygraph Institute published the opinion that the computerized voice stress analysis is an unreliable tool in making a determination as to truthfulness. Yes or no?"

"No."

"Are you aware that the American Association of Police Polygraphists has taken the position that the Computer Voice Stress Analyzer jeopardizes criminal proceedings?"

"No, I haven't seen that."

The depth of McDonough's expertise was being challenged, yet he had accumulated many confessions through the use of his wonderful machine.

"Are you aware that the American Association of Police Polygraphists has found no scientific evidence or research that supports voice stress analysis as a method of discriminating between the truth and deception?"

"If that's the opinion of the polygraphers association, that's fine," McDonough said, struggling to maintain his composure.

"Are you aware of it?"

"No."

Stephan then spoke up, seeking to protect McDonough; she insisted Attridge's questions were not valid. The reports in question had not been presented. But Attridge had already given the reports to the judge.

The judge asked her to proceed.

"You provided me with your resume, is that right?"

"Yes, ma'am."

"You were certified by the National Institute of Truth Verification approximately one-and-a-half years before you interviewed Joshua, is that right?"

"Yes, ma'am."

"And you told Joshua you had interviewed thousands of people, is that right?"

"Yes."

"Is it your testimony that you interviewed *thousands* of people with the Computer Voice Stress Analyzer *in only a year and a half?*"

"That's not how I presented my statement to Joshua."

Attridge referred to the video tapes and continued: "You told Joshua you had interviewed thousands of people, and that he wasn't even close to the results of the tests you've seen, right?"

"That's not the context of my statement to him."

"It's not?"

"I have interviewed thousands of people," the detective said defiantly.

"But not on the CVSA. It appears you were telling Joshua you had interviewed thousands of people on the CVSA and that, in fact, is a lie, because you haven't. Is that right?"

"If that was the context, it could be a mistruth, yes."

"And a mistruth is the same as a lie, isn't it, sir?"

"It could be, yeah."

Blake followed Attridge, and Blake too dwelled on the validity of the

CVSA. He did a superb job of trying to establish that McDonough had preconceived ideas about the case prior to beginning the interviews and the CVSA tests. A CVSA operator is not supposed to know anything about the case, in order to be a neutral examiner. Chris McDonough failed to do so because he admitted being in discussions with the other police officers about the three boys. Watching the tapes, we concluded that McDonough was fully prepped prior to his early encounter—even with Michael. This should have disqualified his entire test results.

Attridge, Blake, and I wanted this procedural breach by McDonough exposed.

"Did Detective Claytor say anything to you about his opinion on Aaron, Josh, or Michael? Anything that gave you a greater picture of how the murder supposedly was done by these three children? A yes or no answer if you could."

"Yes, he kind of did." McDonough was cautious, but at least he gave the answer we wanted. This man was obviously a key to the defense, and the prosecution now knew it. The court knew it too, and so did McDonough. His testimony continued as we tried to expose what we believed was psychological abuse during the so-called interviews.

Stephan knew exactly where we were headed, and she was working hard to prove that the confessions were solid, that the police had merely done their jobs. She was careful to bring forth McDonough's vast experience with young people, and especially with youngsters the same age as Aaron, Joshua and Michael.

From her perspective, this guy was a sweetheart of a cop, teaching classes for his church.

And McDonough had even questioned a five-year-old.

But I asked McDonough if he had ever given the CVSA test to anyone under seventeen years of age prior to those given to our clients, and the answer was "No."

This didn't exactly strengthen our case, but it watered down the prosecution's case somewhat. When I had the opportunity to re-cross, I made the point again. "You never met Aaron before he took his test?"

"No, sir, I never did."

"Never tested a child under the age of sixteen before, correct?"

"That's correct."

I felt this opened a window to apply my own strategy. The moment I had been waiting for had arrived: "If I am a person who is emotionally distraught, whether it be over the death of my sister or over being accused of her murder, and I'm a young child, how are you going to eliminate such emotional impact on me as I am confronted by your questions? How are you, as a tester, going to be able to do that?"

McDonough perked up, his confidence returning. "The instrument doesn't measure emotion. It measures the AM/PM signal from the larynx—the voice box. And that is controlled through the central nervous system, the two branches of the central nervous system."

"If that is uncontrollable, then a person could never deceive the machine?"

"That's essentially why it's so remarkable, and why over seven hundred law enforcement agencies use it," McDonough answered with a not-so-subtle air of defiance.

"That is the particular concept and the sales pitch that is offered, but there's scientific evidence that questions the very foundation of it. And you'll agree there is a scientific foundation questioning it right now?"

McDonough was sharp. His expertise and experience as a witness allowed him a moment of wit. "There's also scientific evidence that questions DNA. I agree with you 100 percent," he said.

At trial, my expert witness on the CVSA was prepared to state that the test was not scientifically validated, so I felt quite at ease on this topic, despite McDonough's confidence. Stephan returned to reestablish the validity of the CVSA and she asked McDonough if there was a federal agency using it.

McDonough answered, "The CIA uses it," referring to a list of agencies that use the CVSA.

Attridge returned to re-cross. "Can you point to where, on your list, the Central Intelligence Agency appears?"

"I can tell the court how that appears," McDonough hedged.

"It is not on this list, is it, sir?" Attridge held up the list.

"On your list, I don't know. Let me look at it," McDonough openly challenged.

"It's not on your list either, is it?" Attridge waited for the detective to see her list.

"I don't know if we have the same list, ma'am." McDonough was defiant, and Attridge sounded belligerent. Both were keeping within the bounds of their professional personas, however, both containing the repartee so that the conflict did not appear personally combative. But Attridge was leaning hard on the detective, and he resented it. The little battle between them did not escape the judge, but Hammes was a wise referee, and as it ended up, it was admitted that the CIA was not on the list of agencies using the CVSA. But it was accepted that the CIA could be on some list of law enforcement agencies that had used it.

The defense objective, of course, was to thoroughly discredit the CVSA.

Later, in my re-cross, I asked this: "Detective McDonough, I reviewed some of the tapes last night, particularly those we watched in court. I noticed that many times you would say to Joshua, 'You're lying to me, you are lying to me. You failed the test.' And Josh would ask what part of the test he failed. And you would say, 'No, let's stick to the issue. You are lying to me.' That's correct isn't it?"

McDonough had a justification for this. "Merely seeking the truth," he said.

However, there were several other subtle discrepancies that crept into the detective's testimony. For example, when I asked, "Wouldn't it be prudent on your part to suggest to the officers"—I was still talking about Joshua's first interrogation and the CVSA test—"'let him go home, bring him back when he's fresh and ask these questions when he's had some sleep, time to eat, time to get out of this environment'? Wouldn't that have been prudent on your part, sir?"

"No," was McDonough's immediate answer. He knew he must stay consistent and protective of everything he'd done during his "interview" with Joshua. "He was in custody, suspected of theft, and I was not going to suggest to the investigators they let him go home for convenience or his own comfort. I was told he was arrested."

"Let's talk about that for a second. He was a minor. Minors who commit petty theft are released home to their parents all the time. You are aware of that, aren't you?"

"Sure, but this dealt with a murder weapon."

"An alleged murder weapon?"

"Yes."

"Or were you told they had physical proof it was a murder weapon."

"I was told the young man had a knife that may have been involved in the murder."

This was important testimony; it reestablished that McDonough had prior knowledge of the case before his interrogation of Joshua. It was not enough to throw the test results out, but it was certainly enough to establish that McDonough presumed the boys were guilty from the start. McDonough had obviously been briefed by Claytor and others at the police station before he even met Joshua, and that is against the CVSA rules. So McDonough insisted he knew only the minimum before he began his so-called interview. In this case, with McDonough having interviewed Michael first, he was no longer an impartial CVSA tester for Joshua.

Stephan returned to ask a few questions designed to uphold the detective's integrity and the validity of the CVSA. Judge Hammes asked a number of her own questions, and then the next witness was called.

Detective Ralph Claytor took the stand and Stephan opened the examination.

What Stephan quickly established was that Claytor and a Detective Ham actually walked from Joshua's house to Aaron's house and then to Michael's. The walk, at normal pace, took an hour and ten minutes (a distance of roughly four miles). This was to show that the boys could have easily met and committed the murder in accordance with Joshua's confession. It also was to establish that the boys could have easily been at Michael's house at the time of the murder. It was a strong point for the prosecution, and one that we defense attorneys could not deny: It was possible that Joshua could have sneaked out of his house and walked to Aaron's place, and that he and Aaron could have gone on to Michael's, murdered Stephanie, and returned home in the space of approximately two and half hours.

Attridge did not dispute any of this, or that it was possible they could have done it at that time of night without being seen. She attacked Claytor, however, for the length of time the boys had been held.

"Are you aware of a Department of Justice guideline that states you are not to interrogate a minor in excess of six hours at a time?"

"We have interdepartmental memos that tell us the Department of Justice would like juveniles out of the facility within a six-hour period."

"So you were aware of the guideline at the time that you interviewed Michael?"

"That's correct."

"Did you know about the guideline when you spoke with my client, Joshua?"

"I did."

"Despite the Department of Justice guidelines, isn't it true that on January 27th through January 28th, 1998, my client was interviewed in excess of eleven hours?"

"Joshua was at the facility for probably that length of time, yes."

The answer had obviously been calculated. Even though the defense knew exactly how long the actual interrogation had taken, Claytor's answer skirted this by saying the boy had been "at the facility" for that long. It was a subtle deception, a meaningless deception in the long run, but a deception nevertheless. Well, it would be naive to think that the police are not protective of their own procedures and their fellow officers. And certainly the court is not blind to this. Indeed, the flaw in even the most devoted system of justice is our very humanity. We human beings are all capable of shading the truth to suit our purposes; we do it all the time.

Attridge next moved her line of questioning back to the subject of the early suspicions the police held.

"Do you recall, specifically on the day of the murder, Detective Sweeney articulating to you his theory that somebody from within the Crowe residence had committed this crime?"

"He was more specific than that," Claytor volunteered. "It was his theory it was the father, Steve Crowe."

"And do you recall the basis for Detective Sweeney's opinion?"

"The discussions going on at that time—actually there were numerous theories—were based on there being no signs that an outsider had come into the residence. And so, with that basis of fact, the discussions gravitated towards family members."

Attridge seized the moment. "At the time of these discussions, you, Detective Sweeney, and the other detectives were not aware of the 911 call that occurred at approximately 9:37 p.m. the night of the murder. The calls were about a prowler being seen near the Crowe residence. Am I correct?"

She had made a courageous U-turn, bringing the focus back on the potential of a third-party involvement again: Richard Tuite, the transient.

Claytor said he couldn't recall when he'd heard first about the 911 call, and Attridge dropped the subject. But she had accomplished her goal.

Attridge began talking about McDonough again. How much information had Claytor given him prior to his interrogation of Michael Crowe? Not even Attridge believed this line of questioning was going to push Claytor into declaring the truth. On the other hand, not to address this would be an unforgivable oversight. McDonough's prejudice before his interrogation, especially of Michael Crowe, was one of our few aces. It was quite apparent to us that he was well aware of the details before Joshua and Aaron entered the list of hunch-generated suspects. Bottom line: this meant that, not only in theory, but in practice, the CVSA had been used as a coercive tool or as a means to turn police speculation into what might be called supposition-based and coerced confessions.

Claytor was obviously not a good witness for the defense. He was not about to jeopardize a verdict of guilty for the three boys, and he was adept at soft-pedaling the truth. For example, Attridge asked him if he had said to Joshua, "The evidence is going to screw you to the wall."

Claytor admitted saying that.

"But you didn't have any evidence that would screw anyone to the wall, right?"

"Not necessarily. I still considered the knife as evidence in the homicide."

"You hadn't processed the knife and you didn't find fingerprints on it, did you?"

"No."

"And you didn't have any DNA evidence, right?"

"No."

"You didn't have any presumptive blood tests on it, did you?"

"No."

Judge Hammes put a stop to this line of questioning. "I think we've covered this," she said, but what we'd heard was that Claytor had a hunch about the knife and so he called it "evidence" to frighten Joshua into thinking there was something unknown that could, in fact, screw him to the wall. Claytor had nicely covered himself, though I felt certain the problems had not passed Judge Hammes unnoticed.

Stephan's next witness was Ms. Franco-Chow, a teacher of both Aaron and Michael in a class for above-average students. According to Franco-Chow, Aaron and Michael were most articulate and advanced. Stephan had already established that the boys' interest was not reading schoolbooks, however, but "fantasy" books. They were both devotees of medieval literature and "killer" video games.

Stephan used this witness to cast doubt on the so-called enmity between Michael and Aaron. Franco-Chow testified that she saw no overt signs of such enmity.

25

• AN UPHILL CLIMB •

Day 181: San Diego, California
July 20, 1998

Claytor returned to the stand and Attridge focused again on the subject of Richard Tuite.

"You were briefed by Detective Sweeney about their interview with Mr. Tuite, right?"

"Yes, that's correct."

"Did you read Detective Sweeney's report?"

"Yes."

"Did you notice that Richard Tuite stated he had not gone into anybody's house on the evening of the 20th?"

"Yes, I did."

"But witnesses stated Mr. Tuite had actually gone inside their homes?"

"One house, yes."

"Did you ever re-interview Mr. Tuite regarding his lie about that one fact?"

"No."

"Mr. Tuite was known to you as a neighborhood nuisance, right?"

"Actually, not to me as much as he was known to others."

"But you know the Escondido police were aware of his mental instability."

"Putting it mildly, yes."

Attridge continued to question the detective about Tuite. He was aware that the transient had been in the neighborhood looking for a young woman by the name of Tracy. He was also aware that Tracy had, at one time, been known for her drug abuse.

"Detective Sweeney interviewed . . . do you have any idea how long he spent with Mr. Tuite?" Attridge asked.

"No. Not specifically."

"He wrote a report that is less than a half a page in length, is that correct?"

"That's correct."

"Would that indicate to you the interview was brief?"

"No. It only indicates that Sweeney wrote a half page. I don't know what to read into that."

"Well," Attridge countered, "is it fair to say that Detective McDonough and his stress analysis machine were never called in to be utilized in an interview of Mr. Tuite?"

"That's correct."

"In fact, Detective Sweeney let Mr. Tuite go on his way."

"That's correct."

"Were you aware that he was subsequently arrested on two counts of annoying and molesting children?"

"Yes, I was aware of that."

Blake followed Attridge, questioning Claytor. After a few questions about Claytor being in charge of the case, Blake narrowed his interest to Richard Tuite.

"There was a resident in the area who came up to your post, I believe, and reported the suspicious activities of Mr. Tuite early that same morning, the morning of the murder, isn't that correct?"

"It was in the morning, yes."

"But you didn't get around to taking any particular action on him until at least a day or two later, is that correct?"

"No," Claytor said, shifting in his seat, "actually that's incorrect. When I found out about the transient, we assigned investigators to follow up and find out what was going on with the calls from the previous night."

The three defense attorneys wanted to create a real option for the court to turn its eyes away from the teenage boys and toward Tuite. These boys, we were sure, were sitting in this courtroom because of a mere hunch by the police, a hunch they attempted to prove by coercing confessions.

During cross-examination, Paul Blake asked Detective Claytor about Dr. Blum's involvement the interrogations. Blum was the psychologist working with the police, the one who offered the opinion that Aaron was a psychopathic killer, "a Charles Manson type with a high IQ."

I followed up with a few questions about Blum myself, but the truth was none of us had constructed more than a loose argument against his absurd observations, which were so unfounded one would think they would be dismissed. Unfortunately, it is never easy to discredit professionals used by the People. I turned to the issue of Aaron's arrest.

"On February 11, where did you contact Aaron and bring him to the station?"

"We found him at Orange Glen High School, told him he was under arrest for the murder of Stephanie Crowe."

"When Gregg Houser came to the station, did you tell him Aaron had been arrested?"

"I believe so, yes."

"Would it surprise you to learn that Gregg Houser says you did not tell him that, but you made vague comments about the knife?"

"Would it surprise me he says that? No."

"Do you think it's the truth?"

"Possibly."

"Did you tell Aaron his father couldn't be present during the interview?"

"No. In fact, his father was there at one point."

"Let me make my point crystal clear: Did you tell Aaron his father could not be with him during the actual interview because he was under arrest?"

"Possibly, I don't recall." Claytor remained cool and calculating in his answers, saying over and over that he could not recall every detail on the videotapes.

"Did you tell Mr. Houser he could not stay with his son, that he had to leave the room while the interview was conducted and the CVSA test was taken?"

"It's possible. Whether I said it in those exact words, I don't know."

"Is it fair to say that the whole purpose of the CVSA test was to get incriminating evidence against Aaron, since you had already arrested him for the murder?"

"No. That's not a fair statement at all."

One thing that turned directly in our favor that day was that Judge Hammes had studied the tapes.

Hopefully she was leaning toward acknowledging that coercion was used in obtaining the confessions. It is hard to imagine how difficult our case would have been in the days before interrogations were routinely videotaped. But even with the videotapes depicting the whole process so clearly, our defense remained weak.

In addition to the confessions, there was also some circumstantial evidence and not a hint of proof that anyone but family members had been in the house the night of the murder. So, to put it mildly, we had an uphill climb—and we all knew it.

Claytor returned to the stand and Stephan returned to January 27, 1998, and asked the detective if he could recall what Aaron had said about his missing knife.

"He said one of his knives was missing, had been for several months. And he implied that Michael Crowe had taken the knife and some money, on Aaron's birthday, October 26th."

This was important testimony for the defense. It again showed Aaron and Michael's relationship was, at best, shaky, filled with anger and mistrust. *Who could possibly believe that two boys who had stopped being friendly would plan and execute a murder together?* A murder, a crime of any kind, takes at least basic trust between the perpetrators. On the other hand, Aaron and Michael were known to be extraordinarily intelligent boys. What a clever plan it would be, to fake a dispute between them, fake the knife stealing even, as part of an elaborate scheme to commit a murder. Elaborate scheming was a key part of the computer games they played, and Stephan was well aware of all the possibilities.

"Detective," the prosecutor said to Claytor pleasantly, "did Aaron tell you about any common activities he had with Michael and Josh?"

"He talked about their game playing, the fantasy games." He added weight to his inference by elaborating: "He mentioned the game called Dungeons & Dragons, but said they went beyond Dungeons and Dragons and developed their own fantasy games."

One could almost hear the voices of these two, Stephan and Claytor, preparing for this testimony, discussing this in advance for maximum impact. As an ex-deputy district attorney in two California counties, I know that this is done routinely. This is legal, and he was her witness. We would do the same coaching of our defense witnesses . . . rehearsal of testimony is all part of the game.

Stephan continued: "Did Aaron describe Michael any further, any more specifically?"

"He did. He also talked about Michael's relationship with his family. He said Mike often made comments about killing people he didn't like. He also said he wasn't very sociable, he normally wore black clothing, hated his family . . . He said that he and Mike talked about moving out when they were eighteen; maybe moving in with Josh."

"Anything else about the Crowe family?"

"He indicated that Michael's family lived in their own rooms and that Michael didn't have many friends. That sort of thing." Stephan then asked Claytor to explain why he thought Aaron's stolen knife might be the murder weapon. Claytor responded by describing the wounds and comparing them to other murders he had investigated.

These answers were apparently upsetting Cheryl Crowe again, so I asked the court if she might be excused. Judge Hammes readily agreed.

Stephan departed from the issue of Aaron's knife and went directly to the subject of Richard Tuite. If there was a weak link in her prosecution it was the transient. He cast a slight shadow over her presentation of the boys' guilt. While there was no evidence or any reasonable motive clearly linked to Tuite, he did represent a possible alternative suspect, so the prosecutor decided to confront the issue head-on.

"Now, detective, could you give us a summary of what efforts were made with regard to the transient Richard Tuite, who had been seen and heard knocking on doors in the vicinity of the Crowe house on the night of the murder?"

"When I first heard about Richard Tuite, the first thing I did was arrange a photo lineup for each individual who had reported seeing Tuite on the night in question. One of the individuals who saw the lineup said they had seen him that night and also more recently, and he gave us a location. That's how we were able to find him. Tuite was asked about his activities on the night of the murder and an evidence technician processed him. He voluntarily gave us his clothes for processing. We obtained fingerprints, photographs, hair samples, that sort of thing, and then we conducted the interview."

"Detective, the general description given by people who had seen Richard Tuite, the night of January 20th—did it comport with his appearance when he was brought down to the police station the evening of January 21st? Was he wearing a red sweatshirt?"

"Yes. Two of the witnesses mentioned the sweatshirt, and he was wearing one."

"Underneath that red sweatshirt, was there any other clothing?"

"He was wearing a white tee-shirt with 'S.D. Jail' on the back of it in black letters."

"A San Diego Jail tee-shirt?"

"It appeared to be."

Stephan quickly changed the subject yet again. "Was it a trick or a plan that you invite Joshua down for a short interview, and then you would book him as a homicide suspect?"

"No. I told Josh's mother I was going to release him. I explained to Josh's father that he was not in trouble and that things had not changed since the January 27/28th interview. And the plan was to get him to the station, clarify the knife issue and turn him loose. We had not planned on booking him for murder that evening. I told him, when I released him on the 28th, he was not in trouble. I didn't lie to him. He was not considered a suspect until events unfolded on February 10th."

Claytor then made it clear that after Michael had confessed, he seemed relieved. With this and other testimony by Claytor and the other detectives, the prosecution had made some strong points.

They were moving forward to their planned end game. Attridge had been making a lot of notes during Claytor's testimony, and she was ready to pounce on the detective, as only Attridge could.

"Some of the persons interviewed by the Escondido police on the 21st identified a photograph of Mr. Tuite as the person pounding on doors the night before, right?"

"That's correct. We were all aware Mr. Tuite was there."

"And you were told by a witness where Mr. Tuite was located, correct?"

"That's correct."

"Mr. Tuite was apprehended as he came out of a laundromat, isn't that right?"

"That's where he was found, yes."

"Isn't it a fact that the Escondido Police Department did not go *into* the laundromat to find out whether or not Mr. Tuite had left any belongings inside?"

"I have no reports to that effect."

"Isn't it also true that the Escondido police failed to ask the owner of the laundromat whether or not there was a continuous videotape rolling while Mr. Tuite was there?"

"I wasn't aware of that."

"Okay, so that never happened?"

"I don't know. I don't have any knowledge of it."

"You don't know if anybody contacted the laundromat itself with respect to either abandoned clothing, or whether or not they had a security tape?"

"That's correct."

"After Mr. Tuite was apprehended, he spoke to Detective Sweeney?"

"Correct."

"However, isn't it safe to say—given the brevity of his interview—he was, in fact, not treated like a homicide suspect?"

"I don't know if brevity is the determination of whether or not a person is treated as a homicide suspect."

"Let's be more specific. The statement you took from Mr. Tuite was that he had not gone into any house near the Crowe residence, correct?"

"I believe that's correct."

"But Detective Sweeney had a report that showed he did go into a residence, right?"

"Yes."

"So it was an inconsistent statement by Mr. Tuite, right?"

"I don't know how the question was put to him. I don't know that was in the report. You'd have to ask Detective Sweeney. I don't know."

"Despite that inconsistency, between Tuite's statements and the statements of the Reverend Green, he was not re-interviewed about this inconsistency, isn't that correct?"

"No, he was not."

"Is this a photograph of Mr. Tuite?" Attridge asked, showing a defense exhibit.

"It appears to be."

"And it was taken by the Escondido Police Department on the 22nd, the date of his interview?"

"I can't see the date on the card, but it's my understanding it was taken on that date."

"He is wearing a red jersey and a white tee-shirt, is that correct?"

"Yes."

"And were you also aware, sir, that Tuite had a cut on his right hand?"

"No, I was not aware of that."

"Were you aware that Mr. Tuite had abrasions on other parts of his body?"

Claytor said he knew Tuite had some scabs, nothing more.

Attridge had made some ground, but Stephan came back strongly. "Detective, with regard to Mr. Tuite, is there anything you knew on January 21st, or anything you've learned since, that would lead you to believe he is, or should be, a suspect?"

"Objection," Attridge exclaimed. "Overruled," said Judge Hammes quickly.

Claytor answered the question: "Going back to the 21st, other than the fact that he was there, I had absolutely no evidence to indicate Tuite had anything to do with the homicide. We were aware he was there, and everybody knew he was reported as a suspicious person, but we had absolutely no connection to the Crowe residence."

"So he was treated the same way everyone else was treated. He was processed and released, the same as the other parties brought to the police station for questioning?"

"Yes. And since that time I've spoke to Mr. Tuite personally. I've reviewed the numerous cases against him and in my opinion he didn't have anything to do with this homicide. I would have to characterize Mr. Tuite as the bungling prowler. There's a common thread throughout all the reports about him: he would go to people's houses and bang on doors and windows. Nothing I ever saw in any of the reports indicates the stealth that would be required to sneak into the Crowe residence, kill the little girl and sneak out again, leaving no evidence. It's my firm belief that Mr. Tuite couldn't accomplish that type of a crime if he tried."

"You describe this crime, based on everything you now know, as a 'stealth' crime."

"Yes."

"Detective Claytor, the incident with the two girls, referred to as the 'molesting the girls' incident, is there any report that Richard Tuite touched those girls physically?"

"Not that I'm aware of."

"So it was a verbal molest?"

"Verbal, yes."

"And the burglary incidents that have been referred to, are those ones where he actually grabs the window screen and shakes it, takes it off in front of witnesses?"

"Yes."

Judge Hammes wanted to know if it had been determined where Tuite slept on the night of the homicide. Claytor said Tuite had told them he slept at the laundromat where he had been found.

The next witness called by Stephan was Tracy Chaffing, the young woman Richard Tuite had been searching for on the night of Stephanie Crowe's murder.

"Tell us when you first met Richard Tuite and how that came about?"

"It was 1990. We met through mutual friends, partied together. Just as friends."

"And how long did you stay friends, or in any kind of consistent contact?"

"About three or four years."

"How often would you see Mr. Tuite during that time?"

"Every few days. We'd party for . . . like a week. Well, four or five days, and then, you know, we wouldn't see each other for a few days, then we'd party again."

"Did you ever live off Valley Center Road?"

"I lived there a few months . . . yeah."

"Did you live with a parent, a father, mother?"

"No. Just me and my son."

"Was there a more recent time that you saw Mr. Tuite?"

"No. Oh, in 1996, when I was living at the ranch, he did show up one time and he came looking for me, I guess. Some of the neighbors told me he was looking for me, and then he showed up one day and wanted to talk. He came into the house. My husband was there. Well, he wasn't my husband at the time, but . . . anyway, he'd been looking for me, and I talked to him. He was a little spaced out, actually, but he ended up . . . My husband told him to leave."

"During the period you knew him, did you tell him to leave sometimes, to leave you alone?"

"There were times when we'd party for a few days and we would, like . . . I'd say it was time to part, you know. I think you should go, or we should just do our own thing. And he would go. I mean . . . that was it."

"Was he ever physically violent towards you?"

"No, not at all. He never even raised his voice."

"And those times when you would ask him to leave, would he react in any violent way towards that?"

"No. Never."

As always, Attridge followed Stephan for cross. "When you knew Richard, you were a brunette?"

"Yes I was."

"Is it safe to say that during the time you knew Richard, you were doing a lot of drugs?"

"Yes."

"And you've recently gone through recovery, is that right?"

"Yes."

"So maybe you weren't observant, not as you are now, because of the drugs?"

"Yes . . . I mean . . . Yes."

"And the drug you used with Richard was speed, right? Methamphetamine?"

"Yes."

"And sometimes you and Richard, and other people I assume, would do speed for four or five days at a time?"

"Yes."

"Were you aware he was a diagnosed paranoid schizophrenic at that time?"

"No."

"If I told you he was in a state mental hospital in the years 1990 and 1991, would that change your estimate of the time frame you used to hang out with him?"

"I suppose it would, yes."

"So you're not real sure which years you hung out with him, right?"

"Not the exact dates."

"Would it surprise you to know that Mr. Tuite was committed to the state hospital in July of 1990 and not released until October of 1991?"

"Yes, it would."

"Because you don't remember that?"

"No, I don't."

"Would it surprise you to know that Mr. Tuite was returned to the state mental hospital after that point in time?"

"Yes."

"Did you know that Richard Tuite was committed to San Luis Rey Mental Hospital at one point in his life?"

"No."

"Were you aware that Mr. Tuite was arrested in 1993 for stabbing somebody?"

"No."

Attridge then showed Tracy a recent photograph of Tuite. "Do you recognize the person in this photograph?"

"Yes. It's Richard Tuite."

"Did he appear that way when you last saw him?"

"No. His hair wasn't so wild. He was a little bit more cleaned up. His hair was combed back. He'd dress a little bit nicer than that."

"Did you ever have a sexual relationship with Mr. Tuite?"

"No."

"If Mr. Tuite was walking around saying things like, 'Tracy, why won't you fuck me,' would you think that was, in fact, out of the blue?"

"Yeah."

"And when Richard did speed with you, he would get weird, true?"

"He would . . . I'd be driving his truck, and I'd be looking in the rear-view mirror and he would ask me what I was looking at . . . he would think people were following us. We were driving this one time and he had come up to some spray paint on the road, graffiti, and he got out of the truck and looked at it like it was some message about someone that was following him, or something, you know. And I told him, 'Get in the truck.' And I tried to bring him back to reality, you know, and I just talked to him like a friend, and just gave him reality. Just talked to him and brung him down, you know."

After Attridge's cross, neither Blake nor I had a question for this witness.

Cynthia Ames was called to testify. She had been driving on the road the night of the homicide and had seen Richard Tuite standing by the side of the road, his hands in his pockets, "Just staring across the street, like a statue," she said. Her testimony reaffirmed Tuite being in the area on the fatal night.

The prosecution then called to the stand George Durgin, manager of the Escondido police crime lab.

He had helped collect and analyze evidence in the Crowe case from the beginning, and had also tested Richard Tuite's shirt for blood or other signs that could link him to the killing. Durgin's testimony was the beginning of Stephan's effort to produce physical evidence against the boys. He was more than willing to tell what a superb job he had done, and he expounded at length on his expertise and credentials. However, what this man's testimony showed was that there was an absence of incriminating evidence in the case. It also showed a remarkable lack of evidence that the house had been entered by anyone from outside.

Durgin, in a way, reflected the state of both the prosecution and the defense positions: how little we each had to offer as evidence that could support our cases. The prosecution kept the edge, though, because they had some circumstantial evidence—*and, of course, the confessions.* The case we had to make was in the methods used (the coercive ways) to obtain the confessions. As I have made clear throughout this narrative, *confessions are extremely high hurdles to cross in the courtroom, regardless of how the police acquired them.* Short of physical abuse, the general view is that even if the police used trickery, in the end, confessions are always volunteered. After all, everyone knows that criminals are going to trick, lie, and deceive, so it is "fair play" in the modern procedures used in interrogation—kind of like fighting fire with fire to get the "truth." This explains the prominence, if not the dominance, of psychological interrogation techniques such as the Reid Technique of interrogation. In any case, Attridge, Blake and I were all worried at this juncture, and with good reason.

Aaron Hahn, who was a salesperson for The Gamekeeper—a large store that sells family games, medieval role-playing games and fantasy games at the University Town Center shopping center in San Diego—was the next witness called by the prosecution. Their game expert, he was there to reveal the sinister nature of the certain games, in particular the violent nature of Dungeons & Dragons and *Final Fantasy VII.* Remember, this was the late 1990s, a time when violent video games were suspected by the authorities of causing young people to act out violent acts.

"Mr. Hahn." Stephan got directly to the point. "These role-playing games, like Dungeons & Dragons, are they scored? Or is it just a game you play without any score?"

"It's not like the game called Ridge, where you have a certain point total you are trying to reach. But over time, players score points. They do this by killing things. Getting objects and solving puzzles, too, but the most common way would be killing things."

"Would 'killing things' include killing human beings?"

"Yes. It can range anywhere from killing wolves to monsters, mythical monsters, and then killing people."

Attridge tried to counter the implication inherent in Stephan's query, that these games were about murder. "So you can play this game according to your own imagination," she said, "for altruistic reasons, right?"

"If you want to, yes." Hahn answered. "But," he added quickly, "most of the points you acquire will come from killing things." He suggested that while some older people played these games, the bulk of players were between fourteen and twenty-four years old.

Blake and I both questioned this witness, but to little avail. These games, no matter how one wanted to whitewash them, were about killing. When you "kill" something, you receive what the developers of the games have termed "experience points." This, of course, fit the scenario the prosecution was constructing. The police had been convinced quite early that Michael, Joshua and Aaron had taken their games out of fantasy and into reality, and it was not an unfounded accusation. At the time, many studies had been done on these games and what role they played in actual violent acts. Had we been keeping score, like the games in question, Stephan would have made high marks here, and she gained ground.

The next witness was Arlynn Charles Bove, who pleasantly noted that his nickname was Sam. He had been with the sheriff's office for twenty-seven years and had spent seven of those years in the crime lab. He retired in 1990 and started his own private business called Forensic Arts and Investigations. He was in court as a witness for the prosecution, and he was there to affirm that Aaron's "Best Defense" knife was a perfect tool in shape, length and blade style to be the murder weapon.

Attridge went on the attack immediately. "You primarily work for law enforcement, is that right?" she asked.

Mr. Bove, good old Sam, was cautious. "I have worked for the defense on a few occasions. Generally out of the area. I have to be careful of conflict of interest."

"Isn't it a fact that you did not compare any other knives to the exhibit, just the 'Best Defense' knife and the compass knife, right?"

"And a scalpel."

"A scalpel?"

"That's correct."

"You didn't endeavor to go out and get other knives, to see whether or not they could make similar impressions?"

"No."

"Am I correct in stating that you used the actual evidence item—Aaron's knife—and you stuck it into some raw pork ribs?"

"Yes, I cut into pork meat with bones in it."

"You were actually at the scene of this homicide, with Robert Cheeseman and George Durgin, is that right?"

"Yes, the sheriff's crime lab was invited to take prints in Stephanie's room."

By the time these tedious exchanges were over, Mr. Bove had gone through a series of responses that ranged from pleasant and cooperative to openly resentful. He was there for one purpose: to make the case for the prosecution that Aaron's knife was *the* murder weapon. But the trick appeared to be beyond his capabilities. I asked him how many times he had to make cuts before he got the type of cut wound he was looking for.

Stephan objected, of course, and Judge Hammes sustained, but that was what it was about, as far as I was concerned.

Further cross-examination showed that the knife used to kill Stephanie had a "hilt guard," to protect the user's hand, and it had left bruise marks as it was thrust into her body. The "Best Defense" knife hilt guard when tested could not leave the same bruise marks when inserted into the pork meat to the same depth and width as the cuts of the murder weapon. The knife blade was just too long. The cut marks just did not match.

Bove had been after the results the police wanted.

Before the proceedings ended that day, Joshua's mother was called to the stand. Tammy Treadway looked gaunt from the entire ordeal and her obvious concern for her son. Attridge's purpose was to establish that Joshua had acquired a facial tic from the stress of his circumstances. All the boys had lost weight by this time, and all three were showing various signs of distress. Nearly five months had passed since they had been confined, and longer yet since the hellish nightmare of the murder.

At this point it is appropriate to comment on Joshua's character. We know that he had quickly confessed and pointed a finger at Michael and Aaron to save himself. Or maybe it was just to comply with the police, who had told him that *this would be a saving grace for him.* We Americans do not like the weak. We have in us a love for heroes, guys who stand firm for family and friends, so Joshua is a natural target for our disapproval. But here was a young boy, barely into his teens, suddenly involved in a murder case as a suspect. He was frightened and cast into a world he only knew from television and movies. He was an artist, with a big imagination, and so who knew how he envisioned prison life?

When we think about all this, we must remember that at any time during the weeks-long Fitness Hearing Joshua could have made a plea bargain and sent Aaron and Michael to their doom. But he didn't. When Joshua fully understood the consequences of his readiness to cooperate, he stood very tall, even at his own cost. The DA's office had offered him a plea bargain, but he didn't take it. Mary Ellen Attridge had approached him more than once with a plea bargain, too. He even refused his own attorney, who had no doubt warned him this was a difficult case to win. There was even talk of a plea with no jail time.

26

· DEFENSE WITNESSES ·

Day 185: San Diego, California
July 24, 1998

T
he hearing resumed with Paul Blake's direct examination of the Reverend Earl Guy. He had been extremely vocal in his belief in the boys' innocence, and this had brought him adverse publicity, even harmed his reputation with members of his church congregation. Some had seen his support as inappropriate, but many others had raised money to help pay for the boys' defense, a refreshing glimpse of community spirit.

"How is it that you know Michael Crowe?" Blake asked the reverend.

"My first association with Michael was through his sister, who was active in our congregation. I met Michael once, maybe twice, at church activities. He attended the youth group once. He wasn't a regular participant there, so most of my knowledge of him was simply as Stephanie's brother. But I met him on occasion. Following Stephanie's murder, I got more involved with the family. Most of my association has been since then."

The minister served the defense mostly as a character witness for the Crowe family. But also he had been summoned to the police station in the afternoon on the day Stephanie died, and he was present during some of the questioning of the Crowe family members. He offered quite a different picture of how Michael responded to his sister's death. He said Michael had seemed tired and withdrawn, and he didn't seem to have a focused sense of what to do.

The next witness was Aaron's mother, Susie Houser. She had been divorced from Gregg Houser for nine years. Both their sons were living with her, Aaron and Adam. I asked Mrs. Houser if Aaron ever hit other boys. She said he didn't, but he had hit his own brother once, when he was five. I asked her how he was with animals.

"He has two cats of his own and babies them, he's very kind." I also asked her about Aaron's speech; the way he talked. The police, the psychologist Blum and the prosecution played heavily on Aaron's seeming calculation of everything he said in his response to questions. As I said early in this book, Aaron was the only teen I ever knew who thinks deeply before he speaks. The prosecution viewed this trait as just another sign of the boy-monster being withdrawn and capable of plotting to kill.

"In regard to Aaron, and how he acts under stress," I asked, "did you overhear his side of a telephone conversation with Joshua?" I was referring to the controlled call set up by Detective Claytor.

"Yes."

"What did you hear in Aaron?"

"I heard a boy who was upset and angry."

"How does Aaron react when he's upset, frustrated or angry? How does he speak?"

"He slows down his speech, lowers his voice, tends to think and choose his words with care."

"Are any of these characteristics similar to Gregg, his father?"

"Yes." This was a subtle point, but important nevertheless. Aaron spoke a lot like his father. While this didn't burst the prosecution's bubble, it at least pointed out that Aaron's way of talking and answering questions was not because of some deeply rooted psychological problem but was rather a natural pattern.

With this established, I asked Mrs. Houser how Aaron had responded after that controlled phone call was over.

"He said, 'I don't know why Josh would say those things, Mom. Why would he?' He was shaking. We had to calm him down."

"Who was 'we'?"

"Adam and me."

Judge Hammes asked about Aaron and Michael's friendship, prior to their breakup. Mrs. Houser said they seldom went to each other's houses, but they talked on the phone once a week. Aaron was much closer to his friend Scott, she said. Hammes was very interested in this topic, it seemed, and her inquiries lasted for quite a time. She went back to December, before the homicide, to Aaron's schoolwork, and to what happened when the police had first gone to their house and the boys were home alone. She asked numerous questions about Aaron's missing knives. Her questions were very thorough and penetrating, although neither the defense nor the prosecution knew exactly what she was after. What we all did know—the defense and prosecution—was that she was on a path over which we had no control. Was it a tack that would help or harm our case? Impossible to tell. As a result, we all just sat there silently waiting for her to finish with Susie Houser.

27

• COERCION AND TRICKERY •

Day 202: San Diego, California
August 10, 1998

A t this point, the Fitness Hearing had been going on since July 7, and the three boys had spent six months jailed in Juvenile Hall.

Paul Blake began with witness Richard J. Ofshe, a professor at the University of California, Berkeley. This man, for more than a dozen years, had been doing research on the tactics and techniques of police interrogations: the way both true and false confessions are obtained. He had been publishing the results of his work since 1989. He was poised, articulate and very well prepared. He said he had studied the interrogation tapes and the transcripts and knew the details of the Stephanie Crowe murder case. Certainly he was well credentialed and held in high esteem by his peers across the nation. He explained that a new work he was completing, a book, included a paper called "The Social Psychology of Police Interrogation: The Theory and Classification of True and False Confessions." There was also one titled "The Decision to Confess Falsely: Rational Choice and Irrational Action," and another, "The Consequences of False Confessions: Deprivations of Liberty and Miscarriages of Justice in the Age of Psychological Interrogation."

He was certainly important to the defense since he had also a long list of professional consultations with police agencies, which meant that while he was definitely involved for the defense in this case, he was esteemed on both sides of the judicial fence.

To emphasize the background and expertise of Dr. Ofshe, Paul took a long time revealing Dr. Ofshe's experiences, studies, and expertise and the results of his efforts to free innocent people, people who had been imprisoned based on confessing to crimes *they didn't commit*. Dr. Ofshe described an exact model of how Claytor, Wrisley, and McDonough—who he referred to as "the Magician"—achieved Michael's and Joshua's confessions. He clearly identified the several ways police use coercion to get the results they want, as opposed to seeking the truth. This was the strongest testimony we had against the confessions, and it gave us a glimmer of hope, but would Judge Hammes also see what we saw? Dr. Ofshe was unambiguous in asserting that the police had, in our own case, falsely and abusively obtained the admissions of guilt from the boys. The judge duly noted these opinions and followed up with a question.

"Dr. Ofshe, are you saying the confessions made by Michael Crowe and Joshua Treadway are false statements, or are you saying, yes, they are coerced, but their reliability is a separate question that depends on other facts?"

"I have no opinion about the truth or falsity of the statements," Ofshe answered. "In order to offer a private personal opinion, or an opinion that someone in some venues might be permitted to testify to, would require an analysis of the post-admission narrative fit, and I haven't examined the facts of the case, so I can't do that."

Stephan then tried to undermine Dr. Ofshe's opinions and conclusions, but she was hard pressed. Ofshe pointed out, citing many cases, a line-for-line account of the questions and answers given during the boys' interrogation, and how intimidation and deal-making was at the core of Michael's and Joshua's confessions.

After Dr. Ofshe's testimony was over, I could sense the positive feelings in the courtroom, but I did not get a good reading on how Judge Hammes had taken it.

Mary Ellen Attridge called Shannon, Michael's younger sister, to the stand. Shannon established the time Stephanie had eaten her salad on the fatal night: 6:30 p.m.

I called Patricia Bolt to the stand, a teacher of Aaron's, who had been teaching for thirty years.

"I coach and run the academic competition, the academic decathlon team and the academics league team, which is styled after the old TV *College Bowl*."

"Have you had occasion to watch as Aaron practiced and participated in that 'activity bowl,' as you call it?"

"You bet."

"What would you call the group that participates in this activity?"

"We call it North County Academic League, but it's countywide. That's just our version of it, but we basically call it an academic league."

"Okay. When you observed Aaron in the academic league, had you had a chance to see him under pressure or stress as he tried to compete and answer questions?"

"Yes. In practice, sometimes he would answer all the questions and nobody else got a chance to even try. So we had to ask him to not answer questions sometimes, so the other kids got some practice."

"How does Aaron act in regards to pressure? When I say 'act,' I'm talking about his emotional state and the way he speaks, the way he acts and reacts."

"He would get frustrated when he knew the answer and we wouldn't let him answer. After everybody else had a chance at it, and couldn't answer, then we'd let him answer it. He would be very slow, deliberative, indicating his frustration. Then we'd all kind of laugh at him, and he'd laugh with us."

I called Adam Houser, Aaron's brother, to testify. Adam is also articulate and intelligent. He was important because I wanted to reaffirm the time Aaron had gone to bed the night of the homicide and show that it would have been quite difficult for him to leave the house without someone hearing him.

"Can you hear the door opening? The one from your room—if you are in there and the door is shut?"

"Oh, yeah."

"And is there another way out of your house, other than that front door?"

"There's a sliding glass door that leads out to the back, and there's a garage and then windows. Other than that, no."

"In regard to the sliding glass door, is there anything difficult about opening and shutting that particular door?"

"It's hard to open and squeaks real loud."

I asked Adam about Aaron's response to the controlled phone call that had been instigated by the police.

He answered, "Aaron was really shaken up by it. He was nervous, and was going, 'Mom, why would Josh say something like this? Why is he doing this?' He couldn't stay still. He was just walking up and down, pacing, really upset."

Adam was very helpful, at least from the defense point of view. He mentioned that Aaron, like he and his father, had the same voice patterns, especially under stress. He had a slow, deliberate articulation and delivery of speech. It was a family trait, and I felt confident Judge Hammes would make note of this. This ought to certainly help to relieve the accusation that Aaron's way of speaking was a symptom of his deep, dark personality—a mentally disturbed psychopath, as the DA's office had concluded.

The last witness called was Gregg Houser, Aaron's father.

"Did you ask to be present for the CVSA test?" I asked.

"I did."

"And what did Detective Claytor tell you?"

"He said, no, it wasn't possible. My presence there would disturb the test."

"In regard to your son's status at the police department, did Detective Claytor tell you he was under arrest for murder?"

"Not until four-thirty that afternoon."

"Did he tell you Aaron was under arrest for *anything?*"

"No."

"Would you have allowed him to take the test had you known he was under arrest?"

"No, I would not. There's no way. If you go under arrest, I know well enough that you seek legal counsel. That's what I would have done."

When Mr. Houser was allowed to leave the stand there was that strange relief a person feels when he reaches halfway up a peak he's climbing and sits down to take a rest. He looks down the mountain and feels a sense of freedom and accomplishment. Then he looks up and realizes the real climb is yet to come. I wondered what Attridge and Blake were feeling. I wondered what Stephan was experiencing.

Finally, the time had come for closing arguments. The hearing was soon to be over and all the *should've-dones* and the *would've-dones* were irrelevant. At a time like this, you look at your client, and you glance at his parents and relatives, and suddenly you want to call up the magic that makes all their pain and worry go away. You want to tell them you have this thing licked, you have saved the day and it's time to go home and celebrate. You want to do these things, but you know you can't.

You simply hope that your best has been good enough.

28

• CLOSING ARGUMENTS •

Day 202: San Diego, California
August 10, 1998

"I think the reason this case has been so hard," Stephan began her summary, "is because it is so difficult for us to accept that there is a face to these three boys that is not what we see right here.

"It is very hard for good people to look at others and see evil. We don't want to accept it. We'd rather turn to some mentally ill demented nobody who has a rap sheet, because that's so much easier for us to grasp and understand." (She wanted to toss Richard Tuite out of the picture, apparently.)

"We don't do the same thing," she continued, "when we look at the face of good, like with Stephanie, the epitome of good, and the absolute contrast to her brother Michael. When we look at her face we don't ask why this child, this twelve-year-old, spends three days a week in church, or why she spends time volunteering at the library. Why isn't she just out chasing boys and having fun, or whatever twelve-year-old girls do?

"But we look at the faces of three intelligent minors, young men, and we cannot accept the fact that there is pure unadulterated evil at work in this diabolic trio, and I do not say that lightly. There is a lot of evidence. But it's been hard to look at the evidence because our initial impression—even mine—was, it can't be so! These three people wouldn't kill a little girl; slaughter her like a lamb in her sleep. Because of what?

"Because Michael hated Stephanie, as a reflection of his hate for his family, and as a reflection of his hate for his own self, for his own failure. For his feelings of not being popular. For being referred to as Stephanie's brother—as he declared to us in complete and full detail in his statement, on tape.

"And they tell you," she pointed at the three of us, 'Oh, that's coerced.' Yeah, right. You can get somebody, maybe for five minutes or half an hour, to describe something that is completely farcical, maybe for an hour. But we have an hour and forty-five minutes of it, at the end of which this young man was sitting back in his seat, drinking his Coke with a complete sense of relief. And why?

"When he was placed under arrest, it was over. The gig was up. The game was over, and he was now feeling like, 'Since I'm going to be arrested anyway, I might as well tell you that this little girl bugged the heck out of me.' And he sat there and did exactly that. As soon as he was placed under arrest, he said, 'I didn't like her anyway.'"

Stephan continued, saying how Michael had openly admitted that he thought Stephanie deserved what happened to her, and how he hated his family. She then turned to the subject of what the defense had represented.

"They tell us, 'But Michael's statement doesn't have details, so it must be false,' ignoring the obvious, even to a bunch of blue-collar people in a jury box, if this were a trial, they would completely understand why Michael would not give details. It's very simple. Not because it's all a lie, which is what everybody wants to believe, but because on January 23rd, his buddy Josh—who he loved like a brother—had not been arrested yet. And Aaron had not been arrested yet either." She paused for effect. "If Michael had given a single detail about the murder, he would have had to give up Josh and Aaron. He could not give details about the murder. He could not tell us why it happened, not without implicating his two friends. That is just obvious."

Stephan was demonstrating in great detail her rhetorical prowess, which she had effectively honed over the last nine years of being a prosecutor. Her words definitely echoed her conviction that these three young boys were murderers.

"So here we sit, and we bring on various experts, and they all miss the very obvious of why we didn't hear details. Because they would be so damning. They would show how horrible, how sophisticated, how planned . . . What he'd rather do, is say, 'Okay, you have me. You're going to arrest me, fine. I'm not going to be so stupid as to give you the details of how premeditated, how planned, how sick and disgusting this murder was. I'm not going to do that.' But it's so much easier to just say that this means it's all false.

"Then we have Joshua and the tremendous, horrible pressure that was put on him by the police on January 27 and 28. But what happened? He went in there, with all this pressure the police put on him, pressure that has been described here in such great detail, and he still had the presence of mind to call a couple of hours before that controlled phone call was made. And why did he call? Because he had not told the police hardly anything. He had given them just the tip of the iceberg: 'I received the knife that was the murder weapon.' That's all.

"All this talk about the police wanting evidence against Michael and what did Josh give them? Not evidence against Michael. He gave them evidence against Aaron. Josh gave them evidence they didn't expect, against Aaron, not Michael. In fact, in many ways, he made Michael's culpability less, by not making him as much the mastermind, the actual killer."

Oh, how masterfully she intentionally wove the "evidence"—all the while ignoring the dozens of hours of excruciating interrogation of the boys.

"So if the police were masterminding this thing, and were feeding him the information, then why is it that he didn't turn out to be a witness against Michael? They already had Michael. But without prompting, Josh provided information that it wasn't just Michael, it was also Aaron. Which, by the way, Your Honor, is exactly what Michael told us, but not in a direct way. Michael told us this early in the game. He wanted to take some of the blame off himself, so he tipped off the police. He went off on how evil Aaron is. How, without Aaron, maybe he wouldn't have done it. And if he were to kill another human being, it would be Aaron. So he was already telling us, in a roundabout way, what Josh finally told us.

"How many times in life do we run across two young men that talk about killing a sister of one of them, the other saying, 'Have you done it yet? Have you killed her yet?' And then the sister turns up dead?

"As the pressure was put on him, Josh repeatedly asked, 'What do you have? What's your evidence? What's going to happen to me?'

"We are not dealing here with three normal boys. We are dealing with diabolic minds, very intelligent young men who committed an adult crime in a very adult way. But because we look at their faces we think they are young and dumb. But that's not what they are, that's *not* what they are. What these three minors did not count on is that no matter how smart they are, how good they are, there is something called justice. And no amount of planning can ever account for that, and that's exactly what happened in this case.

"Not only that—as maybe they have discovered during these proceedings—Stephanie found them out. Stephanie herself let the world know who her killers were. And Stephanie will still win.

"After Susie Houser made her call, reporting a knife missing, it was all over. Now the call came the very next day from Josh. And what did he say to Aaron? 'They took the knife you gave me, Aaron.' We're talking about just the first few minutes, before he was completely tipped off. And Aaron replied, 'What knife did I give you? I don't know what you're talking about. I'm missing a knife. Did you steal my knife? What's going on?' And the next question was even more crucial. And I believe, Your Honor, it reflects a direct admission of guilt in this matter. Josh asked, 'Are we going to get into any trouble?' And Aaron's answer? Remember, this was before he was tipped off. Aaron said, 'Okay Josh, listen up. Right now they probably think this is separate from what is going on with Mike.'

"What Aaron was saying is very clear: The police probably thought the knife theft incident was completely separate from what was going on with Mike. And what was going on with Mike right then? He was being charged with murder. There was nothing else going on with Mike. Nothing.

"So what Aaron was doing here was . . . he was comforting Joshua, telling him the police probably thought this had nothing to do with the murder, or with Michael. 'You are just looking, at most, at a misdemeanor,' he said. 'So keep your mouth shut and let's go on with the plan.' That's what Aaron was telling him.

"The next thing is very important, too. In that controlled phone call, Aaron was telling Josh, 'Now listen, listen, Josh. You know Michael and I hated each other, basically.' He was feeding him. What was Josh supposed to say? He was feeding him a defense again. I mean this whole conversation, now taken in the context of what we know to be the facts, there was no hatred for Michael. This was just a beautiful thing Aaron devised as soon as Michael was arrested.

"All of a sudden, on the twenty-seventh, when Josh was interviewed, one of the first things out of his mouth—I'm talking about the interview before he was arrested—was, 'And you know that Aaron and Michael hated each other, or had a falling-out.' That was so irrelevant at the time, but all of a sudden he wanted to inject it. He wanted to help Aaron.

"Now we know from the controlled phone call that Joshua did not steal Aaron's knife, but Aaron actually gave Joshua the knife. Why would somebody admit to the theft of something—a minor offense? Why would you admit that unless you were trying to avoid something a lot bigger?

"Josh gave us the accurate information on the twenty-seventh about what his role was. He didn't give us the whole thing, but he gave us the right information. He was the designated weapons man. Why? Well, it makes a lot of sense. Aaron was going to do the killing. Michael was going to help in the killing. They had to make sure Josh was in it as deep as they were, not just as a lookout.

"And how do we know Josh was the designated weapons person? Well, he didn't have just one knife; he had two that were both strangely acquired. The Scott Colegrove knife and the knife that was actually used in the killing—Aaron's knife.

"I think there were two turning points in this case. Two that made the plan not work. One, I talked about Stephanie herself. These three did not for a second think they had left a breath of life in that little girl. When Michael told the police, three or four different times, that her door was shut and there was nothing amiss at four-thirty in the morning, he told them that with complete confidence. He knew, or thought he did, that his sister had drawn her last breath on the bed. They walked out of that room, shut the door without making a noise, but they didn't close it entirely. It was open just enough for her little fingers to claw at as she scratched her way out of the bed and to the doorway. I tell you, Your Honor, those five, ten minutes of her life . . ."

Again she paused for maximum effect.

"There is not any amount of punishment these three men can get in their entire lives that will make up for those ten minutes when Stephanie crawled her way out of the bed. When she crawled her way to that doorway she wanted to make sure the world knew these men killed her.

"After they murdered Stephanie, around midnight, Michael never came out of his room, because he would have seen her body. And then he wouldn't have told that stupid story. But he thought she was still in her bed, and because the grandmother was already awake, the mother and father were already awake, he had no idea that maybe nobody moved her off the bed and down to the floor, where he saw her.

"The mother said goodnight to Stephanie between nine-thirty and ten o'clock. At ten o'clock Stephanie was still on the phone with a friend, which means that . . . and I also don't want to go through Shannon's testimony about the salad, because it is irrelevant. And even if you believe this child to say she remembers, although she didn't remember at the time that her sister ate a salad at six-thirty, that would mean Stephanie would have to be dead at nine o'clock, but we know she was alive. But this is irrelevant, because we know that twelve-thirty was the time of death. The killing time given by Josh is consistent with the medical testimony, especially the fact of the rigor mortis. He could have given many other times, if innocent, but he didn't. And from there, he described on four different occasions that the plan came about rather like the way they would discuss their games. It would be in the context of how they would play Dungeons & Dragons. 'We could do this; we could do that; we could do this. This is how we could do it. You could be the one to do this. I could be the one to do that.' Natural enough, since the three of them were so into these fantasy and role-playing games."

Stephan then came to the words "Kill Kill" scribbled on Stephanie's windowsill. She indicated strongly that this had been identified as Michael's handwriting. Both Attridge and I objected immediately, on the grounds that she was misstating the testimony, but the objection was overruled. She continued, saying these words suggested part of the game playing the boys included in their masterminding the murder.

No matter how many times you sit and listen to an opposing attorney build a final argument, you never truly lose the impulse to interrupt and say, "Hey, wait a minute, let me explain that." You don't do it, of course. You can't. At those times you have to remind yourself that while it is generally agreed that many good attorneys are great speakers, the best attorneys are always great listeners. And so you listen, and you contain your own convictions. If you don't, you are lost; and your clients invariably end up losing too. I would have my opportunity, and the prosecutor would then have to sit and listen to me—to us.

Stephan continued, reiterating key points from Joshua's "confession" that explained why no one heard Stephanie scream and why the police found no blood on the boys' clothing.

"They walked out of Stephanie's room, *then* the mess started. When she crawled out of her bed, she made the mess, but it was a *clean* scene at the time of the stabbing. There's no way Josh could have known that. There is no way, making up a story, trying to please the officers, that he would not have added, 'He had some blood on him, on his hands, on his clothing.'"

Stephan then went to the subject of Aaron's knife. She attached great significance to how the blade matched those of the wounds and the cuts through Stephanie's comforter. She made the point that the knife had fluoresced as a presumptive test for blood, even though that was inconclusive.

"I've gone through clothing, method and planning. The murder weapon is right because it's consistent in every way, according to what we see in the pictures. . . . In addition, Joshua gave us the time of the death, the time of his walk, and he further gave us the person who did the actual stabbing, which is very interesting because he could have picked one or the other. But he picked the one who had the most training in the use of knives. He picked Aaron.

"Now, Your Honor, as in every case, there are things killers are never going to tell us about. We're never going to know if Josh was actually stand-ing there, watching this girl die, for instance. But he had a lot of personal knowledge about things nobody else knew, not even the police, like the time of the death, the method of killing and the method of their entry into the house . . . Michael opened the laundry room door for Joshua and Aaron.

"I want to briefly address the issue of the transient. This case started off with the defense saying they could prove the involvement of Mr. Tuite. He had stabbed somebody in the throat before, and at twelve-thirty that night was seen in the neighborhood. But all of this information proves nothing. First of all, the house was not broken into."

A reminder to readers: A sliding glass door at the rear of the Crowe home was not locked, and it was found slightly open when checked the morn-ing after the killing. This door was considered by police an unlikely entry point simply because they felt the blinds and the door itself would make too much noise if used for entry. Based on this flimsy assumption, the police and the prosecution seemed blindly convinced there was no intruder. And the authorities never really considered Cheryl Crowe's (and Michael's) state-ment about hearing a thumping noise in the night. Most important was Mrs. Kennedy's son, who was at the Crowe house the evening of the murder. He had been asked to lock the door behind him when he left. Did he do so? Or was the door left open—accidentally—or unlocked? Just so inconveniently, the police never talked about how secure the door, which everyone used, was or whether it was subject to jimmying.

The prosecutor continued her summary: "We know from the evidence that the assailant would not be bloody because Stephanie was stabbed with a comforter on top of her. She crawled out of her bed later, so the assailant would not be bloody, and the people who hugged Stephanie's body, later, would be the ones most likely to have any sort of blood on them.

"We know that Richard Tuite was in the area, knocking on doors, saying, 'Hello, I'm Richard, is Tracy home?' We know he would look for Tracy all the time. Tracy came to court and told us that you say 'boo' to this guy and he just backs off. He's never been violent toward her. So what do we have on this? He was seen wearing the red shirt, and underneath it—the white shirt, the jail shirt. He got out of jail five days earlier. And we know he had no contact with Stephanie Crowe. What would the defense have us believe? He took off his shirt and somehow Stephanie spit on him, or sweated on him without him knowing? You can use any logic you want, but it doesn't fit the case.

"Richard Tuite was such an easy target. If the police were really in a hurry to solve this case, and to get someone for it, Richard Tuite would have been the perfect target, the perfect one to pick up and arrest. And you know what? Maybe someone could coerce him to confess. He would have been such an easy target for the police, but *he didn't do it.* So the police went to much harder targets, but that's how our system is supposed to work. They are not supposed to look at how ugly a face Richard Tuite has versus how pretty these minors are. They are supposed to do the investigation in an objective way, without prejudice.

"It is our position that these three minors are presumptively ineligible for treatment as juveniles. They must be treated as adults. So, Your Honor, when we look at these factors, when we look at the gravity of this case . . . the slaughter of a child in her sleep, and the planning and sophistication that went into it, that this is a very adult crime. They should be held to answer as adults. The murder of Stephanie was much more serious than some game, and justice is going to be done. Thank you, Your Honor."

Summer Stephan had completely committed herself to the case against the boys. This was her case—lock, stock, and barrel. As she finished, I frankly thought to myself that this was her chariot to fame and promotion. The one case every prosecutor looks for to make their career. But, at what cost? The lives of three boys.

Mary Ellen Attridge delivered the first defense summary.

"If the Escondido Police Department had not made a hasty and unwise decision, we would not be here today. They would have not endeavored to make a case out of whole cloth against these three boys, because they had the suspect already. They had the person who did this, right there in their holding cells. Summer Stephan has argued that we desire to pick on Mr. Tuite because he's a disenfranchised kind of guy, and an easy target. Well, we didn't invent Mr. Tuite. Mr. Tuite was there . . ."

She continued, covering the lack of evidence, and then she went deeply into the technology of the stab wounds and the knife and its precise measurements. She struck hard on the coercive elements of the interrogations. When she was nearing the end of her statement, she said, "And so, Your Honor, it seems what this case comes down to is whether or not the Escondido Police Department initially dropped the ball and mishandled a murder case. This is not a particularly popular accusation to make, but certainly there's evidence against Mr. Tuite that cannot be disregarded. I find it particularly freakish that a couple of days after the girl was killed, Mr. Tuite was in the parking lot of a motel, telling police officers the reason he was there was to talk to the family of the kid who died. Why would Richard Tuite want to talk to the Crowes? They didn't know him. That is more than a mere coincidence.

"If you take the alleged coincidences surrounding Mr. Tuite and stack them one on top of the other—the seven eye witnesses, the prior stabbing in the same location of the body, the fact that he was essentially stalking this family a couple of days later, and having him in that same remote area knocking on every single door on that night—the odds of all of those things happening are astronomical. Most importantly, the condemnation of a juvenile offender to adult court is the worst punishment the system is empowered to inflict."

Attridge finished late in the day, so Paul Blake and I were relieved that we'd have more time to prepare our own closing summaries. The next day would be the day of reckoning.

The fate of Aaron, Joshua, and Michael would be in the hands of Judge Hammes. And the hearing, which had begun five weeks earlier, would at long last be over.

29

• RESTLESS THOUGHTS •

Day 202: San Diego, California
August 10, 1998

I didn't sleep much that night.

I rolled and tossed, thinking no matter how well we had represented our clients, the cards remained heavily stacked against us. I had been a prosecutor. I knew the strength of having the system's support in such cases. I knew the emotions and the psychology of the prosecution. Summer Stephan's desire to win was evident. She had called the boys "diabolical" and "evil," and she wanted them punished, isolated from society and enslaved behind the walls of a prison for life. We—Mary Ellen Attridge, Paul Blake, and I—wanted them free. We believed in their innocence, and we did not want to lose them. Certainly their parents and relatives did not want to lose them, and this lay heavy on my mind.

That night I tried to put a final hypothesis together. I had been going over what might have happened the night of the murder ever since Tuite had come into the shadowy picture. I will share my thinking here, for the reader's contemplation:

Assume that Richard Tuite walked up the Crowe driveway sometime after nine that evening. He had been going from house to house, looking for Tracy. He had been searching for hours and was tired and frustrated,

The back entry to the Crowe house.

but he remained fixated on finding Tracy. She had lived in his mind for months . . . for years.

She was part of his good memories, a time when life was better, with lots of parties, lots of highs, and no one had been nicer to him. We knew a little about how this fixation had affected him. Then she was out of his life. He had seen Tracy's image in two small girls, had called them Tracy, asked them to have sex with him. How many other females he projected Tracy's image onto we will never know, but he saw Tracy in female strangers everywhere, that is a given.

Assume that after the Reverend Gary West told Tuite that Tracy did not live at his house, Tuite walked north, up the driveway to the Crowe home. It would have been around 9:30 p.m. by this time. Assume that he walked around the house, looking through the windows before knocking at the door, as he had done at a number of other houses, but he saw no one in the dining room or the kitchen. Then he reached Stephanie's bedroom window.

She was on the telephone. He watched and he listened. She was talking about a movie, *Titanic*, and maybe about boys. Maybe he couldn't hear very much, but there she was: Tracy. *She'd been in this house all the time, hiding from him. Why?* They had been friends and he trusted her, but now she was talking and laughing with someone else. He wanted to tell her how much he missed her, how he kept her image in his mind . . . and she would understand. They would sleep together. He had always wanted to have sex with Tracy.

Tuite hurried back to the door he had passed earlier, the south-facing backdoor leading into the laundry room. The door was unlocked so he opened it and walked in. He stood, frozen for a few moments, wondering what to do. Then he leaned against the door, closing it behind him. At this very moment the policeman, responding to the 911 call from Reverend West, had driven his cruiser up the same dark country driveway. He saw the door close and assumed the people inside were locking up for the night. Things looked otherwise normal. The transient was not in sight.

Assume that Tuite was confused, didn't know quite what to do. *What if Tracy would be angry at him for coming in? Maybe she'd been hiding from him, avoiding him all this time.* We can't know what he had in his mind. We can't say how the paranoia, the fear of rejection, might turn into hate, or God knows what emotions might swarm through his psychotic head as he stood silently inside that house.

In my mind, I assumed that he crept through the house, passed the kitchen, opened and shut the door to Steve and Cheryl's bedroom, and quietly walked on to Stephanie's door.

The thought of this psychotic man creeping through the house, checking each room, sent a chill through my body. A coldness that grew as I thought back about the testimony of how Tuite entered other homes that night, and how he persistently followed those two young girls—girls Stephanie's age.

There he stood, listening to Stephanie and in his mind hearing Tracy. She was so happy, so aloof from him, talking about boys she liked, laughing with her friend on the phone.

Was she laughing at him? Was she inside the bedroom with some other lover?

We are left with nothing more than this kind of speculation. But if we assume Tuite was in the house, it follows he would be in some odd state of delusion.

He waited in some timeless state, wallowing in his own mental confusion, listening to voices, some real, some inside his head, watching images pass by in the darkness . . . images from times gone by; images that are created by drug-induced hallucination. The thought of killing Tracy came to his mind. To murder someone is the ultimate act of control.

When he finally stole into Stephanie's bedroom, one to three hours after he had entered the house, she was asleep. Maybe this, too, stirred rage in him. Or maybe he looked at her and thought he would keep her from hiding from him again. Maybe he had no thoughts at all, no calculations. Maybe he didn't even know she was sleeping. Maybe she was just laughing at him, or having romantic thoughts about someone else. Schizophrenia can cause a person to project all kinds of realities onto their world; they can spend hours lost in the chasms of their confused mind, where angels or devils can beckon them deeper and deeper into their own morass. *If Michael Crowe could have a demon alter ego, as the police assumed, then why not a proven drug abuser with schizophrenia?*

My mind raced aimlessly, conjuring every possible action, thought, or reason this man could have had. Always, I came back to the little girl and the reality of the knife attack.

I thought to myself, Stephanie regained consciousness after the attack. She pushed herself up and out of bed. She wanted to call out, but her throat was too damaged, so she crawled to the door and banged her fists against it (or the wall), making an attempt to get help. Both Michael and Cheryl Crowe heard this pounding, but it sounded so distant that no one got up to investigate. Stephanie would have used her remaining strength struggling to open her door, then died just inside the doorway of her bedroom.

Judith Kennedy, Stephanie's grandmother, said she had stepped into Stephanie's bedroom before touching something with her foot. She looked down and turned on the light, discovering her granddaughter lying on the floor. The paramedics reported that they had to pull Mrs. Crowe away from Stephanie, she was hugging her dead daughter so tightly.

What if, as the paramedics attempted to pull her away, Stephanie's body was moved further into the door alcove? By the time the police arrived, they could easily conclude—and did—that it would have been much easier for someone to see the body as they passed her bedroom in the night, as Michael had done earlier.

Even if Stephanie had been just inside her bedroom doorway when Michael got up at 4:30 that morning, people do not necessarily look toward the floor when they enter or exit a room. And if they have a painful headache, as Michael did, or are half asleep, they may not look at anything. On his return trip to his bedroom there would be no reason to look toward Stephanie's bedroom door at all. He would have simply walked down the hall, turned into his own room, and gone back to bed. The idea that Michael had to have seen the body was speculative at best, yet it was a major focus by the police and the prosecution.

• • •

Granted, all this mental rambling was pure speculation on my part—one more effort to make sense of what happened and find a loophole in Stephan's theory. What we defense attorneys were sure of, however, was that Richard Tuite had found his way into the Crowe home and into Stephanie's room.

The prosecution claimed we were reaching out for anything that would take suspicion off the boys. If the bumbling Richard Tuite had committed the crime, the prosecution said, where were his fingerprints? Further, why wasn't he covered with blood?

And anyway, two of the boys had confessed.

30

• LOOSE ENDS •

Day 203: San Diego, California
August 11, 1998

The day of the final arguments, as I got dressed, my mind was still filled with recurring thoughts about the case. What worried me most were the several loose ends. I knew, as did Mary Ellen Attridge and Paul Blake, we had not tied things together well enough to be assured the confessions would be deemed coercive. And if they were not, all our arguments would fall on deaf ears. If the confessions held, the boys would be certified to adult court and would, in all likelihood, be convicted.

What we really needed was hard evidence. Any single, tiny piece of something substantial that would place Tuite inside the Crowe house. Such evidence would give the judge pause; it would make the confessions even more suspect. *Why had Tuite been searching for the Crowe family at the motel, where the police had housed them three days after the murder?* Was it the morbid curiosity of a "nut case," or had he realized he had not murdered Tracy but another girl, and was tempted to make some sort of contact to ease his conscience? Or who knew what else? That too was the problem. Who knew what? We had nothing with which to build a case against Tuite; we had nothing regarding Tuite to present to the court.

But the prosecution had no hard evidence against the boys either. Without the confessions, the prosecution would have nothing.

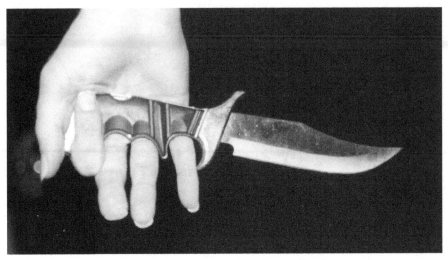

Aaron Houser's "Best Defense" knife.

The "Best Defense" knife was the purported murder weapon, but to grip the knife by the finger grooves meant that the blade and hilt did not match the murder wounds. On the other hand, if Tuite did the killing, where was the weapon he used? Certainly it is not difficult to dispose of a knife. But circumstantial evidence against the three boys was strong enough to make the question of how confessions were obtained less critical.

Blake went ahead of me in presenting his closing argument. He had been conservative throughout the hearing, compared to Attridge's flamboyance. He was difficult to read at times and never exposed his feelings. But on this day he expressed something I also felt.

"Your Honor," he began, "we seldom see a case like this, but when we do, we are reminded why we went to law school and why, perhaps, you became a judge. We search for the truth, for justice, and to protect the innocent. Your Honor, my client, Michael, is innocent. So innocent, I can't stand the thought of what has been done to him and his friends." He kept his summary brief, covering the same key points, and we took a brief recess after he was finished.

When we returned to the courtroom, at ten after ten that morning, I began my closing argument: "It is my pleasure to summarize the proceedings and the evidence. Last night I was trying to think what I might say to a court that is very thorough, very well prepared, and very attentive to the proceedings. Since I'm the third one to speak for the defense, and the court has heard so much from Ms. Attridge and Mr. Blake, I think the best thing for me to do is summarize the points most pertinent to Aaron Houser. I agree with and take the same position on the legal points raised by Ms. Attridge and Mr. Blake on the evidence.

"In particular I will address the confessions, the alleged confessions the police extracted from these children. I believe this court has the power to take action and bring this to an end, simply because of the way in which these so-called confessions were extracted.

"This is not an easy job for me. It unnerves me, because we have so much at stake here. These three boys are at their formative age, when they should be enjoying themselves. Instead, what are they doing? They are incarcerated, waiting for the system—we adults, who have been entrusted to care for them and protect them and structure their future—to do the right thing. This court has the power to act now and stop this."

I proceeded with my closing argument and started to feel relieved as I spoke; relieved, but a long way short of relaxed. I made the key point that there would be no case at all if it were not for the confessions. Confessions that anyone could plainly see were coerced. It was a major point, but was it enough?

I concluded by saying, "You are a good judge of people, Your Honor, and I trust you, as do the parents of these children. I trust you, specifically, for Aaron, and I hope you will let him go home. He's innocent, and he has suffered enough. Thank you, Your Honor."

Stephan began her rebuttal. mostly a rehash of the evidence she had presented earlier, but she concluded by saying: "The defense urges you to look at Michael, but they do not want you to look at him during the hour and forty-five minutes when he was describing his motive, his venom, his reason for killing Stephanie. They don't want you to look at his face as he was chewing and drinking water during the interrogation. They don't want you to look at Joshua as he was sitting there, crying, saying, 'I hope Aaron doesn't kill me.' They don't want you to look at him as he's giving the two-hour rendition—after *Miranda*—to Detective Wrisley, relaying all the facts of the crime. How relaxed he was, for someone being charged with murder.

"So, Your Honor, you have a case where two have confessed: Michael and Joshua. You have a case where the third person has a hypothetical explanation that is eerie . . . and I believe the People have met their burden fully, and I ask you to do the right thing."

"Thank you counsel," Judge Hammes said. "We're going to take a five-minute recess, and then I'll deliver the court's opinion."

Part Four

Conclusions, Vicious Circles

31

• SMALL VICTORY •

Day 203: San Diego, California
August 11, 1998

Five minutes can seem like such a long time . . . but Judge Hammes finally returned to deliver her ruling. This shockingly short amount of time left me, Attridge, and Blake believing the three teenage boys were on their way to adult court and a probable life behind bars.

"I'm going to cut to the chase," the judge said. "You have all waited long enough. I find that the People have established a prima facie [sufficient] case against the three accused. I will release these minors on their own recognizance, pending trial as juveniles in the Superior Court. But I have a strong suspicion that their involvement in this crime is nowhere near beyond 'reasonable doubt.' If this were a trial, these boys would be not guilty."

I looked at Attridge and Blake in disbelief. The looks on their faces must have mirrored my own as we all broke into cautious smiles. *This was a small but wonderful victory!*

Judge Hammes went over her reasons for the ruling. The key factor was that she saw the confessions as coerced.

Stephan looked upset. As soon as she could, she excused herself and made a dash out of the courtroom. She went directly to the adult arraigning Superior Court department to schedule an immediate arraignment, so that the boys would be kept in Juvenile Hall.

Once certified to adult court, minors had to be rearraigned. She intended to use the arraignment to reestablish bail—a high enough bail to keep the boys incarcerated until the trial. This is one way the prosecution can deal with a losing case. As long as the suspects remain in custody, there is still a chance of them folding to a plea bargain offer, but back in their homes, they gain strength and support. Stephan knew this, so her fervent hope was to lock up the boys and trap them into a bargain for a reduced sentence.

This was her way of not losing without winning.

Summer Stephan was career minded, and losses were not on her agenda. Aggressiveness is not a flaw, but the law should be devoid of politics. What this means is that the district attorney's office, the police departments, and the other law enforcement agencies should not be pressured to solve crimes and get convictions for murders or other felonies, just for budgetary or public relations purposes.

The purpose of the American judicial system is justice. There should be no accolades for prosecutors who win at any cost. But for those who uncover the truth no matter where it falls, all praise and glory should be garnered.

I am not saying that Stephan would put innocent boys away just for her own career progress. I'm sure she felt she was doing the right thing. But how could she not see the ominous nature of the confessions?

How could this happen?

The answer is in the way the system works. Prosecutors invariably build their case from the belief that a person arrested must be guilty. But while most people who end up standing before the court on criminal charges are guilty, not all are. It should not be forgotten that the very purpose of our judicial system is not to punish the guilty so much as to protect the innocent. This euphemism is lost more often than not.

• • •

Paul Blake, Mary Ellen Attridge, and I were ecstatic over the ruling. The boys' parents and relatives were all much relieved, of course, and many wept. The boys themselves stood silent, not understanding what had happened. We explained that they were going home, and all three showed expressions of joy that I cannot begin to describe but will remain etched into my memory forever.

When Attridge walked out of the courtroom, she raised Joshua's hand high in triumph. There were a number of frowns about this open expression of victory. The brows of bureaucrats narrowed, seeing it as an indignity not proper for an attorney. But I thought it was a great: She had beaten the odds. We all had, but she was the most triumphant one because her client was Joshua, who was the key to the fate of the other boys.

Viva Attridge, I thought, and I thanked God.

We thought what would happen next is that the district attorney would drop the case, assuming Tuite's guilt, or at least concede on the boys' innocence. Instead, Paul Pfingst said this to the press: "The judge found that there was a strong suspicion these three young men butchered a twelve-year-old girl, and yet she let them go home. That is extraordinary." He was being political. He was not thinking that the boys might be innocent, only that his office had lost. I can think of nothing sadder or more egocentric than this kind of response.

From this, however, came a vast show of community spirit that we are apt to think is a mere relic of the past. Twenty families—some of whom had never even met the Crowes, the Housers, or Treadways—put their own homes up for collateral to raise bail, which we got reduced to $250,000 for each boy on appeal. And while many who made this sacrifice refused to be interviewed, I managed to convince Ron Sealey, a local resident who put up his home, to speak out. Extracts from the interview with him follow:

"You took a tremendous financial risk, sir. We do not think of people being so heroic these days. Why did you risk your home to help these boys? What inspired you?"

"My wife is a very generous person. And I didn't believe they had the right kids."

"I was amazed to discover you were a seasoned peace officer, a deputy sheriff. As the court hearing showed, the Escondido police officers had a *hunch* Michael was guilty from day one. Starting then, they did all in their power to prove that hunch was correct."

Mr. Sealey paused in thought and said, "As a cop, you work with hunches of course. Hunches get you through, sometimes. But you have to have some objective reasoning behind it. You have to work it through, and if you can't *disprove* what your hunch tells you, then you have something."

"That sounds reasonable," I commented, "but what they did over at the Escondido Police Department is ground their investigation on their hunches as if the objective of the case was to prove the hunches correct."

"Those guys, Claytor and Sweeney . . ." Emotional, Sealey paused. "I'm not saying the entire Escondido Police Department is bad, but what Claytor and Sweeney did was inconceivable; it's not even good police work in my opinion. We went through countless pages of interrogation transcripts. Now there's a joke. And I'm still shocked when I think how intrinsic Chris . . . what's his name? McDonough? He should not be a police officer."

"Speaking of McDonough, Aaron said that all his life he had trusted the police; thought they were someone to turn to. And then he met McDonough and Claytor and, well you know what happened after that."

"Yes. Aaron knew me when I was a cop. And that's the thing. You teach your kids if they're in trouble they should go to the police. Aaron thought this, and . . . Sweeney should never have allowed it to happen. And the way they tried to get around *Miranda*. You don't have to get around it. You use it. But these guys failed to meet the minimum. Read the reports, you can see the incompetence. And anyway, I cannot condone a cop lying."

"Do you recall they started by telling Michael—on the same day his sister was murdered—he had a demon inside him?"

"Yes. The first thing I'd do as defense attorney is rip those officers from one side to the other for that. It was a comedy of errors. Durgin, the head of their crime lab, is a joke. It goes on and on . . . I'd not want my son confronted by such people; it's scary to think about. That's why my wife and I were willing to help. We didn't want to see any kid go through such hell. But we were not alone. A lot of people gave their hearts to these boys and their parents. We were not the only ones to risk our home, and we were certainly not the only ones to believe in the boys' innocence."

We both stood, and I shook Ron Sealey's hand, then added, "I can't think of anything more touching, especially in this day and age. What you all did, standing up to what you deemed a miscarriage of justice, reminds us all that when push comes to shove, a strong community spirit prevails."

Among others who reviewed the interrogations was Mr. Richard A. Leo, one of the foremost authorities on false confessions and the co-author of *The Consequences of False Confessions: Deprivations of Liberty and Miscarriages of Justice in the Age of Psychological Interrogations*. He is a scholar and author of many studies and papers on the subject of crime and confessions and is highly respected in his field. When I asked him his opinion on the methods used, his conclusion matched that of Sealey: "People like Claytor, Sweeney, and Wrisley should not be police officers. McDonough," he said, "was arrogant, perhaps the worst of the bunch."

Because of his own background in psychology I was tempted, but reluctant, to ask Dr. Leo to comment on Lawrence Blum, the Orange County psychologist who had watched the interrogations on a TV monitor and concluded that Aaron was a "sociopath, a Charles Manson with a high IQ."

"Look," my question began, "I hesitate to ask your opinion about a colleague in your field, the psychologist Blum, who deemed Aaron Houser a sociopath. But would you care to offer a comment about him? A quote I can use?"

Richard Leo is an articulate, intellectual and thoughtful man. I knew I had put him on the spot. There was a pause, then came the unequivocal reply: "Blum is a fucking idiot. No one can make that kind of a diagnosis without ever meeting and working with a person. There are essential tests. He made the conclusion from watching videotapes. What does that tell you?"

What the Crowe murder case shows is that Claytor, McDonough, Sweeney, Wrisley, and Dr. Blum got caught up in their own zeal and investigative techniques. They stopped questioning the facts and pursued internal hunches, which were nothing short of biases. They did not understand the three boys they persecuted, children they could not relate to, so they assumed the worst. This is disgraceful and frightening when one thinks of the implications for the children in this or other cases.

When I think about the ramifications of this entire ordeal, it becomes essential to not narrow our responses merely to the mistakes or ruthlessness of the Escondido police; consider also the politics of the San Diego District Attorney's office. The DA blatantly placed public image and re-election at the top of the agenda, not the pursuit of justice. Just look at what occurs across the nation. Even as this case was in progress, two boys, seven and eight years old, were interrogated at a Chicago police station for six hours and persuaded to confess to killing an eleven-year-old because they wanted her bicycle. As it turns out, after months of terrifying experiences, semen was found by a lab test and a thirty-year-old man was charged with the terrible crime. And this is just one example of many.

Is this the type of police work we want in our society? When dealing with children, do we really want this kind of blatant pressure and brow beating as a substitute for careful forensic investigation?

We must wonder how the police draw confessions out of innocent people, adult and juvenile.

It's an unequivocal fact that the interrogation "techniques" used in this case were a form of psychological torture. Any expert in psychology will tell you that if you terrify a young subject, and keep them sleep deprived, hungry, thirsty and needing to use the restroom for hours on end, they will probably confess anything—even to assassinating Lincoln—to relieve their fear and discomfort.

Many of us think that when someone confesses, they simply must be guilty: *why on earth would an innocent person confess to such a heinous crime?* But false or coerced confessions continue to occur all the time, for a variety of reasons and under a myriad of circumstances. This case should send a chill down the spine of every American parent, because the terrifying fact remains: *This could happen to anyone.*

What if it was *your* child?

• EPILOGUE •

The duty of a prosecutor is to seek justice, not merely to convict.
—American Bar Association Standards for Criminal Justice
3-1.2(c): The Function of the Prosecutor

Irrespective of Judge Hammes's ruling at the Fitness Hearing, Summer Stephan and Paul Pfingst were determined to proceed with their prosecution against the three boys. They decided that Joshua would be tried first. Stephan's strategy was, if Joshua were convicted, then the district attorney would try to strike a deal with Mary Ellen Attridge for Joshua's cooperation and testimony against Michael and Aaron in their trials. Prior to the Fitness Hearing, Stephan had offered Joshua no jail time for his plea and cooperation.

A month before Joshua's trial, Judge John Thompson threw out most of Michael's interrogation statements and all of Aaron's interrogation statements. However, Joshua's second interrogation—with its detailed account of the plot to kill Stephanie—was ruled admissible and would come in at his trial. Judge Thompson did rule that Joshua's confession could not be used against Michael or Aaron. The Crowe family and the Houser family breathed a sigh of relief.

I was faced with the prospect of Joshua going to trial first. This presented several different strategic options to my defense of Aaron. The defense team had not yet tested the clothing Tuite had been wearing on the night of the murder. I had mentioned to Attridge early on that we should test his clothing for blood. There was no way the stabber would not have gotten blood spatters on him with such a close personal attack. She wasn't receptive to the idea at all. I didn't blame her for the cold reception. After all, Tuite was the only suspect the defense could point a finger at as the true murderer. Find no evidence on his clothing connecting him to the Crowe house, and there goes the phantom-of-the-opera crazy-killer defense.

However, the circumstances were now different. If Joshua is convicted, he becomes a potential knife in the back of Aaron and Michael. His testimony affirming his detailed confession in exchange for leniency at sentencing would seal the fate of the other two boys. I would end up having to attack the credibility of a boy who had sat next to Aaron since arrested and at the defense table during the 707 Fitness Hearing. Pictures of the three boys together at all hearings had been plastered all over the newspapers and media for nearly a year. Under such circumstances, Tuite as the real killer would not sell very well to a jury. It was time to pressure Attridge into testing Tuite's clothing.

During one of the pretrial hearings, I pulled Attridge aside and told her that we had to test the clothing Tuite was wearing on the night of the murder to see if there was any evidence connecting him to the Crowe house and Stephanie. Attridge was once again hesitant.

She calmly stated, "If the clothing comes back negative, it will weaken our argument that Tuite was the real killer."

"So what," I argued. "No evidence was found on the boys or their clothing connecting them to the murder. If we don't," I said, looking Attridge right in the eyes, "we will be guilty of malpractice for not doing so. And that is exactly what any good appellate attorney will argue when Joshua's conviction goes up on appeal: failure of the trial attorney to provide an adequate defense—sheer incompetence.

"You do not want your career to have that label," I said with a shake of my head in frustration at her lack of response. Attridge just looked at me as though I wasn't making sense.

Thinking I had lost, I concluded, "I certainly don't want that moniker on me. If you will not make the motion, I will. I would prefer to do so with you and Paul."

Attridge finally spoke. "Let me think about it. I may want to look at the clothing first."

What did she mean by "look at the clothing first"? What could she tell by looking at the clothing that the police hadn't already seen? Would she agree and make the joint defense motion? Frankly, I didn't believe she would. As a consequence, I began preparing to make the motion on my own.

To my surprise, Attridge, at Joshua's next pretrial hearing, stood up and informed the court that she and Stephan had agreed to test Tuite's clothing and that the district attorney's office and Attridge's Alternate Public Defender's (APD) office would send the clothing to a San Francisco Bay-area laboratory for independent testing. Both the DA and the APD's office would share the costs of the testing. I was flabbergasted. Once again she acted on her own. This time it fit my defense.

Planning for the worst, I began to analyze Joshua's confession. To do so, I studied various interrogation techniques. Having been a deputy district attorney, I was familiar with police interrogation tactics. The defense had experts Richard A. Leo and Richard J. Ofshe who we would call to testify to the coercive nature of the interrogations. But if the jurors in Joshua's trial do not believe their testimony and convict Joshua, then I would need another approach.

I decided to reverse the tables on the interrogators by having our experts not only talk about the coercive nature of the interrogations—the lies, long hours of isolation, constant questioning, and mind games—but how the boys' answers and body language indicated they were telling the truth about not killing Stephanie.

There's no doubt the interrogation techniques used on Michael, Joshua, and Aaron were psychological in nature and heavily reliant on the Reid Technique of interrogation. But all psychological-based interviews rely upon the interrogator's interpretations of a suspect's responses to questions and accusations of guilt. If I could show the interviews as coercive, but more importantly convince a jury that Michael and Aaron's actual responses showed their denials of guilt were truthful, then I would have a plausible defense even in the face of Joshua affirming his confessions. I believed that neither Attridge nor Blake had thought of this approach yet. I decided not to disclose my strategy, and I even contemplated contacting John E. Reid himself. My plan was to ask him to review the interrogation tapes and tell me if he felt the officers abused his technique of interrogation. It was worth a shot. If he said the officers used his techniques appropriately, I would not call him as a witness. If he objected to the way his technique was employed, I might call him as a witness. Either way, the prosecution could not call him or someone associated with his company, John H. Reid and Associates, Inc., as a witness, since I had retained him as a consultant. Well, that was a possible plan.

One day into jury selection for Joshua's trial, the Bay Area independent lab called. They had found three spots of Stephanie's blood on Richard Tuite's red sweatshirt. The Escondido police had run tests on Tuite's white T-shirt but not on his red sweatshirt. Later, a state crime laboratory would further find Stephanie's blood on the hem of Tuite's white T-shirt. Late that afternoon, Attridge called me at my law office with the news. We were both ecstatic. I congratulated her on her bold move to resist any plea bargain and to try the case. Most importantly, I praised her decision to test Tuite's clothing.

We decided to press for dismissal of all charges against the boys.

Stubbornly, Stephan would *still* not concede that Richard Tuite was the murderer. She put forth several *theories* as explanations for the blood being found on the red sweatshirt. She theorized the Escondido police had co-mingled other bloodied evidence with the red sweatshirt—despite the fact that Tuite's clothing was collected after the murder and packaged separately from all the other evidence. Further, Tuite's clothing was tested many months after the evidence in the house had been examined, so co-mingling of the evidence was improbable at best. Moreover, no evidence implicating the three boys, whether DNA or not, was ever found at the murder scene.

Desperately grasping at straws, she then suggested that Tuite had rummaged through a garbage can where the real killer had thrown bloodied items from the slaying of the little girl.

All the while Summer Stephan and Paul Pfingst ignored the evidence staring them in the face. The day Tuite was found in the laundromat and taken to the police station, the detectives confiscated his belongings. In his pockets they found three one-dollar bills, loose change, a Smith Brothers cough-drop wrapper, a Snickers candy wrapper, and two white matchbooks. Cheryl Crowe would later state that she typically had Snickers bars in the house for the family. More important, a bag of Smith Brothers cough drops were seen in a police photo of the Crowes' kitchen countertop. The photo had been taken the morning of the murder.

Finally—six weeks after the discovery of the blood droplets on Tuite's shirt—the district attorney dismissed all charges against Michael, Joshua, and Aaron. However, the dismissal was without prejudice, leaving open the possibility that the boys could again be prosecuted sometime in the future. The angst felt by the boys and their families was palpable. *Who could live with the possibility of having that horror shadowing them with no definitive end in sight?*

Not wanting to admit that they had been wrong, the Escondido Police Department, for more than a year, refused to arrest Richard Tuite for the murder. Finally, the case was handed over to the San Diego County Sheriff. As the evidence mounted against Tuite, so did the political pressure against Paul Pfingst.

Finally, the district attorney recused his office. The prosecution of Tuite was turned over to the California attorney general's office.

In 2004, after a three-month-long trial—and six and a half years after Stephanie's brutal murder—Richard Raymond Tuite was convicted of voluntary manslaughter. He was sentenced to a mere fourteen years in prison.

In another weird twist, on September 8, 2011, the United States 9th Circuit Court of Appeals, in a 2–1 vote, said Tuite was entitled to a new trial simply because a sole witness was not cross-examined by the defense.

In May 2012, fourteen years after Stephanie's death, San Diego County Superior Court Judge Kenneth So made the extremely rare ruling that Michael, Joshua, and Aaron were factually innocent. Judge So concluded that the evidence showed *beyond a reasonable doubt that the teens were innocent.*

In yet another mind-boggling turn of events, on December 6, 2013, Richard Tuite, in his retrial, was found *not guilty* of the murder of Stephanie Crowe. The jurors reached their decision after two days of deliberation. Richard Raymond Tuite walked free from prison at the age of forty-four. However, he is required to register as a sex offender for lewdly harassing, following, and attempting to enter the apartment of the two Escondido girls, ages twelve and thirteen, shortly after Stephanie's death.

District Attorney Paul Pfingst was defeated at the polls by Superior Court Judge Bonnie Dumanis, who campaigned against Pfingst's mishandling of the Crowe murder case. She served as district attorney from 2003 to 2017. Surprisingly, Dumanis decided not to finish her last term of office, and she resigned. Her early retirement meant that an interim district attorney would need to be appointed for the remainder of that term, serving up until the next district attorney was elected in 2018.

In a "you wouldn't believe it if you saw it in a movie" moment of judicial madness, Summer Stephan was appointed interim district attorney in June 2017. Then in June 2018, running against a criminal defense attorney, she was elected to a four-year term as San Diego County District Attorney.

Meanwhile, the Crowe family filed a civil rights action against the Escondido and Oceanside Police Departments and won an award of $7,250,000 in 2011, nearly fourteen years after Stephanie was stabbed to death. Aaron Houser and his family won a similar award of $4,000,000. The Treadway family also filed a lawsuit but gave up their claim in order to find peace and finality to their tragic ordeal.

But neither the defendants nor their families will ever truly have peace of mind. Having been ground through the cruel machinery of systemic injustice, no amount of money will ever replace what was stolen from them.

And at the end of the day, the murderer of young Stephanie Crowe still walks free.

· AFTERWORD ·

When a Government lawyer, with enormous resources at his or her disposal, abuses power and ignores ethical standards, he or she not only undermines public trust, but inflicts damage beyond calculation to the system of justice. This alone compels the responsible and ethical exercise of this power.

In re Doe, 801 F. Supp. 478, 480 (1992)

My cause in writing this account of the Stephanie Crowe murder case is supported by Ken Armstrong and Maurice Possley, who said this in their *Chicago Tribune* article, January 1999: "With impunity, some prosecutors across this country have violated their oath and the law, committing the worst kinds of deception in the most serious cases. They have prosecuted black men while hiding evidence the real killers were white. They have prosecuted a wife, hiding evidence her husband committed suicide. They have prosecuted parents, hiding evidence their daughter was killed by wild dogs. They do it to win."

Not all prosecutors fall into these traps, of course, and not all cops make the mistakes that Claytor and company did. Not every detective who interrogates people "McDonough-izes" their suspects. Or wrongly utilizes the Reid Technique of interrogation. But it is well known that men, women, and children have been jailed and imprisoned simply because the authorities have hidden evidence, destroyed evidence, even lied to construct or distort evidence.

Worse yet are tactics that produce coerced confessions. The Crowe case is certainly not an isolated incident. It is just one more example among the many. There are books, such as the ones that Leo and Ofshe have produced, filled with stories of false confessions leading to false convictions. In case after case, prosecutors have lied, covered up evidence, or suborned coerced confessions, resulting in innocent people being sentenced to death, all in their zealous need to prove their gut feelings or suspicions and *win*.

As I stated earlier, in this era of protests against the use of excessive physical force by police and calls for police reform, the psychological aspect of the criminal investigation and prosecution of juveniles should not be overlooked.

Michael Crowe, Joshua Treadway, and Aaron Houser were lucky to be born into white, middle-class families. Friends and neighbors mortgaged their homes to raise bail money and hire attorneys, and used their influence—their "white privilege," if you will—to organize a defense effort that even then barely prevailed.

It doesn't take much to imagine what the outcome could have been had the three teenagers been born to parents of color. In all likelihood, they would be living out their lives behind bars, wrongly convicted of a crime they did not commit, after having been battered psychologically until they "confessed" and then tried as adults.

This is exactly what happened in New York City to the Central Park Five—five Black juveniles, ages 14 to 16, who in 1989 were tried for the rape and brutal beating of a white female jogger. They maintained their innocence but were convicted of attempted murder, rape, and assault, in part, on police-coerced confessions. The five Black males spent six to thirteen years in prison before being exonerated in 2002, when DNA evidence confirmed the guilt of the true rapist and he confessed to the crime. They were awarded a $41 million settlement in 2014, although the City of New York denied any wrongdoing.

These examples illustrate the decadence and lack of responsibility in our justice and law-enforcement systems. There is a dishonorable thread running through the very fabric of the law itself. The Supreme Court must come to grips with the fact that the latter part of the twentieth century and the beginning of the twenty-first century have seen a dilution and stripping of the safeguards the accused and their lawyers need in order to ensure that the innocent are not wrongly convicted.

As our country—even the world—re-evaluates the role, behavior, and protocols of police departments and the legal system, we should also address the lawful techniques and procedures that may result in false confessions, not only from adults, but particularly from easily manipulated juveniles.

Adopt a Children's Bill of Rights, as I have laid out in Appendix II. Bring back the preliminary hearing as a meaningful barrier to screen out the weak cases and preserve the rights of the accused. Michael, Joshua, and Aaron would have been tried separately and probably convicted if California Welfare and Institutions Code section 707 had not existed. The Fitness Hearing stipulated in this code served as a preliminary hearing and afforded the defense attorneys in the Crowe murder case the opportunity to challenge the prosecutor's case before going to trial.

Finally, prosecutors who break the code of ethical procedure must be brought to justice, just like others who break the law. They must never lose sight of their goal to seek convictions, of course; that is not my point. They need to be freed from having their drive for conviction—the winning of a case at all cost—as the dominant criterion for their public image. The criterion for determining success as a prosecutor should be how well he or she follows due diligence—a diligence that must include seeking the *proof of innocence as well as the proof of guilt*. In the far reaches of this effort, losing a case should be as rewarding as winning a case, for this compelling reason: the objective of a prosecution is to see the truth prevail.

The challenge is complex, because in pursuing their common purposes, the police and the prosecution invariably become bedfellows. And this results in the prosecution being subject to the prejudicial view that the suspect who has been arrested is to be tried, so the suspect must be guilty. Just as obviously, when a confession is obtained, both the prosecution and the courts are generally convinced this is an admission of undeniable guilt. But confessions can be and sometimes are coerced. This is a shameful example of human action.

In ancient times, torture was the process for obtaining confessions. Not so many years ago, a process called "the third degree" was used. Today, we are more humane, right? But how much more humane? To revisit Michael Crowe one more time, can you imagine being fourteen years old and, on the day of your sister's death, you are told that *a demon lives within you and that demon killed her, then the demon made you forget your terrible deed?* I doubt that you, or anyone, can know what that would be like. It is beyond comprehension.

During the many weeks of the 707 Fitness Hearing, there came a day when Joshua Treadway felt he had to say something to Aaron and Michael about his confession—specifically about saying they had planned and carried out the crime.

"You know what happened to me, right?" he said.

Michael simply said, "You're fine, Josh. Don't worry," and the boys felt a renewed closeness, a rekindled friendship that perhaps is deeper, more mature than ever before. We are left to wonder what the future holds for these three boys, now grown, free men. Or are they free? They are innocents, but they are lost. Their lives have been impacted in brutal ways that will affect them as long as they live. After their terrible interrogation ordeal, followed by their arrest and incarceration, they then had to sit together while Deputy District Attorney Summer Stephan declared in open court that they were "evil," and "cold-blooded murderers." Mrs. Treadway said the vision of Summer Stephan looking at the boys during breaks was an image she will never forget. "It was this awful, cold and icy stare," she said.

While Michael, Joshua, and Aaron may never escape the images of what happened to them, I believe that we, as a society, must not close the book on this unfortunate incident. We must remember, always, that these children might have been our own.

In a very special way, they are.

• • •

For additional information about this case and videos of the police interrogations, go to: donaldmcinnis.com.

APPENDIX I

• COERCED CONFESSIONS •

Law enforcement officers have the obligation to convict the guilty and to make sure they do not convict the innocent.

—Justice White, *United States v. Wade,*
388 U.S. 218, 256 (1967)

For centuries, torture has been a standard in interrogations. In the 1800s and early 1900s, physical abuse of suspects by police was routine in America. In 1936, the United States Supreme Court in *Brown v. Mississippi* ruled that confessions obtained through violence could not be introduced as evidence at trial. The case involved three black men who were accused of killing a white farmer. The three were whipped and beaten, and one was even hung by the neck, until they confessed.

Following the *Brown* decision, the police refined their interrogation methods into what was depicted in the movies as the "third degree"—a use of physical abuse that many times did not leave marks or disfigurement, as suspects were yelled at, threatened, blinded by bright lights, and punched, and had their heads shoved in toilets.

In the early 1960s, ex-police officer/polygraph expert John E. Reid and lawyer/criminologist Fred E. Inbau collaborated on a psychological method of interrogation called the Reid Technique. This method of interrogation would usher in a new era in accusatory interrogation. This new model is based on psychological manipulations utilizing isolation, confrontation, and minimization of culpability and consequences.

The accusatory method establishes control over the suspect by leaving them alone in a small claustrophobic room before interrogation, has the interrogator ask accusatory and close-ended questions that reflect the police theory of what happened, and has the officers evaluate body language and speech, in order to determine if the suspect is lying.

Here is, in simple, plain terms, the Reid and Inbau Third Stage of interrogation, and its nine steps of psychological examination:

Step One: Direct Confrontation of the Suspect

The direct interrogation of the suspect is usually conducted by a team of officers, each playing a different role. However, there may be instances where one officer will do the entire interrogation. In the Crowe murder case there was a team of police officers from the Escondido Police Department and an officer from the Oceanside Police Department, a psychologist from Orange County, and at times, an observing deputy district attorney from San Diego County.

In Stage Three, the interrogation is very accusatory, with the officer telling the suspect that the investigation clearly shows they committed the crime. The entire interrogation is primarily a monologue of accusations with supposed evidence indicating the suspect's guilt. This typically involves presenting the suspect with false evidence of guilt. Such false evidence could include claims of a co-defendant having confessed, physical evidence existing connecting the accused to the crime, or lying about the results of a polygraph test (or, in the Crowe murder case, the results of a Computer Voice Stress Analyzer test). Thus, deceit is an essential part of the Reid Technique of interrogation.

While so confronting the suspect, the interrogator or team of officers will be observing the suspect's behavioral reactions. A passive reaction to the accusations is usually viewed as evidence of guilt or deception by the suspect. Spontaneous, forceful, and direct denials are considered indicators of innocence.

Step Two: Theme Development

Police interrogators are taught that they must present a moral justification or theme for the offense in an effort to shift the blame away from the suspect to some other person or set of circumstances. The interrogator presents, in a sympathetic, monologue manner, the themes which contain reasons that will psychologically justify or excuse the crime. The reason could be as simple as the youth of the accused. The objective is to give the suspect a way to accept responsibility for their wrong by either avoiding blame for their actions, or by allowing the suspect to minimize the seriousness of their actions. This kind of theme development is most effective with people who have a guilty conscience for some non-criminal reason, are emotional, had a bad childhood or upbringing, or are just young or immature or psychologically can't handle the situations they are in.

Step Three: Handling Denials

Denials by a suspect must be stopped. Every time a suspect starts to deny or tries to explain their denial, the interrogator must interrupt, pointing out the ridiculousness of the denial, or accusing the suspect of not listening to the evidence the police have gathered. If necessary, the police officer should change the subject, e.g., point out another piece of evidence of guilt. To not interrupt the suspect's denial gives the advantage psychologically to the accused.

To accomplish Step Three, the police will usually use a good-cop/bad-cop type of role playing. The purpose of the role playing is to get the suspect to be open and responsive to the friendly officer. This technique works well with quiet or unresponsive subjects.

Step Four: Overcoming Objections

When attempts at denial do not succeed, the suspect will often give various objections or reasons in support of their innocence. For example: "I would never steal from my company because I love my job." Such logic-based denials give the interrogator an opportunity to turn the denial against the suspect. Further, most police officers believe an innocent person will continually give the same denial or reasons, while a guilty suspect supposedly will continually attempt to reason their way out of the accusation. Once the accused sees their reasons are not being accepted, the suspect will usually start to withdraw and cease responding to the interrogator. For the psychological interrogation to be successful, this must not be allowed to happen.

Step Five: Retention of Participation

When the suspect becomes passive or starts to withdraw, the accused is at their lowest point psychologically. The interrogator looks for signs of surrender: an emotional outburst, the suspect placing their head in their hands, or shaking their head without speaking. In this moment of hopelessness, the officer reaches out to the suspect as an understanding ally. One way the interrogator can do this is to close the physical distance between the officer and the suspect. A simple consoling touch, along with reassuring statements of sympathy and understanding of why the crime was committed, will draw the suspect back to the officer. The officer should always look the suspect in the eyes and, using their first name, try to get the accused to re-engage.

Step Six: Handling the Suspect's Passiveness

As the interrogator re-engages with the suspect, the central theme of why the suspect committed the crime should be emphasized, along with statements of sympathy and understanding of why the crime was committed. The suspect should be told to tell the truth, be remorseful, and confess, because it is the right thing to do. Every effort will then be made to break down the suspect's remaining resistance, such as going through the evidence against them.

Step Seven: The Presentation of Alternatives

At this point, the interrogator presents two alternatives as to why the suspect committed the crime. The first alternative is more callous and socially unacceptable. The other alternative is more understandable and face-saving but just as incriminating. Here are examples:

1) Isn't it true you needed the money because you could not find a job? or

2) Isn't it true you did not plan the crime out; it just happened spontaneously? or

3) Isn't it true you need psychological help to overcome the evil inside of you?

The interrogator may follow the more face-saving alternative with a supporting statement that encourages the suspect to choose the more understandable alternative. In any event, the suspect's choice is a confession and psychological acceptance of the interrogator's theme as to why the accused acted criminally.

Step Eight: Suspect Orally Confesses

The initial acceptance of either alternative, no matter how small the acceptance may be, must now be developed into a full confession. The police are taught that they should immediately respond with a statement acknowledging the admitted facts. The officer should then engage the accused in a basic review of the crime's events, obtaining statements which corroborate the validity of the accused's confession. The officer may make a suggestion as to how the crime was committed. This process may continue for as long as it takes to get a solid confession. It is important that the suspect is alone with the interrogator during this time. The presence of another person may discourage the suspect from talking about the crime.

Step Nine: The Written Confession

Since many suspects later deny their confession or say it was coerced, the police must attempt to get a signed written confession. In a court of law and to jurors, a signed confession is considered to be stronger than an oral confession. When the suspect appears averse to a written confession, the officer may ask the suspect to write a letter to the victim asking forgiveness for the crime committed.

Analysis

A key element of the Reid Technique is the interrogator's ability to detect when a suspect is lying. Thus, the emphasis is on getting to know the suspect and his or her background through a period of non-confrontational interviews and the necessity to observe how the suspect reacts throughout the period of interrogation.

However, various studies challenge the ability of a person, even a trained investigator, to discern truth from lying. This is particularly important when dealing with the young, the poorly educated, those under great stress, or suspects who have been traumatized. The mentally ill can be especially difficult to read, due to the inability to understand the motivation of their responses.

Reid and Associates responds by challenging the method of those studies and the motivation of the test subjects to lie. Further, Reid and Associates believes that police officers through training and experience have an increased ability to detect truth from lies, as opposed to social scientists conducting controlled studies.

Another element of the Reid Technique is the investigator's suspicion that the suspect is guilty. Such an assumption may affect the investigator's interpretation of the suspect's responses and what is the truth or a lie.

Other critics challenge the coercive nature of the interrogation process through psychological manipulation and the contamination of the interview due to misrepresentations or outright lies about the existence of incriminating evidence. They conclude that these efforts may lead a suspect to incorporate such information into a confession.

Reid and Associates responds to such criticism by stating that false confessions are the result of the investigator not following the tenants of the Reid Technique. By way of example, Reid and Associates cites situations of police making promises of leniency in return for the confession, threatening or intimidating the suspect, or excessively long periods of interrogation as factors which will cause a suspect to give a false confession.

To read further, see Richard A. Leo, *Why Interrogation Contamination Occurs.* 11 Ohio State Journal of Criminal Law 193 (Fall 2013); Timothy E. Moore and C. Lindsay Fitzsimmons, *Justice Imperiled: False Confessions and the Reid Technique.* 57 Criminal Law Quarterly 509 (2011); John E. Reid and Associates, Inc. (website), www.reid.com. For a detailed defense of the Reid

Technique, see John E. Reid and Associates, Inc., *Clarifying Misinformation about The Reid Technique*, www.reid.com/pdfs/20120311.pdf.

Other Methods of Interrogation

There are other types of psychological methods of interrogation that are not as confrontational as the Reid Technique and do not use deception.

The **Kinesic interview method** has some similarities to the Reid Technique in that it requires the interviewer to analyze the suspect's behavior in order to determine if he or she is lying. Kinesics is communication through human body motion and was first used by anthropologists to study human posture, gestures, and movements. In 1970, Professor Ray L. Birdwhistell published a book titled *Kinesics and Context*. From this publication and subsequent research, the Kinesic interview method of analyzing nonverbal human behavior was devised.

Author Stan B. Walters, in his book *Principles of Kinesic Interview and Interrogation, Second Edition* (CRC Press, 2003), describes four fundamental stages of a suspect's interview: (1) orientation, (2) narration, (3) cross-examination, and (4) resolution (Id. at 25-29).

During the orientation and narration period, the interrogator studies nonverbal communication traits of the suspect. Walters refers to this phase as the "Analysis Phase." The interrogator uses information gathered during this phase in order to tailor the confrontational cross-examination stage. Walters describes thirty-some human traits as guides to evaluating a suspect's responses. These body language movements help the police determine when the suspect is lying. According to the Kinesic method, denials by the suspect should be confronted with only real or circumstantial evidence, not lies.

To read further, see D. Glenn Foster, *The Kinesic Interview Technique*, International Due Diligence Organization, www.international-due-diligence.org/ wp-content/uploads/2015/08/IDDO-The-Kinesic-Interview-Technique.pdf

The **PEACE method of interrogation** is taught in England through the College of Policing, which refers to itself as "the professional body for everyone who works for the police service in England and Wales."

PEACE stands for Preparation and Planning, Engage and Explain, Account, Closure, and Evaluate. Under the PEACE method of interrogation, the suspect is presumed innocent and, as a consequence, is allowed to tell his or her story without interruption or accusations. The investigator may ask the suspect questions about the narration in order to clarify what is being told. The investigator then confronts the suspect with inconsistencies or contradictions between the suspect's version of events and the evidence. The investigator may even point out the implausibility of or inconsistences in the suspect's own statements or story. However, in the PEACE method, the officer is prohibited from deceiving the suspect.

To read further, see College of Policing (website), www.app.college. police.uk.

For a comparative analysis of interrogation techniques, see Christian A. Meissner, et al., *Interview and interrogation methods and their effects on true and false confessions.* Campbell Systematic Reviews (2012; 2013).

APPENDIX II

• CHILDREN'S RIGHTS •

After reading this book, you may be thinking: How could this happen to these three boys and their families? Why weren't the parents told that their children were being detained and interrogated? Why weren't the parents told they could be present with their child during interrogation? And why weren't the parents told they had a right to consult with an attorney prior to their children being interrogated?

You may be wondering: How can children's rights be best protected? What are those rights? And can a child under eighteen years of age really understand and give up their rights, while appreciating the full consequences of what they are doing?

Regrettably, these same questions arise across this country on a daily basis as children are confronted by authority figures. The Crowe murder case is just one example, and not the last, in a long history of children confessing to crimes they did not commit. We adults must make sure that care is taken when the state deals with children.

The United States Supreme Court established four basic safeguards against self-incrimination in its 1966 decision of Miranda v. Arizona:

1. You have the right to remain silent.

2. Anything you say can be used against you in court.

3. You have the right to an attorney.

4. If you cannot afford an attorney, one will be provided for you.

These safeguards became known as the Miranda rights warnings. The specific wording of the warning varies, depending on the state, or federal, jurisdiction. However, the basis is the same for all jurisdictions. A confession is invalid unless a suspect, in custodial interrogation, is informed of their Miranda rights prior to questioning.

Today these Miranda rights are read to children prior to in-custody questioning. However, studies have shown that minors—children and adolescents—lack the mental capability to fully comprehend the meaning of the rights; therefore, minors cannot make a "knowing and intelligent waiver of their constitutional rights" as required by law.

In an effort to improve children's comprehension of their constitutional rights, the language of Miranda rights as read to adults should be simplified, and additional rights must be added for minors' protection. To this end, the following Miranda-based safeguards should be read to suspects under the age of 18.

• CHILDREN'S MIRANDA WARNING •

1. You have the right to remain silent. This means you do not have to say anything or answer my questions or any other officer's questions.
2. Anything you say may be used against you. This means what you say can be used against you in juvenile court or, if you're charged as an adult, in adult court. In other words, what you say can get you in trouble.
3. Before and during all questioning, you may have your parent or guardian present, and you may talk privately with your parent or guardian. So before you say anything, you may talk with your parent or guardian.
4. You or your parent or guardian may talk to an attorney, free of charge, before talking to us.
5. You or your parent or guardian may stop the interview at any time.
6. You or your parent or guardian may, at any time, have a free attorney with you during questioning.

Do you want to talk to your parent or guardian?

Do you want to have a lawyer present?

Do you want to talk to us?

Miranda rights are effective only if those rights are fully understood. To advance the understanding of those rights, a Children's Bill of Rights is proposed:

• CHILDREN'S BILL OF RIGHTS •

1. A child shall have the same constitutional rights as an adult.
2. A child has the right to be advised of his or her Miranda rights when detained and questioned in a manner suited to his or her intellectual development.
3. A child shall have present, before and during any questioning, a parent or guardian or legal caregiver ("Custodial Parent") who shall exercise the child's Miranda rights in the best legal interest of their child.
4. A request by a child to talk to a Custodial Parent shall constitute the invocation of the child's Miranda right to remain silent.
5. No child or Custodial Parent shall waive the Miranda rights for a child 14 years or younger without first talking to an attorney, who must agree that the child's Miranda rights may be waived.
6. A child 15 years or older may waive their Miranda rights only after the child and their Custodial Parent first consults with an attorney.
7. If the child or their Custodial Parent cannot afford an attorney, one shall be provided before the child is questioned, at no cost.
8. The child, the Custodial Parent, and their attorney shall be advised of the nature of the matter being investigated and why the child is being questioned.
9. When the Custodial Parent is suspected of committing a crime, an attorney shall be provided, at no cost, to represent and advise the child regarding the child's Miranda rights, and be present during questioning of the child.
10. If the child is suspected of a criminal offense, the child's attorney shall advise the child and the child's Custodial Parent that the child may

be charged as a juvenile offender, subject to detention and rehabilitation under juvenile law, or, when allowed by law, may be charged and sentenced as an adult, including a sentence of life in prison.

11. All questioning of a child who has been detained shall be video recorded. The recording shall be preserved for use in a court of law, irrespective of whether the child is charged with a criminal offense.

12. A child shall not be questioned for more than 4 hours in a 24-hour period, and shall be allowed to eat and rest 8 hours between periods of questioning.

The rationale behind the Children's Bill of Rights is that the law recognizes a child as a legal person. As such, minors should have the same rights as adults, from the moment they are born. Parents, courts of law, and the community recognize that minors lack the intellectual development and life experiences that allow an adult to understand and exercise independent judgment to protect their rights and best interests. This is why minors should be afforded special protections when being detained and questioned by persons of authority. This is particularly true because a child's life, and the environment in which they are raised, is structured and completely controlled by adults. As a result, children are extremely vulnerable to psychologically coercive interrogations, and are much less resilient than adults when dealing with the criminal justice system.

If we are to nurture each and every child to their maximum potential, the criminal justice system should be structured in a way that protects children while rendering justice for society. The Children's Bill of Rights and the Children's Miranda Warning will go far toward accomplishing this end.

For further reading on a child's ability to comprehend and knowingly and intelligently waive their constitutional rights and on how they respond to custodial interrogations, see: National Juvenile Justice Network, "Using Adolescent Brain Research to Inform Policy: A Guide for Juvenile Justice Advocates," September 2012, www.njjn.org/our-work/adolescent-brain-research; Allison D. Redlich, "The Susceptibility of Juveniles to False Confessions and False Guilty Pleas," 62 Rutgers Law Review 943 (2009);

NES Goldstein, LO Condie, R Kalbeitzer, JL Geier, "Juvenile Offenders' Miranda Rights Comprehension and Self-Reported Likelihood of Offering False Confessions," National Center for Biotechnology Information, U.S. National Library of Medicine (Dec. 2003, 2005), www.ncbi.nlm.nih.gov/pubmed/14682482; Mary Beyer, "Recognizing the Child in the Delinquent," Kentucky Children's Rights Journal, vol. 7 (Summer of 1999); Catherine C. Lewis, "How Adolescents Approach Decisions: Changes over Grades Seven to Twelve and Policy Implications," Child Development, vol. 52 (1981); Steven Drizin and Richard A. Leo, "The Problem of False Confessions in the Post-DNA World," 82 N.C. Law Review 891 (2003-2004).

• ABOUT THE AUTHOR •

DONALD E. MCINNIS is a criminal defense attorney who represented Aaron Houser in the Stephanie Crowe murder case.

Mr. McInnis has specialized as a litigator trying criminal and civil cases. During his four-decades-long legal career, Mr. McInnis experienced both the prosecution and defense side of the criminal law. Early in his career, he served as a Research Attorney for the California Superior Courts. Later he became a Deputy District Attorney for two different counties in Northern California and a Deputy Public Defender in San Diego County, and is thoroughly familiar with all aspects of police and prosecution practices.

He has also served as a Superior Court Judge Pro Tem, been an arbitrator for the American Arbitration Association, and a referee/arbitrator for the California Superior Courts. Mr. McInnis is admitted to try cases before all state and federal courts in California.

Mr. McInnis is Of Counsel to the Law Offices of Hamilton & Associates, APC, serving all Southern California counties.

AWARDS AND RECOGNITIONS

- Who's Who in American Law
- Who's Who in California
- Member of the Mexican Academy of International Law, Mexico City, Mexico

- Bachelor of Arts Degree, San Jose State University
- Juris Doctorate Degree, Santa Clara University Law School
- International Law Diploma in European Integration Law, Europa Institute, University of Amsterdam

PUBLICATIONS

- Money & Politics, Citizens Initiative: Who Shall Govern, 59 Santa Clara University Law Review 69 (2019). Available at: digitalcommons.law.scu.edu

- Children rights: *The Evolution of Juvenile Justice: From the Book of Leviticus to Parens Patriae: The Next Step After In re Gault*, Loyola of Los Angeles Law Review, Volume 53, Number 3, Spring Edition, 2020.

- Juvenile law: *Children and the Law: Time to Fulfill the Promises of Miranda and Gault*, Dartmouth Law Journal, January 2021.

• ACKNOWLEDGEMENTS •

There will always be a warm place in our hearts for Aaron Houser, Josh Treadway, Michael Crowe, and their beleaguered families and their community of friends. This story and its ending could not have occurred without the strength of their love and the character of their beliefs.

In particular, I wish to thank Aaron for trusting us with his life. I have never met such a mature, intelligent, and thoughtful young man. His willingness to endure many months of solitary confinement, knowing the prosecution wanted to plant an informant as a roommate, showed a strength of character that most adult men are not capable of, much less a 15-year-old boy.

I wish to thank my co-defense counsel, Mary Ellen Attridge and Paul Blake, whose professional cooperation and legal talents provided a sterling defense for the three teenage boys. This story is as much theirs as it is mine and our clients.

I will be forever beholden to Jack Marlando whose research, writing skills, and commentary struck a chord of truth that allowed this book to tell the full and truthful story of the murder of Stephanie Crowe.

To Chantal Boccaccio I give a thunderous applause for her dedication to the publication of this book and the cause it represents. Without Chantal's steadfast belief in the innocence of the boys, her research, and writing contributions, the reader would not have experienced the emotional trauma of this tragedy.

To Erin Willard, David Wogahn, Fauzia Burke, attorney and professor Richard James LeVine, and in particular Larry Edwards, I give thanks, for without them this story would not have the quality and professionalism of a real-life crime drama.

Most importantly, I thank Judge Laura P. Hammes for her dedication to truth and justice. Without her insightful and judicious handling of the three boys' hearing, the truth as to who killed Stephanie Crowe would not be known.

No attorney is an island unto themselves. We would not exist if it were not for the causes we champion and the clients we defend. Justice is a cumulative effort of many people and their talents, just as this writing is a accumulative effort of many talented people dedicated to the ethos of a just and humane society.

Made in the USA
Las Vegas, NV
12 January 2023

65464337R00203